CASTELLS IN AFRICA
Universities & Development

Edited by
Johan Muller, Nico Cloete & François van Schalkwyk

Published in 2017 by African Minds
4 Eccleston Place, Somerset West 7130, Cape Town, South Africa
info@africanminds.org.za
www.africanminds.org.za

Chapter 3: 'Universities as Dynamic Systems of Contradictory Functions' first published in 2001 by MaskewMiller Longman in *Challenges of Globalisation: South African Debates with Manuel Castells* edited by Johan Muller, Nico Cloete and Shireen Badat.

African Minds is a not-for-profit, open-access publisher. In line with our goal of developing and fostering access, openness and debate in the pursuit of growing and deepening the African knowledge base and an Africa-based creative commons, this publication forms part of our non-peer reviewed list, the broad mission of which is to support the dissemination of knowledge from and in Africa relevant to addressing the social challenges that face the African continent.

This work is published under a Creative Commons Attribution 4.0 International License (CC-BY).

ISBN Paper 978-1-920677-92-3
ISBN eBook 978-1-920677-93-0
ISBN ePub 978-1-920677-94-7

Orders
African Minds
4 Eccleston Place, Somerset West 7130, Cape Town, South Africa
info@africanminds.org.za
www.africanminds.org.za

For orders from outside South Africa:
African Books Collective
PO Box 721, Oxford OX1 9EN, UK
orders@africanbookscollective.com
www.africanbookscollective.com

Contents

Acknowledgements iv
Preface v
About the editors viii

SECTION 1: FRAMING CASTELLS IN AFRICA
1. Castells in South Africa 3
2. Universities and the 'new society' 17

SECTION 2: CASTELLS IN SOUTH AFRICA
3. Universities as dynamic systems of contradictory functions 35
4. The role of universities in development, the economy and society 57
5. Rethinking development in the global information age 67

SECTION 3: PUTTING CASTELLS TO WORK IN AFRICA
6. Roles of universities and the African context 95
7. Universities and economic development in Africa 113
8. Research universities in Africa? 135
9. African universities and connectedness in the information age 159
10. Contradictory functions, unexpected outcomes, new challenges 187

Afterword 2017 by Manuel Castells 197

Appendices 202
References 208
Index 217

Acknowledgements

This book is the culmination of a 17-year engagement with Manuel Castells and his ideas. We first encountered his paper for the World Bank on higher education and development (an abridged version appears in this volume), and the application of his ideas and their possible relevance for higher education in Africa was underway. We want to thank him, as a scholar and friend, for the unparalleled stimulation and comradeship he has provided, and not least for the unfailingly courteous manner in which he did it. (The more formal relationship between Manuel Castells and several supporting organisations and initiatives – Centre for Higher Education Trust (CHET), Higher Education Research and Advocacy Network in Africa (HERANA) and Stellenbosch Institute for Advanced Study (STIAS) to name a few – is described in detail in Chapter 1.)

This book would not have been possible without the financial support provided by CHET by way of two of its projects focused squarely on the role of universities in knowledge production in Africa: the HERANA project funded by Carnegie Corporation of New York, with initial support from Ford Foundation; and the project 'Factors that Affect Research Productivity at Universities' funded by DST-NRF Centre of Excellence in Scientometrics and Science, Technology and Innovation Policy (SciSTIP). Our thanks also go to Angela Mias (CHET) and Linda Benwell (Millennium Travel) for arranging the three meetings that contributed both to the conceptualisation and the completion of this book.

Preface

In addition to publishing three seminal contributions made by Manuel Castells during his time in South Africa, this volume brings together new and previously published insights on how Castells has shaped research and thinking on higher education and development in Africa.

What was previously published has been edited and, in some cases, substantially reworked to fit the ambit of the collection.

The new material is to be found in Chapters 1 and 2, as well as in the concluding chapter. Chapter 1 traces the trajectory of Manuel Castells's association with Africa, mediated in the main by the Centre for Higher Education Trust (CHET) since 1998. The chapter also provides the reasoning behind the publication of this volume. Chapter 2 focuses on a few key Castellian concepts to show how, when brought together, they might shine some light on how universities function in the present time, particularly in relation to development. The chapter brings into relief what Castells augured globalisation would mean for higher education (and development) – trends to which most policy-makers, analysts and researchers simply did not pay sufficient attention.

Chapters 3, 4 and 5 present Castells's own thinking on the role of higher education globally and in Africa. Chapter 3 was first published in 2001 in *Challenges of Globalisation: South African debates with Manuel Castells*. It is republished in this volume with minor corrections. Chapters 4 and 5 are transcripts of two public lectures delivered by Manuel Castells in South Africa. The first lecture, 'The Role of Universities in Development, the Economy and Society', was delivered on 7 August 2009 at the University of the Western Cape in Cape Town. The second public lecture, 'Reconceptualising Development in the Global Information Age', was delivered at the Stellenbosch Institute for Advanced Study (STIAS) at Stellenbosch University on 5 June 2014. Both chapters are edited transcripts of these lectures.

The remaining chapters are versions of previously published chapters, edited to speak more directly to the ideas and concepts that emerged from Castells's lectures and his interactions with higher education scholars in South Africa.

Chapter 6 is an edited version of 'Chapter 1: The Roles of Universities in the African Context', originally published in *Knowledge Production and Contradictory Functions in African Higher Education* (see Cloete & Maassen 2015). The chapter traces how African universities have been grappling with the Castellian functions by situating them in the historical context in which African universities were established and steered.

Chapter 7 comprises edited excerpts from the first two chapters of the publication *Universities and Economic Development in Africa* (see Cloete et al. 2011). The chapter draws on empirical evidence to establish what the predominant notions of the roles of African universities are – both at institutional and government levels. It shows that the notions are mixed and often not in alignment within higher education systems, and even if there is a strong notion of the development role of the university as knowledge producer and/or system-level alignment, the knowledge production aspirations are not matched by the realities at the coal-face.

Chapter 8 includes selected sections on the role of research in African universities from several chapters in *Knowledge Production and Contradictory Functions in African Higher Education* (see Cloete et al. 2015). The chapter has been updated to include previously unpublished data, and draws on the empirical evidence to explore how universities are managing their contradictory functions, particularly as a group of elite African universities aspire to elevate the role of research. It provides a more in-depth analysis of the research policies and processes at African universities, and brings to the fore the need for system-level differentiation to ameliorate the tensions inherent in single universities – traditionally orientated towards training – attempting to strengthen research.

Chapter 9 was originally published as the chapter 'University Engagement as Interconnectedness: Indicators and insights' in *Knowledge Production and Contradictory Functions in African Higher Education* (see Van Schalkwyk 2015). The substantially rewritten version of the chapter in this collection examines how current project-based research activities are failing to strengthen the knowledge production function of African universities, in so doing, curtailing their ability to participate in globalised knowledge networks. Unlike preceding chapters that honed in on the relationship between the university's function as knowledge producer and its contribution to development, Chapter 9 explores the university in Africa in the context of Castells's network society.

Chapter 10 provides a synthesis of the empirically-focused Chapters 6 to 9, and concludes that universities in Africa are struggling to balance the contradictory Castellian functions; all the more so when they are expected to emphasise research. The chapter explores who should shoulder the blame for the slow pace of progress towards research-led universities in Africa. And rather than concluding on a sombre note, the chapter reminds us to keep putting Castells to work in order to better understand the systemic and structural impediments hampering the transformation of African higher education.

The Editors
June 2017

About the editors

JOHAN MULLER is emeritus professor of curriculum, and senior research scholar at the University of Cape Town. He is a visiting professor at University College London Institute of Education, and extraordinary professor in the Centre for Research on Evaluation, Science and Technology (CREST) at Stellenbosch University. He is a sociologist of education and has published in the area of curriculum theory and policy, focusing on schooling as well as higher education.

NICO CLOETE is director of the Centre for Higher Education Trust (CHET) in South Africa. He is a guest professor at the University of Oslo, an extraordinary professor at the Institute for Post-School Studies at the University of the Western Cape, and extraordinary professor in the DST-NRF Centre of Excellence in Scientometrics and Science, Technology and Innovation Policy at Stellenbosch University. He was general secretary of the Union of South African Democratic Staff Associations (UDUSA), and the research director of the South African National Commission on Higher Education (NCHE).

FRANÇOIS VAN SCHALKWYK is an independent researcher working in the areas of higher education studies, open data and scholarly communication. He holds masters degrees in education and publishing, and is currently reading for his doctorate in science communication at Stellenbosch University in South Africa.

Section 1: Framing Castells in Africa

Chapter 1

Castells in South Africa

Nico Cloete & François van Schalkwyk

One can seldom say precisely when or where an intellectual thread started. An elusive starting point certainly applies to the idea of bringing Manuel Castells to South Africa. Most likely, it was one of the first policy acts of the post-apartheid Department of Education that triggered the idea to invite Castells.

Soon after the first democratic elections of April 1994, the Department announced its intention to establish a National Commission on Higher Education (or the 'NCHE' as it is commonly referred to in South Africa). The NCHE, established by a proclamation of then president Nelson Mandela in December 1994, was charged with advising the government of national unity on issues concerning the restructuring of higher education by undertaking a situation analysis, formulating a vision for higher education, and putting forward policy proposals designed to ensure the development of a well-planned, integrated, high-quality system of higher education in South Africa. Nico Cloete was Director of Research for the NCHE and was to become the director of the Centre for Higher Education Transformation (CHET) which was established when the NCHE had fulfilled its duties.

The terms of reference of the NCHE stated that restructuring South African higher education should address the inequalities and inefficiencies inherited from the apartheid era, as well as respond to the social, cultural and economic demands of a globalising world. The extent to which these two worthy aims were in tension was quite unrecognised at the time.

The challenge for the NCHE was that the 'system' as it was then, was fragmented and modelled on an outdated version of the post-school education system in the United Kingdom (UK). This model had by then been radically revised and massified in the UK. This is, of course, a frequent dual problem in post-colonial societies: both the irrelevance of the 'borrowed' model and its obsolescence back in the 'mother country' (Cloete & Muller 1998).

There was a tension in the NCHE; some NCHE commissioners saw the main problem as redressing apartheid's inequality, while a minority regarded a fundamental restructuring of the system as the main task. This tension was never fully resolved.

The NCHE report of 1996 proposed three principles for a transformation framework. The first was increased participation, specifically, to increase the size of the system with a primary focus on equity. This was a proposal for massification which the government rejected. Instead it opted for the Department of Education's planned growth strategy. The second principle was heightened responsiveness within higher education to societal needs; namely, a shift from a closed to a more open system. The third principle was increased cooperation and partnerships in governance structures. The NCHE framework focused heavily on equity and democratisation, while paying virtually no attention to development, to research and to innovation.

A major problem with the transformation discourse in South Africa at the time, including that of the NCHE, was that the single-minded focus was on equity and democracy as counters to the social damage done by apartheid. But the legacy of apartheid was only one major problem, the other being that the transformation discourse needed to be connected to development – particularly the globalising knowledge economy and South Africa's participation in it. But it wasn't. The NCHE and subsequent policy papers did not take as their point of departure reflections on the roles and functions of a higher education system to propose a new tertiary education system that would include equity, democratisation and development as key principles. Knowledge production and innovation, and the key role that higher education could play in economic development, were largely ignored.

After the publication of the final report of the NCHE in September 1996, the newly-formed Centre for Higher Education Transformation, aware of some of the key issues not addressed by the NCHE, resolved to strengthen the knowledge base on the role and functions of higher education in South Africa and in Africa by combining traditional higher education studies with more general scholarly reflections on the change dynamics of higher education. The first foray in this direction led to a series of seminars and presentations by prominent scholars such as Kwame Anthony Appiah, Mahmood Mamdani, Peter Scott and Carol Schneider, and by practitioners such as Malegepuru Makgoba, Ahmed Bawa and Donald Ekong. The series of seminars resulted in the book *Knowledge, Identity and Curriculum Transformation in Africa* (see Cloete et al. 1997).

The book addressed two key challenges facing post-apartheid South Africa, namely, knowledge and identity. In the concluding chapter, 'Citizenship and Curriculum', Johan Muller identified the citizenship skills required as political (mediatory and democratic), cultural (navigating difference) and economic (productive and problem-solving). While the main focus of the project was to discuss knowledge and citizenship skills for a revised curriculum (the NCHE had decided not to address curriculum transformation directly), the chapter that had considerable influence on the direction of CHET's future work was by Peter Scott: 'Changes in Knowledge Production and Dissemination in the Context of Globalisation'.

Scott had come to the attention of the NCHE via two of his books – *The New Production of Knowledge* (with Gibbons, Nowotny and others in 1994) and *The Meaning of Mass Higher Education* (1995) – both of which arrived in South Africa in photocopied form. These texts directly influenced the NCHE's proposal on massification. However, neither the government nor the NCHE grasped the importance of his analysis that massification and knowledge production in a context of globalisation was not simply more students and staff, but a radical restructuring of higher education that accompanied changes in managerialism and marketisation, as well as the production of knowledge itself in terms of consumption, circulation and conservation; exponential growth of information and communications technology; the shift away from knowledge that is academic, disciplinary, homogeneous and hierarchic to knowledge that is applied, transdisciplinary, reflexive and horizontal; the demise of the enlightenment model of knowledge as coherent, autonomous and self-referential; and the simultaneous globalisation and fragmentation of academic disciplines, so that disciplinary expertise is no longer unitary and cohesive but diffuse, fluid and opaque. Some of these prognostications remain contentious.

In his chapter in the book *Knowledge, Identity and Curriculum Transformation in Africa*, Scott refers to a number of theorists reflecting on globalisation, including Beck, Eagleton and Fukuyama. While these authors all had interesting things to say, what triggered our interest was the discovery, via Jamil Salmi, then senior fellow in the World Bank higher education division, of a paper that Manuel Castells had presented at a World Bank Seminar on Higher Education and Development in Kuala Lumpur in June 1991.

The paper, 'The University System: Engine of development in the new world economy', approached higher education via sociology in a very different way to the other theorists. In 1998, Johan Muller and Nico Cloete met with Martin Carnoy, one of the world's foremost comparative education economists and as one of Castells's long-time friends and intellectual collaborators, Carnoy introduced the pair to the 'trilogy' – *The Rise of the Network Society* (1996), *The Power of Identity* (1997) and *End of Millennium* (1998). Carnoy suggested that if CHET wanted to understand the relationships between globalisation, higher education and development, it should invite Castells who, according to Carnoy, was very interested in Africa, but had paid little attention to our continent in the trilogy owing to an absence of reliable data. We received an enthusiastic response to our invitation letter, but were informed that due to the interest around the trilogy, Castells's diary was full until June 2000.

The delay turned out to be a blessing – CHET was better prepared in 2001 than it would have been in 1998. By 2000, Castells was one of the five most cited social scientists in the world. Even South Africa's President Mbeki was familiar with the trilogy and announced to his Cabinet that Castells was the Karl Marx of the 21st century. Castells regarded this as a huge compliment, and a huge misunderstanding.

CHET coordinated Castells's first visit in collaboration with representatives from the National Economic Development and Labour Council, the Council on Higher Education, the Development Bank of Southern Africa, the Human Sciences Research Council, the Universities of the Witwatersrand, Natal and Cape Town, and the Presidency. Castells was accompanied by Carnoy and the visit consisted of six seminars in Johannesburg, Durban and Cape Town, and two meetings with President Mbeki. In addition to academics and students, there were participants and presenters from government, business councils and trade unions, and the public meetings were well-attended. Much to Castells's irritation, many participants kept regarding him as a promoter of globalisation, instead of an analyst of globalisation.

Such was his resonance at the time, that Castells was being referenced by politicians in parliament. Ben Turok, in a debate in the National Assembly on financing for development and a new paradigm of economic and social development designed to eradicate poverty (19 September 2000) commented: 'Only a few weeks ago, Manuel Castells, the very distinguished Spanish professor who visited South Africa, said to us – and he met the President – "Either South Africa sinks or swims." You either swim in the tide of technology or you sink as a country. He went on to say [...] that the world brand of capitalism is implacable and cruel. Globalisation is sundering the world into two groups: One, with dynamic information-based economies and the other with the vast deteriorating old economies dominated by informal and survivalist activities, and Africa is the latter case. He said that if we – Africa and South Africa – do not join this new technicological [sic] age we will be obliterated.' And the Minister for the Public Service and Administration in the National Council of Provinces (26 September 2002) declared: 'Prof. Manuel Castells, a world-renowned sociologist, is part of this Council and he was present last year. He said – and has done so in various lectures – that the availability and use of information and communication technology is a prerequisite for economic and social development in our world. It is the functional equivalent of electricity in the industrial era.'

While the higher education community had latched onto Castells's unique and compelling approach to the role of the university, his early interactions with the Mbeki government were centred on the importance of information and communication technology (ICT) infrastructure as a determinant of the country's ability to participate in the global networked economy.

After one scheduled meeting, Mbeki insisted on a second day with Castells, from which emerged the decision to form the Presidential Information and Communications Technology Advisory Council, established with remarkable speed in October 2001. Its main aim was to accelerate efforts to establish South Africa as an advanced information-based society which would be the engine for a knowledge economy, moving South Africa away from its endemic dependency on mined resources.[1]

The new Council was a high-powered group consisting of chief executives from global companies such as Oracle's Larry Ellison, Carly Fiorina of Hewlett Packard, Thierry de Beauce of Vivendi Universal, Rajendra Pawar of NIIT Technologies, Esther Dyson of Edventure, Reza Mahdavi of Cisco Systems, Sten Fornell of Ericsson, Veli Sundback of Nokia and Valentin Chapero of Siemens. It also included Mark Shuttleworth (South Africa's IT billionaire) and, from government's side, Mbeki himself plus a number of ministers and directors-general. Manuel Castells was the only academic on the Advisory Council.

---

1   http://www.dirco.gov.za/docs/2002/ict1004.htm

The group did have some influence on the establishment of the Presidential National Commission on Information Society and Development which was tasked to develop a government policy framework for ICT, strategies to make government a model user of ICT, and the preferred models for creating an information society.[2]

By 2006 the Commission fragmented with Cisco withdrawing due to possible conflicts of interest because they were advising and doing business with government.[3] There were also rumours about lack of implementation and that Mbeki had lost interest as conflicts within the ANC, particularly with Deputy President Zuma, escalated. At a workshop with Castells at STIAS in 2011, the previous head of policy and government communications responded to a question about the failure of the grand ICT ambitions by saying that the HIV/Aids fiasco had had a negative effect on Castells's visit. Mbeki had, as he had done in the case of ICT, established a Presidential Advisory Aids Panel.[4] The Aids Panel included denialists such as Peter Duesberg, incidentally also from the University of California. Considering how this debacle had embarrassed the government, many Cabinet members were apparently deeply sceptical about the 'information society', which they saw as another Mbeki folly with Californian advisors.

Many authors have highlighted the importance of the state in developing countries if countries are to realise the potential of ICTs for development (Grace et al. 2001; Heeks 2002).[5] Notably, Castells provides an historical analysis of the changing role of the state in a globalised world and explores its ability both to constrain and enable agencies. In his seminal three volumes on the *Information Age: Economy, society and culture*, Castells (1996; 1997; 1998) does this in relation to technology and innovation.

Castells's consideration of the reconfiguring of the nature and

---

2   http://www.gov.za/sites/www.gov.za/files/23107_0.pdf
3   http://www.balancingact-africa.com/news/telecoms-en/4158/cisco-withdraws-from-mbekis-international-technology-advisory-group
4   http://www.csicop.org/si/show/aids_denialism_vs._science
5   This section draws extensively on the work of Gilwald (2009).

role of the state as a result of global pressures from the nation state in the industrial era to what he calls the 'networked state' in the informational era provides a backdrop for understanding the impact of globalisation on the state and society, and the necessity for countries to develop their information infrastructure and human capital to meet the challenges arising from this.

The unevenness of this global development, according to Castells (1996; 1997; 1998), reflects the relative ability of social institutions, such as the state, to enable the mastery of strategic technology. This, he argues, can propel a society into the new economy. He sees the changes in the mode of production as revolutionary technological developments distinguishing this informational era from the previous industrial era. Castells (1996: 7) contends that while knowledge and information have been central to the process of production in previous eras, it is only in the informational mode of development that the 'action of knowledge upon knowledge itself' is the main source of productivity. In this epoch, knowledge generation, processing and transmission become the fundamental sources of productivity and power.

While originating in the productive process, the technology and its associated relationships, according to Castells (1996; 1997; 1998), spread throughout society, so influencing the concentration and distribution of power. It is not that technology *per se* determines historical evolution and social change, but the technology (or lack of it) that embodies the capacity of societies to transform themselves as well as the uses to which societies decide to put their technological potential. It is for this reason that Castells (1996; 1997; 1998) contends that the state should play a central role in developing a forceful supply-side policy through investment in education – critical to the citizens' ability to adjust to change brought about by technological innovation – and in the necessary infrastructure such as telecommunications.

Despite being tarred by the vagaries of South African politics, by the time Castells left Africa for the first time, he had put firmly on the national policy agenda the following: the increasing centrality of knowledge and information to production and development in a globalising world; the key role of societal learning, or 'learning to learn', in keeping these productive goods vital in the social body; and the deep influence the network society would have on our senses of personal and collective identity. This took the debate several leagues beyond the NCHE.

For higher education in particular, his chapter 'Universities as Dynamic Systems of Contradictory Functions' (Castells 2001) drew on the 1991 'engine of development' paper in terms of the four functions of universities, and added new insights and reflections on higher education and development policy in the third world (particularly in Africa and Latin America). One important insight, which started to affect South African higher education by 2015, was that 'the demand for higher education has reached the status of a social need, regardless of the actual functional requirements of the economy or of the institutions' (Castells 2001: 211). The tension that Castells was pointing to, between 'social needs' and 'functional requirements', was not visible to South Africans at the time of Castells's first visit.

Three strands of the work that CHET pursued post-Castells 2000 are captured in subheadings of Castells's (2001) 'Universities as Dynamic Systems of Contradictory Functions' published in *Challenges of Globalisation: South African debates with Manuel Castells* (Muller et al. 2001): (1) 'Universities in the Third World: From dependency to development', (2) 'Higher education as development policy: The new frontier of international aid', and (3) 'Universities at the crossroads of a new international order'.

The first direct intellectual contribution of Castells to this work was realised in the book *Transformation in Higher Education: Global pressures and local realities* (published in South Africa in 2002 and by Springer for the international market in 2006). The subtitle comes from Castells's chapter in *Challenges of Globalisation* titled 'Think Local, Act Global'. The conclusion of this review of transformation in South Africa focused on new international trends and responses by the South African government and other social institutions. A major novelty was a deeper understanding of the limits of policy, bracketed by both local and global realities. Castells's theory that universities cannot specialise in only one function, and that in order to combine and make compatible various (sometimes contradictory) functions, both academic and governance capacities were needed, shaped the work of CHET for years to come in terms of institutional performance and differentiation.

The second thread related to international development aid and led to the publication of a report on the topic as it relates to higher education in Africa (Maassen et al. 2007) as well as in a follow-up chapter (Maassen & Cloete 2009) on the disconnectedness of the university as a policy issue in development cooperation in a book titled *International Organisations and Higher Education Policy: Thinking globally, acting locally* (Basset & Maldonado-Maldonado 2009).

The third thread, with funding from NORAD and the newly-formed US Foundation Partnership for Higher Education in Africa (which was part of the study on development aid), was to support the establishment of the Higher Education Research and Advocacy Network in Africa (HERANA). HERANA drew on Castells's network notions, his assertion that the recruitment of elites and professional training had been the main functions of universities in third world countries, and that in order to move from dependency to development, a greater focus on the research and knowledge production function is needed in African universities. The important advice to development aid agencies and governments was the need for 'selective aid, either concentrating resources in the best of the existing academic centres and/or creating new universities supported by national governments, private firms and international institutions' (Castells 2001: 217).

Castells returned to South Africa in 2009, this time hosted by the Stellenbosch Institute of Advanced Studies (STIAS). During his 2000 visit, Castells was impressed by the larger Cape Town metropole's combination of natural beauty, winelands and the sophistication of its four universities within a radius of 50km. He proposed a Princeton-type Advanced Studies Institute to be shared by the universities. The leadership at the Universities of Cape Town and the Western Cape showed no interest, but Stellenbosch University had already started to talk about such an institute, and in 2005 the Stellenbosch Institute of Advanced Studies (STIAS) was established with the support of the Marianne and Marcus Wallenberg Foundation.[6] STIAS is now well-established and has hosted a number of Nobel prize winners as fellows. Castells is counted among the Institute's enthusiastic fellows, and he spent time there during 2009, 2011 and 2014.

During his 2009 visit Castells delivered a special lecture on higher education at the University of the Western Cape. In this lecture, he combined the four main functions with the NCHE's proposals about equity, responsiveness and citizenship formation.

Castells's third visit was in 2011 to host, in collaboration with STIAS and CHET, a seminar series on informational development. The topic signals strong links with the arguments presented in 2000, particularly those on identity and the critical contribution of education in informational development. The seminars were a precursor to the book *Reconceptualising Development in the Information Age*, edited by Manuel Castells and Pekka Himanen (2014), that includes a chapter on South Africa co-authored by Nico Cloete and Alison Gilwald (Cloete & Gilwald 2014).

Soon after this visit, the HERANA project, which included eight flagship universities in sub-Saharan Africa, published the book *Universities and Economic Development in Africa* (Cloete et al. 2011). The main findings of this project provided empirical support for Castells's assertion that the focus of African universities had been on elite formation and training, and that 'research production at seven of the eight institutions (University of Cape Town excluded) was not strong enough to enable them to build on their traditional undergraduate teaching roles to make a sustainable, comprehensive contribution to development via new knowledge production' (Cloete et al. 2011: 165). The book concluded that in none of the countries was there a coordinated

---

6   http://stias.ac.za/about-us/overview/

effort between government, external stakeholders and the universities to systematically strengthen the contribution higher education can make to development, as was happening at the time in near-East countries like South Korea and Singapore.

HERANA Phase 3, launched in 2012, aimed at promoting data-informed planning at the eight 'flagship' African universities, and improving knowledge production in support of the continent's development challenges. The focus shifted to a set of indicators that dealt with postgraduate production, staff capacity and research output. The major output from this project was the publication of *Knowledge Production and Contradictory Functions in African Higher Education* (Cloete et al. 2015).

The launch of *Knowledge Production and Contradictory Functions in African Higher Education* at the Africa Higher Education Summit in Dakar in March 2015 was the only contribution that was based on empirical research at African universities. The book also made a significant contribution to the formation of the African Research Universities Alliance, a tangible demonstration that there is an emerging interest in Africa strengthening knowledge production as a core university function. Castells commented that the book 'demonstrate[s] the essential role of higher education in the development of Africa and of the world at large' (on the cover of Cloete et al. 2015).

In 2014, Castells returned to South Africa for a fourth time to host another seminar and, this time, to launch *Reconceptualising Development* (Castells & Himanen 2014). On 5 June 2014, in the lead up to the seminar, Castells delivered his third public lecture in South Africa. The lecture focused on the need to reconceptualise development, acknowledging the role of universities in a new development paradigm.

***

In 2002, not long after Castells's first visit to South Africa, CHET transformed from a typical, increasingly bureaucratic non-governmental organisation located in Pretoria into a much leaner networked organisation, and relocated to Cape Town. CHET became an organisation with only one full-time employee; all the other expertise and skills required, including for doing research, were contracted in as and when required. The administrative, accounting, communications and event management functions were also outsourced to a network of expert service providers.

The Pretoria CHET bears little resemblance to Cape Town CHET but three striking strategic consistencies remain. The first is CHET's ability to organise forums for linking academic researchers to higher education policy-makers. The second is the ongoing pursuit to bolster empirically the argument for the role of knowledge and, by implication, the role of the university in development, while always acknowledging the tensions between the four functions of universities brought to CHET's attention by Castells. The third is CHET's continued commitment to publishing its research.

CHET has self-published many of its reports and books, but it has also partnered with local publishers – with Maskew Miller Longman and Juta in the early days and, more recently, with open access academic publisher African Minds. Castells's first contribution was published as five chapters alongside commentaries by Martin Carnoy and others in the edited volume *Challenges of Globalisation: South African debates with Manuel Castells* (Muller et al. 2001). CHET produced transcripts of his 2009 and 2014 lectures, and published them on its website. This frustrated many scholars eager to locate these contributions on the content-saturated world wide web and ready to reference Castells's contribution to their work appropriately. Adding to the frustration, *Challenges of Globalisation* went out of print some years ago, and the electronic files could not be recovered to publish the book online as an ebook.

Alert to the ongoing interest in Castells's work by scholars of higher education studies and others, and to the limited access to his contributions, African Minds undertook to publish the out-of-print chapter and the two public lectures. Initially, the plan was to publish the three contributions 'as is' without an introduction or any accompanying commentary. However, in discussions with Nico Cloete (CHET) and with Johan Muller, two of the editors of the first Castells publication, it was agreed that the publication presented an opportunity not only to make Castells's contribution to higher education more widely accessible but also to showcase the contribution that Castells has made to higher education research and thinking in Africa fifteen years after his first visit to South Africa.

While the starting point of Castells's visits to South Africa may be shrouded by fading (and ageing) memories, it is hoped that by publishing his three seminal contributions on the university, and by supplementing them with chapters that make explicit how Castells has shaped the research agenda, the effects of bringing his big-picture thinking to bear on the university in Africa will remain indelible.

Chapter 2

Universities and the 'new society'

Johan Muller

Introduction

The current times have not been kind to globalisation. It was not always so. When Manuel Castells first came to the attention of all but a tiny handful of South Africans in 2000 on the occasion of his first visit to the country, South Africa was newly liberated, the future was unimaginably open, and globalisation seemed the right partner for national reconstruction and development. Castells was its avatar. While warning of the tensions and currents that globalisation could unleash, Castells was seen as bearing the optimistic message that globalisation could be a powerful positive force if it was managed correctly.[1] By 2016, that hope, at least in its simplistic form, had been mauled in dramatic fashion, though some would say its dark side could have been predicted if not averted had we paid more careful attention. What is unequivocally clear is that, as we put together this second book of Castells's contributions, a wave of anti-technological modernisation and anti-globalisation is sweeping through the traditional West, and

---

1   The title of the book was *Challenges of Globalisation* (Muller et al. 2001). It is true that the Introduction warned explicitly against seeing Castells as primarily a globalisation theorist; but that was like expressing scepticism about Mandela at the time – not a thinkable proposition.

a virulent populism is everywhere on the rise. The times are not propitious for the global cosmopolitan project.

But it would certainly be a grave mistake to think that globalisation has little to say and contribute to higher education today; the universal dismay of the UK universities to the strictures that Brexit will bring is indicative of the widely shared nostrum that universities need access to world networks to thrive (Corbett & Gordon 2017). But how are we to think that nostrum in a developing country that has a fledgling higher education system and too many patchy institutions? What are the opportunities and threats to higher education in the shadow of 2016? How might Manuel Castells illuminate the path today?

Re-reading his key text from that time, published again here for its prescience and foresight, and with the wisdom of hindsight, one can see he was warning against certain trends that we in South Africa simply didn't pay sufficient attention to. Take 'massification', for example, something invested with a charge of moral rightness hard to resist at the time. After all, black students had for too long been denied the fruits of education in general and higher education in particular. Who would deny their moral right to higher education, a right enshrined in the Freedom Charter and the Constitution? Massification was the necessary vehicle to deliver this right, and we were encouraged in this belief by other luminaries visiting in the early 1990s, like Sir Peter Scott (Scott 1997). What we took away then from Castells's magisterial essay was that development required four explicit functions to be effectively performed by the university system. What we did not notice as clearly was that a further implicit function, the pressures for access 'regardless of the actual functional requirements of the economy' (Chapter 3: 41) – massification for massification's sake – though indubitably a legitimate social demand, had to be carefully managed if it was not to render the delivery of the explicit development functions ineffective, if it was not to 'suffocate' the development potential of the universities. Castells could not have been clearer: if access to universities is opened

CHAPTER 2 Muller: Universities and the 'new society'

and the university is unable to separate out this function from its legitimate functions, conditions for high-level research become tenuous, then impossible, and the best graduates will leave, or simply not return after getting their PhDs in the metropoles, an endemic situation in African universities further to the north of South Africa. The students who remain behind get frustrated, and lose respect for the science function – a bell ringing loudly on the campuses in South Africa in late 2016 as the students fought not only for free education, but took the fight to, and against, their professors. Neither the education function nor the science function can properly thrive in such an environment.

The implications of the Castellian schema are thus not undilutedly optimistic, though Castells has more often than not been taken for a techno-optimist. The reasons lie in the architecture of his theoretical apparatus. This apparatus contains structural conditions as well as agents, powers to produce and powers to dominate, contradictions that have to be managed, and this can be done with wisdom or with folly. As against the rather smug narrative of universities being, next to the Church, the most durable of institutions, he tells a different story that includes at least the following: first and foremost, do universities have faculty capacity to attract good students and to do globally recognisable research? Have they produced a recognisable track record and reputation? Can the faculty, and the university as an institution, plug into global networks? Above all, can the university balance the historically specific form of the contradictory functions and adapt to its historical place and role and thrive? It is by no means a foregone conclusion.

This seems a rather large message to extract from Castells, whose main contribution to the sociology of universities in development can fairly be said to lie in the three pieces printed here. There is only one index entry to 'universities' in the famous trilogy, for example. This should not be taken to mean that his work does not speak to universities, and powerfully so. To get beneath the skin of Castells will require a little digging.

On power, knowledge and capacity

The aim in this brief introduction is not to provide a comprehensive review of Castells's theoretical reach. Rather it is to focus on a few key concepts and show how, in connecting them up, they together might shine some light on how universities function in the present time, particularly in relation to development.

A strong case can be made that the central concept in social science is power, and Castells places this concept centrally in his work. Starting with Poulantzian Marxism (Castells 2009 is dedicated to him), by the time of the trilogy, Castells's theory of the state and of political power is more orthodoxly Weberian (see also Castells 2009: 44). That is to say, power is the imposition of the will of one upon another, and the state, sovereign since the Treaty of Westphalia throughout Europe, has a monopoly on the lawful exercise not only of power but also of violent power. At the height of the power of the nation state, say up to the Second World War, might determined what was right.

In the networked world, this power changes subtly but decisively. Under globalisation, states can be said to lose power, but not *influence*. They can shape outcomes, but they can no longer determine them in the same way. This is because, in addition to the traditional three layers of power of the nation state – the local, the regional and the national – a fourth supra-national layer emerges, which now conditions, and places limits on, the traditional power of the territorially bounded entity. Castells names the two new forms of power in this new network configuration *rule-setting* (or governance by standards) and *governance in networks*. A higher educational example might be helpful.

Take the case of transnational qualifications frameworks. The European Qualifications Framework as an exemplar of a supra-national standard-setting body has created a set of parameters to which all qualifications in the Eurozone must conform in order to be registered. Castells would say that of the two kinds of new agent wielding power in the global networks, here the *programmers* hold sway – the group of early-joining representatives, principally in

CHAPTER 2 Muller: Universities and the 'new society'

this case those from the Irish qualifications authority – since they were able to set the criteria for the standards which control the rules for inclusion and exclusion to the qualifications framework. This has meant that for the late-joining countries, the wiggle room to negotiate their terms of inclusion is considerably reduced, although there too other considerations prevail: for late-joining Norway, a relatively influential country although not legally part of the EU, wiggling gained some concessions; for even later-joining Estonia, with lower standing in Europe, the terms of entry were simply accepted as if set by edict (see Elken 2016). The UK, by contrast, with their impending Brexit, are betting that they have sufficient alternative networks to join to mitigate the costs of exit. Time will tell whether they will opt to switch from the European Qualifications Authority to which they presently belong. Everything turns on the alternatives available. Castells calls the power to be able to join comparable alternative networks switching power, which, alongside programming power, circumscribes the range of new powers operating in the network society.

Although Castells doesn't refine this new set of powers much further, political science at large has tried to capture them, and the somewhat diminished form of power Castells calls influence, in what Nye has called the new paradigm of 'soft power' (Nye 1990, 2011). 'Soft' power is exercised via persuasion, and entails the ability to shape preferences through appeal and attraction, where credibility becomes a key resource. By Nye's own admission, this notion of power is descriptive rather than normative, or even really rigorously conceptual. This has not stopped it being seized upon by the would-be standard setters, or would-be programmers, to construct global rankings from this rather soft notion – the 'Soft Power World Rankings' (for which Nye writes a Foreword) and the 'Monocle Soft Power Survey'. For a more rigorous conceptual account, a brief look at Steven Lukes (2005) is instructive.

Lukes is well known for his thesis about the three faces of power. These 'faces' are conventionally seen as on a continuum from empirical enactments of the exercise of power ('A exercises power over B') identified with the empirical study of power by political scientists like Dahl; through more indirect exercises of power where power can be seen as for the common good, identified with sociologists like Parsons; to a radical form, where power shapes preferences in such a way as to circumvent the affected agent's freedom and rational self-determination. In revising his thesis in 2005, Lukes comes increasingly to lean on the distinction made by Spinoza, between *potentia*, which is roughly glossed as 'power to', or the ability and capacity to do something; and *potestas*, roughly 'power over', which is the traditional notion of power as domination of one agent over another. *Potestas* is always deformative, it withdraws or deprives, it places another in your power, constraining their choices, securing their compliance; *potentia* is productive or creative, it extends horizons, it imagines new futures. As Giddens (1979: 348) says with customary clarity, 'Power in this broad sense is equivalent to the *transformative capacity* of human action.' It involves the capacity to achieve something of value. In this sense, as we will see, highly specialised knowledge as produced by universities confers a very specialised capacity to its holders, which is where universities and development come in, but more on this later.

Lukes draws several lessons from this seminal distinction. First, power as capacity weans power from its exercise: one may possess power, but that is separate from exercising it. One may decide not to exercise it, or to exercise it badly – or, in more Castellian vein, in a non-networked field or site, which means its force is blunted or diminished. Secondly, following Spinoza, *potentia* is the more encompassing notion; all power is a capacity, *potestas* just a special case of it. In fact, Lukes would advocate that we shift entirely to what he calls a dispositional account of power, an account in terms of capacities, an account he allies to Sen and Nussbaum's capabilities approach. Castells will have none of it. Although he cites the distinction between 'power over' and 'power to', which he attributes to Parsons (Castells 2009: 13), he goes on to say that 'the power to do something [...] is *always* the power to do something against someone' (Castells 2009: 13). That is, for Castells 'power to' is also always 'power over'. On this point, Castells is himself highly consistent, as we commented in the conclusion to the earlier volume.

Fortunately, we do not have to arbitrate between Lukes and Castells; in any case, we agree with Castells. It is enough to say that, as we enter the networked spaces of informationalism, the dispositional dimension of power comes more insistently into view. We can see this in the way that Castells defines the powers of programmers and switchers in terms of their abilities and capacities. We also commented on this when we commented on Castells's oft-misinterpreted notion of knowledge in our earlier volume (Muller et al. 2001). This bears a brief re-statement.

Commentators persist with the cavil that Castells didn't take knowledge seriously. Maton (2014: 2), to cite just one recent example, complains that Castells 'relegates' knowledge to a footnote, and concludes that, like other mainstream sociologists, he treats it as a 'black box'. What is quite true is that he does not treat knowledge as a factitious object or structure, as Maton and others do, for instance; for him, as we have already seen, it is a productive capacity. As we pointed out earlier, Castells regards the data and information as 'bits' out there, while knowledge as a capacity is the ability to assemble the data into information with which to assess, make informed guesses and expert hypotheses, and integrate the most robust of these into theories that relate in determinable ways to the existing theoretical corpus.

The bottom line then is that, while Castells (and others in the political economy tradition) treats knowledge as a *capacity* of knowledgeable agents, educators tend to treat knowledge as the *existing knowledge corpus* as well as the new knowledge which can be demonstrably added to it. For the economists, knowledge is an expert capacity 'in here'; for educators, knowledge is an expert commodity that can be treated as 'out there'. There are good reasons for both approaches to knowledge.

The educators need to focus on two issues that economists take for granted. The first is they need to conceptualise the 'what' of learning in terms of a specifiable curriculum. The question they must be able to answer is: what is the knowledge that must be selected into the curriculum and sequenced and paced in a determinable fashion? Attempts to design a curriculum in terms only of capacities (educators call them 'competences'), in terms of what learners should be able to *do*, are currently favoured by outcomes-based approaches to curriculum (like the European Qualifications Framework mentioned earlier), but their greatest drawback is they signal rather poorly what teachers and learners are expected to cover over a specific period. Specifying the end point of learning doesn't tell one how to get there. Educators cannot avoid a certain degree of treating knowledge as 'out there'. The second issue educators focus on is: what is the individual scholar's, or institution's, contribution to new knowledge? Here the outputs 'out there' are treated as proxies for their (the scholar's) productiveness. To answer both of these questions requires treating knowledge as 'out there' in some sense or other.

Economists by contrast have a different question to answer, one related more directly to labour power and labour productivity. Knowledge is treated here as a productive asset. In this sense, labour units are treated as *already capacitated*, so the need to specify the curriculum, or to count output units, falls away. It is not so much that the 'out there' doesn't count, as some sociologists of education have concluded; it is that what is 'in here' counts far more for the future value-adding activity of the concern. To see why that is, a brief detour into what Castells means by 'development' is in order.

Towards the 'new society' (Castells 1998: 360)

The place where Castells is clearest about this capacity is in his distinction between two forms of labour power and their relative value. 'The most fundamental divide in the network society, albeit not the only one, is between self-programmable labour and generic labour' (Castells 2009: 30). Castells continues, and it is worth quoting him at length:

> Self-programmable labour has the autonomous capacity to focus on the goal assigned to it in the process of production, find the relevant information, recombine it into knowledge, using the available knowledge stock [...] the more what is required from labour is the capacity to search and recombine information [...] in terms of value-making (in finance, in manufacturing, in research, in sports, in entertainment, in military action, or in political capital), it is the self-programmable worker who counts for any organisation in control of resources. (Castells 2009: 30)

The second form of labour, generic labour, may well possess skills of a fairly specialised sort, but they are not what Castells would call 'informational' skills, they do not lend themselves to being autonomously renewed in the workplace – once trained, always trained so to speak. So when innovation and production requirements change – and they will increasingly do so at an ever-greater pace in the network economy – the self-programmable worker can self-renew, while the generic worker must either be replaced by another more skilled worker, or by automation. In the remorseless logic of the network world, they do not have the key capacity to self-renew and are therefore replaceable.

The name 'network world' though masks the dynamic that drives it. Castells draws a distinction between the mode of *production* and the mode of *development*. The two main modes of production have been capitalism on the one hand and statism/collectivism on the other. The network society has tilted the balance towards capitalism, but not without hybrid modes emerging; the Chinese and Russian societies are just two that come readily to mind, not to mention the East Asian ones, about which more below. In a sense, the old tension between these still sits at the heart of modes of production.

It is in the mode of development that the greatest change is to be discerned, from industrialism to a post-industrial mode that some have called the 'fourth industrial revolution' and Castells calls 'informationalism'. It is this mode of development that has been the topic of discussion in this introduction, and which heralds Castells's 'new society', bringing with it decisive changes in the social relations of production, experience and power.

This view of development might seem quite conventional, but what Castells is trying to do is show how the concept of informationalism as a mode of development marks a break with both dependency theories of development and neoclassical economics in the field of development theory, usually called 'neo-liberalism' for short. The four Asian Tigers taken together, for example, confound both theories (Castells 2009: 250). Dependency theory predicted that economic development under capitalism in formerly dependent countries was not possible; and neoclassicism predicted that success would depend upon the market winning out over the state in directing the economy. The Tigers have been successful under capitalism, but they all had states that had intervened systematically in their strategic guidance of national firms and multinational corporations. They have also repressed or limited democracy in one or other way, concentrating on the improvement of living standards rather than citizen participation (Stalder 2006: 119). This too goes against the neoclassical grain.

Two other factors were crucial to their spectacular lift off. These were low labour costs and a large, well-educated and skilled labour force. For all of them thus, the *'availability of educated labour, able to reskill itself during the process of industrial upgrading, with high productivity and a level of wages that was low by international standards'* (Stalder 2006: 274, italics in original) was the key. This gave the labour force the flexibility to adapt to the informational paradigm – to science, hi-tech and R&D. Castells is at pains to stress the role of the state in producing 'high-quality labour' (Stalder 2006: 276). All of this stands in stark contrast to most if not all other postcolonies, where poor quality education and high wages, driven up by second and third industrial revolution unions, created the opposite set of conditions, with their consequent costs.

We may speculate then that where the proportion of self-programmable to generic labour is tilted positively in favour of the self-programmables, conditions are propitious enough that a country can dig itself out of the dependency trap. Where the balance is tilted the other way, the path to independence is much more arduous. The differential between the two forms of labour will only increase under informationalism. The factor making the difference is education, especially and increasingly higher education: 'The critical quality in differentiating the two kinds of labour is education, and the capacity of accessing higher levels of education' (Stalder 2006: 361). This underlines the critical role of universities in effecting the 'new society', the post-dependency thriving economy and society.

The empirical chapters in this volume that follow the three benchmark papers by Castells examine this Castellian legacy. Theoretically, they do this mainly by invoking the 'four functions' schema Castells introduces in his first paper. It is in their empirical realisation of Castells, though, that a larger conceptual debt becomes apparent. Their main empirical target is knowledge production, and their main indicator is the publication output of universities, their research productivity, including doctoral graduates. Of course, in a purely empirical tradition, the amount of research produced is correlated with the amount of innovation in the national innovation system. But the authors are operating here at least implicitly in a Castellian vein. The capacity to do research signifies the specialised capacity to manipulate symbolic systems, the result of which, in many key cases, has material payoffs and consequences. This is the symbolic capacity that is the basic condition for self-programmability. It is not only transmitted through induction into research, but this is the university's pre-eminent way of transmitting it, at least at a high level. The PhD is the proxy indicator that signifies the summit of self-programmability.

A research-productive institution is an environment where symbolic manipulation is a constant backdrop to other academic labours, and smart graduates need such an environment to flourish, and thereby to contribute to it with their own research outputs, patents, software programmes and other symbolic value-producing products. The amount of research output an institution produces is thus not only an index of its contribution to the present innovation economy, but through its magnetic inductive pull on good graduates, produces the producers of the future health of the innovation system as well.

It is frequently said that universities have to educate for the middle sectors of society as well, and Castells has incorporated the training of the civil service and bureaucracy into his fourth function of universities. There was a time in the postcolony when this, along with the ideological function and the training of dominant elites was all that universities did, at least in Africa. In too many cases, that is all they still do. But to train a skilled civil servant, it is no longer sufficient to teach the skills of concentration and procedural accuracy, along with the social virtues of attention to detail, loyalty to the state and sobriety. Most of these fairly repetitive skills are now swallowed up by software programmes. So, it is thought, what those in the service professions now most need are social skills like interpersonal and communication skills.

From the view developed here, the skills civil servants will also increasingly need are the skills of symbolic manipulation – drawing up and managing procurement and performance plans, strategic planning, performance management and the like. While much of these too are available as software, adapting them to the particular needs of the institution requires higher-level skills than before. To coin a phrase, these skills have the potential to create a *knowledge or informational dividend*; they are able to generate new value. The procedural and communication skills do not have this potential.

The twin themes of this book – universities and their role in development – are now in focus. Universities are, self-evidently, the privileged social institution for the inculcation of high-level expertise (what Castells calls in these essays the 'education' function) and the development of self-programmable, innovative or inventive capacity (what he calls here the 'scientific' function). It is the latter, though intimately dependent on the former, which counts most under informationalism. As we will also see in the chapters below, the dependence goes both ways: if an institution focuses on the education function to the neglect of the scientific or research function, the expertise level purveyed by the institution runs a real risk of slowly dropping down the scale from informational towards generic. On the other hand, if another institution develops a grand policy to be a research-led institution but neglects to employ the highly skilled scholars to do the research, the policy will remain empty. A theme of Castells's is that each needs the other in order to thrive.

In order to see this connection more clearly, a second link back to our first volume (Muller et al. 2001) may be helpful. In that discussion, we highlighted the fact that the ubiquitous term, 'learning to learn', was an institutional capacity rather than an individual capacity. Distinguishing with Eder (1999) between 'rule learning' and 'substantive learning', we argued that in order for an institution to be productively or creatively adaptable to challenges of the network society, it had to have the capacity to 'learn to learn', that is, to adapt to challenges and mediate contradictions. In the first paper, Castells is concerned to outline two sets of contradictions that adaptable institutions are able to mediate: that between the divergent demands of the extrinsic four functions of universities; and that between the four extrinsic functions and the intrinsic social function of expanded access. *These contradictions must be mediated in order for the two key functions, the education and science functions, to flourish, for success in the network world.* This is the core challenge for the would-be developmental university, particularly in the developing world.

There is a connection between the idea of self-programmability, a capacity at the individual level, and 'learning to learn' or what Castells calls here 'adaptability', the commensurate capacity at the institutional level. These capacities must run in tandem. It does not help if an institution has excellent high-level self-programmable staff, but, in a burst of moral conscience, throws open its doors so that these high-capacity staff are swamped and the science function of research consequently smothered. Nor does it serve if an institution espouses the fine ideals of becoming a research-led institution but does not invest in the kind of staff that can deliver the desired research. These mismatches are well illustrated in the data presented in the chapters that follow, mismatches considerably illuminated by Castells's perspicacious theory in the bracing chapters that precede them. These highlight the growing pains of developmentalism, as universities in Africa struggle to discover what it is to be a developmental university in a developing country. As the theory predicts, and as the empirical chapters that follow show, not all of them will make it.

It remains to connect this account back to the two faces of power, the productive face and the face of domination. As we commented earlier, Castells is insistent that productive power is not the 'good' power, and domination the 'bad' power. The two always come together. As we saw with the example of the European Qualifications Framework, two faces of 'power over' can be observed here. They are exclusion and inclusion. Those with power can so define the standards, or rules for inclusion, that some can be kept out, others let in. But as we also saw with that example, that the way the programmers can wield power is not only exclusionary; they also do so by determining the rules of inclusion and the terms of participating once in. Once the criteria have been set – be they data protocols, intellectual property regulations, or criteria for university rankings, there is always less than optimal wiggle room; how much depends on the relative power of the actor entering the network. Once in, and once the regulations are binding, the only counter-power is to switch, a strategy dramatised by Brexit. Only rarely can the rules be effectively challenged from within.

Again though, care must be taken to see both sides. University rankings confer distinct network advantages over those not ranked or lowly ranked. Castells's theory urges us to see both sides of the coin, not just one, an injunction not always easy to heed, as numbers of the South African responses to Castells in the earlier volume can attest. At Davos in January 2017, this message was underlined from an unlikely source, the secretary general of the Chinese Communist party. In his keynote, Xi Jinping stressed that globalisation is a 'double-edged sword', continuing to say,

'It is true that economic globalisation has created new problems. But this is no justification to write off economic globalisation.' He went on to make a telling analogy: 'Pursuing protectionism is like locking oneself in a dark room. While wind and rain may be kept outside, that dark room will also block light and air' (Xi 2017; see also Gui 2017). Indeed. This betokens a flexibility many did not suspect the mandarins of the Chinese command economy possessed; but, as the third essay of Castells's below will show, he spotted it earlier than most. It is for this, amongst many other shafts of perspicacity, that we continue to return to these neglected pieces, and is why they are published here.

Section 2: Castells in South Africa

Chapter 3

Universities as dynamic systems of contradictory functions

Manuel Castells

Universities are institutions that in all societies, throughout history, have performed basic functions that are implicit in the role that is assigned to them by society through political power or economic influence. These functions, and their combination, result from the specific history of education, science, culture and ideology in each country. However, we can distinguish four major functions at the theoretical level whose specific weight in each historical epoch defines the predominate role of a given university system and the specific task of each university within the overall university system.

Firstly, universities have historically played a major role as ideological apparatuses, rooted in the European tradition of Churchbased universities, either in the statist version of the French, Italian or Spanish universities (closely linked to the religious orders, to the Roman Catholic Church and to the national or local states) or in the more liberal tradition of theological schools of Anglo-Saxon variety, ancestors of the liberal arts colleges. The formation and diffusion of ideology has been, and still is, a fundamental role of universities, in spite of the ideology of their ideology-free role.

However, we must consider this role in the plurality of ideological manifestations. Ideological apparatuses are not purely reproductive machines, as seen in the functionalist theory exemplified by Pierre Bourdieu (1970). They are submitted, as Alain Touraine has shown (1972), to the conflicts and contradictions of society, and therefore they will tend to express – and even amplify – the ideological struggles present in all societies. Thus, both conservative and radical ideologies find their expression in the universities, although the more the ideological hegemony of dominant elites is established in society at large, the more conservative ideologies tend to be predominant in the university, with the expression of radicalism being confined to a minority of the student body as well as to some 'official radicals' among the faculty members, tolerated on behalf of the necessary flexibility of the system. On the other hand, the more the sociopolitical rule of society relies on coercion rather than on consensus, the more universities become the amplifiers of the challenge to domination in society at large, as is often the case, for instance, in Latin America (Nassif et al. 1984). In such cases, universities are still predominately ideological apparatuses, although they work for social change rather than for social conservatism.

Secondly, universities have always been mechanisms of selection of dominant elites. Included in such mechanisms, beyond selection in the strict sense, are the socialisation process of these elites, the formation of the networks for their cohesion, and the establishment of codes of distinction between these elites and the rest of the society. The classic liberal arts college in the Anglo-Saxon tradition, including the Oxbridge version of theological schools, or the state-based European universities, played a fundamental role in the formation of the new elites of the proto-industrial and industrial societies, as family heritage was eroded in its legitimacy as the sole source of social power. Without substitution for the ideological role of universities (and actually frequently overlapping with it), elite selection and the formation of social networks became the backbone of the leading institutions of the university system, actually constructing the internal hierarchy of such systems on the basis of a scale of proximity to the values and standards generated in such institutions. The English system, built around the undisputed dominance of Oxford and Cambridge, is probably

CHAPTER 3 Castells: Universities as dynamic systems of contradictory functions

the quintessence of this elitist role of the university, an extremely important function in any society. But the role played by Ivy League universities in the United States, by the University of Louvain, based on the influence of the Catholic Church in Belgium, or by the University of Moscow in the Soviet Union, is in fact very similar, and reproduces the process of elite selection and formation, while adapting it to the historical and cultural characteristics of each society.

The elite selection function should not be associated necessarily with private universities oriented toward the aristocratic or bourgeois elites. For instance, in France, where the service of the state was traditionally the noblest function, carrying with it the highest power and prestige, the elite university is fully institutionalised in the system of the *grandes écoles*, loosely connected to the university system, but largely independent from it. As is well known, the *grandes écoles* prepare exclusively for civil service, with the graduates committing themselves to at least ten years of service to the state. At the top of the technical *grandes écoles*, the École Polytechnique is technically linked to the French Army, and although the great majority of its graduates have probably never touched a gun, they keep climbing in the hierarchy of army officers, since their 'active duty' generally takes place in the technocracy of the French state.

As a sign of the dominance of the state over private firms in France, the elite of industrialists (but also of leading managers) is often recruited among former graduates of the *grandes écoles*, after they have accomplished their 'tour of duty' in government. Thus, elite-oriented universities are linked to the specific history and composition of elite formation in each country.

The science-oriented university came, in fact, very late in history, in spite of the practice of science in universities in all times, including the achievement of fundamental scientific discoveries in universities that were by and large ideological apparatuses. The first universities focusing on science and research as a fundamental task were the leading German universities in the second half of the 19th century, although there were a few early transfers of the science university model to the United States, particularly the Johns Hopkins University, built around the Medical School.

What seems today to be the third and most obvious function of the university, that is, the generation of new knowledge is, in fact, the exception throughout the world. In many countries it had not yet been fully recognised as a fundamental task by the political institutions and private firms until the coming of the current technological revolution, when the examples of the decisive influence of American science-oriented universities in the new processes of economic growth (the 'Silicon Valley syndrome') won the reputation of being 'useful and productive' for the universities of the Information Age. However, this shift in the conception of the university's role should not overlook the fact that in most of Europe, research has been institutionally separated from higher education and confined into scheduled 'National Scientific Research Centres' of the French, Spanish or Italian type, while the German model (still operating on the principle of separation between teaching and research) has been somewhat more flexible in the interaction between the two functions. Many European governments have assumed the functions of scientific research in specialised institutions – not trusting the universities, which are considered too vulnerable to student pressures. In other areas of the world, particularly Japan, private firms have also distrusted universities as research-oriented organisations, and many have their own in-house research laboratories supported by government funds, directly linked to these firms' needs and orientations.

The popularity of the research-oriented university came from the success of such models in the American university system. Both private universities, modelled after pioneering engineering schools such as the Massachusetts Institute of Technology (MIT), Stanford or Caltech, and public universities endowed by Land Grant policies, particularly in the Midwest and California, played a fundamental role in generating new knowledge and in using it to usher in a new era of industrialisation on the basis of new technologies (Veysey 1965). But, while this model is now vastly

CHAPTER 3 Castells: Universities as dynamic systems of contradictory functions

imitated throughout the world, it is very specific to America (although, as mentioned, it originated in the German university experience), and remains the statistical exception among universities, even in the United States where only about 200 of the 3500 universities and colleges can be considered as knowledge producers at various levels.

The science university in the United States received a major boost from the military needs of government, during both World War II and the Cold War, since new technologies became critical to assess the American military hegemony in the second half of the 20th century. However, the interesting fact is that the science university model became fully developed in America only as an expansion of the role of another model of university, centred on a different function: the professional university.

The professional university is the university focused on a fourth function, perhaps the largest and most important nowadays: the training of the bureaucracy. This has always been a basic function of the university, since its days as a Church school when it specialised in the formation of the Church bureaucrats. And it was certainly the focus of the Napoleonic model of university that inspired most European universities, or of the traditional Chinese university system, structured around the preparation of the Imperial system of examinations as a form of access to the state bureaucracy, and a model that certainly inspired the Japanese and Korean systems. The training of the bureaucracy, be it the Imperial service or the plethora of lawyers that populated the Italian or Spanish administrations, was (and is) a fundamental function of the university in most countries.

Thus, much of the university system is rooted in a statist tradition. However, when the process of industrialisation required the training of a mass of engineers, accountants, economists, social workers and other professions, and when the expansion of the health and education systems demanded millions of teaching staff and medical personnel, universities were called upon to provide both general and specialised training for this massive, skilled labour force. At the same time, they had to equip themselves to accomplish this function, thus becoming large consumers of their own production. The professional university, focusing on the training of the labour forces, was particularly successful in those countries where it was close enough to the industrial world to be useful for the economy, but not so close that it would lose its specific role vis-à-vis the short-term interests of particular segments of the industry.

Thus, the Land Grant universities in the United States created by state governments to fulfil the development tasks of the regional economy were the exemplary experience that opened the path for future professional universities. The agricultural schools of California and Wisconsin or the engineering schools of Michigan and Illinois, generated a culture of close interaction between the university and the business world, providing the ground for the expansion of the role of these universities in the whole realm of science, technology and the humanities, but always closely linked to their original developmental tasks. The American university experience is better represented by the professional model epitomised by MIT or Wisconsin than by elite universities such as Yale or Stanford, regional varieties or reproduction of social elites. The science-oriented university came later, and developed both on the basis of the elite university and of the professional university, until forming a more complex structure in which several functions interact with each other.

However, for the purpose of the analysis presented here, the important fact is that it was the professional university that gave birth to the science university as the needs of the economy made research increasingly important as a strategic tool to enhance productivity and competitiveness.

The ability of universities to generate research while disseminating it into the industrial world was critical for the university to keep its training function together with its scientific function (Wolfe 1972). On the other hand, those universities, as in the socialist countries, that became completely submitted to the needs of the labour market in the context of a planned economy were, in fact, unable to perform their training function, even less their

CHAPTER 3 Castells: Universities as dynamic systems of contradictory functions

research function (Peper 1984). This was because in a world where technology is rapidly changing, the critical training for engineers and technicians is the one that enables them to constantly adapt to new technologies. Engineering training that was obsolete as soon as the young engineer would quit the school, actually making him or her entirely dependent on his or her training on the job – that is exactly the contrary function that the university is supposed to perform, although practical experience is always critical in adapting and applying general knowledge. These four functions (generation and transmission of ideology, selection and formation of the dominant elites, production and application of knowledge, training the skilled labour force) represent the main tasks performed by universities, with different emphases on one or another according to countries, historical periods and specific institutions.

But universities as organisations are also submitted to the pressures of society, beyond the explicit roles they have been asked to assume, and the overall process results in a complex and contradictory reality. In many societies, and certainly in the West, the demand for higher education has reached the status of a social need, regardless of the actual functional requirements of the economy or of the institutions.

This social need, as expression of the aspiration of all societies to upgrade their education, has led to the so-called 'massification of the university system', as the institutions respond to excess demand by downgrading some elements of the system and transforming them into reservoirs of idle labour, a particularly useful function if we consider that this idle labour is in fact formed by potentially restive youth. Thus, an implicit function of modern university systems is that of surplus labour absorption, particularly for those lower-middle class sectors who think their children are entitled to social mobility through the university system. But the more a university system is able to separate this 'warehouse function' from the rest, the more it is both successful and unjust. The more a university system is politically or socially forced to make coexist the implicitly excluded segments with its productive functions, the less effective it is, actually disintegrating into various organisational systems that try to recreate social segregation outside the formal institutional system. Indeed, the critical element in the structure and dynamics of the university system is their ability to combine and make compatible seemingly contradictory functions which have all constituted the system historically and are all probably being required at any given moment by the social interests underlying higher education policies. This is probably the most complex analytical element to convey to policy-makers: namely, that because universities are social systems and historically produced institutions, all their functions take place simultaneously within the same structure, although with different emphases. It is not possible to have a pure, or quasi-pure, model of the university.

Indeed, once the developmental potential of universities has been generally acknowledged, many countries try to build 'technology institutes', 'research universities' and 'university–industry partnerships'. Thus, after centuries of using universities mainly as ideological apparatuses and/ or elite selecting devices, there is a rush of policy-makers and private firms toward the university as a productive force in the informational economy. But universities will always be, at the same time, conflictual organisations, open to the debates of society, and thus to the generation and confrontation of ideologies. The technocratic version of a 'clean', 'purely scientific' or 'purely professional' university is just an historical vision sentenced to be constantly betrayed by historical reality, as the experience of the rather good quality Korean universities, never tamed by the government in spite of its political control, clearly shows. The real issue is not so much to shift universities from the public arena to secluded laboratories or to capitalist board meetings, as to create institutions solid enough and dynamic enough to withstand the tensions that will necessarily trigger the simultaneous performance of somewhat contradictory functions. The ability to manage such contradictions, while emphasising the role of universities in the generation of knowledge and the training of labour in the context of the new requirements of the development

CHAPTER 3 Castells: Universities as dynamic systems of contradictory functions

process, will condition to a large extent the capacity of new countries and regions to become part of the dynamic system of the new world economy.

To assess the role and tasks of Third World universities in the development process we must first consider their specificity against the background of the analytical framework presented in this paper. It is certainly simplistic to consider altogether the diversity of institutions and cultures that are included in the ambiguous term of the 'Third World university'. Yet, with the important exceptions of China and Thailand, the specificity of the university system in the Third World is that it is historically rooted in its colonial past. Such specificity maximises the role of universities as ideological apparatuses in their origins, as well as their reaction against cultural colonialism, but emphasises their ideological dimension in the first stage of their post-independence period.

Indeed, in the case of the British colonies, the report of the Asquith Commission (1945) set up the conditions for the organisation of universities in these colonies around the model of the British civic university. In the case of the French colonies in Africa, a meeting in 1944, held in Brazzaville by the French provisional government, saw the universities as an extension of the French university system, and organised them as preparing the best students to follow their training in the metropolis (Sherman 1990). An even clearer expression of direct cultural imposition is the case of Zaire, where the Louvanium University Centre in Congo was an extension of the Catholic University of Louvain.

Even modern universities today, such as the University of Hong Kong, appear to the visiting faculty members, including this author, as pure British exports, keeping all the imperial flavour of Kipling's writings. As for Latin America, the much earlier independence date makes the origins of universities appear less directly relevant to their current role. However, the statist-religious character of the colonial foundations of the university system still permeates the structure and ideology of contemporary colleges, emphasising ideology and social status over the economic and labour functions of most Latin American universities (Solari 1988).

The recruitment of social elites, first for the colonial administration, later on for the new political elites created with independence, became the fundamental function of universities in the Third World. Because the political regimes were unstable for a long time, universities – in Latin America for two centuries and in Asia and Africa in the second half of the 19th century – became the social matrix of conflicting political elites, conservative, reformist or revolutionary, all competing to lead and shape the nationalist ideology of cultural self-determination and political autonomy. Thus, in many countries, for a long time, the political function of the university (what is called the 'militant university' in Latin America) – merging the ideological function and the formation of new social elites – has been predominant, to the detriment of the educational and economic tasks that the university could have performed. As several university leaders have proclaimed, the 'political preconditions' had first to be set up for universities to be able to proceed with the accomplishment of their specific role. The intellectual and personal drama of some of the best college professors in the Third World is that in order to pursue their academic endeavour, it had to be closely linked to the university system in the dominant countries, thus denying to some extent their cultural identity and taking the risk of being rejected by their own societies and considered alien to their problems and struggles. The contradictions between academic freedom and political militantism, as well as between the drive for modernisation and the preservation of cultural identity, have been a fundamental cause for the loss of the best academic talent in most Third World countries.

Nevertheless, when countries had to face the development tasks in a modern, increasingly integrated world economy in the last 30 years, the need to train skilled labour gave a new impetus to universities as educational institutions. Furthermore, the extension of the traditionally important middle class in Latin America, and the formation of a new professional class in Asia and Africa, both giving priority to the education of their children at the highest possible level, led to a massive expansion of university

CHAPTER 3 Castells: Universities as dynamic systems of contradictory functions

enrolment. In fact, the new nationalist governments used the creation of universities and the increase in the number of students as a substantial measure of their development efforts. The number of university students has dramatically increased in recent years in most countries.

However, much of this increase has taken place in traditional areas of education (law, humanities and social sciences) since the first task of the university system continued to be to recruit and train the administrative and managerial classes on which the political system continued to rely. Along with it, in the most socially oriented regimes, this took place in the expansion of careers destined for social services, particularly education and health. Indeed, educational workers (mainly school teachers) have become one of the most important occupational groups in the lower-middle-classes of developing countries.

There have also been substantial attempts in a number of countries to increase the level of training in the scientific and technical professions, particularly in engineering and in agriculture-related degrees. Yet, such efforts have faced three major obstacles:

- The lack of trained faculty in sufficient numbers who are able to instruct the students in the most recent technology;
- The lack of an adequate level of funding to train students in experimental sciences and professional schools, leading to a teaching programme dominated by verbal communication and excessive numbers of students in the classroom, undermining the quality of the technical training;
- The well-known vicious circle: there are few highly skilled jobs for engineers and scientists in developing countries, because few firms can operate in these countries at a high technological level, because of the lack of skilled manpower.

The net result is that much of the increase in university recruitment goes to careers without direct impact on the development process because they are less expensive, and the failures in the training are less visible. In addition, the quality of technical training is generally very low, not enabling countries to take their place in the world at large. There is of course the possibility of breaking the vicious circle by a deliberate policy of investment in technical higher education. In fact, countries that have engaged in such a policy have received substantial pay-offs. This is the case of South Korea, of China, Taiwan, and to a lesser extent, of Singapore and of Malaysia. The policy involves the recruitment of foreign faculty and/or the recruitment of highly trained nationals attracted to their home country from their positions in more advanced university systems. There is a definite trend in the last decade towards the creation of new 'technology institutes' in a number of countries to emphasise the need to train skilled engineers, scientists and technicians. However, only some of these institutes live up to the expectations generated by their flashy names and their brand new buildings: those investing enough resources in good faculty and modern equipment to update the quality of their training. Thus, only relatively rich countries are able to provide the necessary resources to upgrade their labour force, creating a new gap within the Third World.

While the training function of Third World universities is slowly making progress, at least in some areas, the science function is increasingly lagging in relationship to the acceleration of scientific research in the advanced countries, particularly in research and development in the critical areas of new technologies. This is both for structural reasons and for institutional causes linked to the specificity of Third World universities.

Structural reasons have to do with the cumulative character of the process of uneven scientific development. Centres of excellence that take the lead attract the best researchers who obtain the best equipment and material conditions, being able to attract the best students who end up forming a closely connected network. Thus, most of the best Third World scientists migrating to the United States or Europe (or staying in these countries after completing their doctorates) do so because it is the only way for them to continue to do research in the cutting edge of their speciality.

CHAPTER 3 Castells: Universities as dynamic systems of contradictory functions

In fact, salary and working conditions appear to be secondary factors in relation to the basic condition: to belong to an advanced scientific milieu. This is partly linked to the amount of resources devoted to research and development by advanced countries. But there are also important institutional conditions, linked to the specificity of Third World universities, that make difficult their performance as centres of generation of knowledge. The need to preserve cultural identity, and the tensions created by the extreme politicisation of universities in overcrowded conditions, make it extremely difficult to manage the co-existence of the ideological and political functions with the scientific activity of the university. The necessary distance and independence of academic research vis-á-vis the immediate pressures of political conflicts become literally impossible when students, and some faculty, are engaged in changing the world or in affirming themselves as their main goal. In addition, the existence of large segments of the university population that are simply treated as surplus labour makes it rather difficult to maintain the respect for scientific activity (whose pay-offs are necessarily in the long term) on the part of students and faculty who are relatively marginal to the society or from university administrators whose main concern is to keep order and maintain the system operating in formal terms, regardless of its actual output in the generation and transmission of knowledge.

The inability to manage contradictory functions within the same system has led a number of countries to concentrate their efforts in a few technical universities (many of them of new creation), while leaving much of the existing university system to its own decomposition. This can be a short-term solution for the training of some technical personnel in certain specialities, but it will hardly respond to the needs of the scientific university. One of the key elements in the development of the universities as centres of discovery and innovation is precisely the cross-fertilisation between different disciplines (including the humanities), together with their detachment vis-á-vis the immediate needs of the economy. Without the self-determination of the scientific community in the pursuit of the goals of scientific research, there will be no discovery. There is certainly a major need for the linkage between science, technology and industrial applications. But it is only possible to apply the science that exists. And there will only be scientific discovery, and connection with the world centres of scientific discovery, if universities are complete systems, bringing together technical training, scientific research and humanistic education, since the human spirit cannot be piecemealed to obtain only the precise technical skills required for enhancing the quality of regional crops. Thus, the refuge of the productive functions of the university system in a few, secluded technical schools can only be a temporary measure to rebuild a complete higher education system on the basis of additional resources, better management and adequate connections with the world's scientific centres, in respect of the identity of each culture.

Universities in the Third World are making dramatic progress in quantitative terms but are still unable by and large to perform their developmental function. Even university systems with great scientific excellence, such as the Indian or Chinese university systems, are falling behind those systems that have been able to manage the interaction between science, technology, economy and society. The ideological and political origins of most Third World universities cannot be ignored but should not be permitted to suffocate the necessary evolution of the university toward its central role in modernisation and development. If Third World countries are also to enter the Information Age and reject an increasingly marginal role in the world system, development policies must include the impulse and transformation of higher education systems as a key element of the new historical project.

If the substantial enhancement of university systems is critical for the development process in the new world economy, and if most countries are unable to mobilise the necessary resources to that end, it follows that the new frontier of international aid passes through the territory of higher education. However, the effectiveness of such aid will be conditioned by the ability to design policies that take into account the specificity of universities as institutions, and are able at the same time to link the science

CHAPTER 3 Castells: Universities as dynamic systems of contradictory functions

and training functions closely with the needs and goals of the economy and society.

It would seem that in most countries, university systems overwhelmed by numbers and handicapped by lack of resources and excessive ideologisation cannot be restructured in their totality in the short term. Thus, this imposes the notion of selective aid, either concentrating resources in the best of the existing academic centres and/or creating new universities supported by national governments, private firms and international institutions. Yet, in both cases it is crucial that universities are conceived as complete academic centres of learning and research, with all levels of training (undergraduate and graduate, including doctorate) and with as many areas of study as possible, certainly mixing science, technology, humanities, social sciences and professional schools. The cross-fertilisation between different areas of specialisation, with flexible programmes that emphasise the capacity of students to think, find the necessary information, and be able to reprogramme themselves in the future seems to be the most effective pedagogic formula according to most experts of education who are open to the new characteristics of technology and management in the advanced economy. At the same time, the co-existence of different levels of training (graduate and undergraduate) makes possible the interaction between advanced students dedicating themselves to research and teaching, and professionally oriented students, future skilled workers, who will receive some of their training from innovation-oriented teachers, able to open up their horizons beyond the current state of specialised knowledge.

The new Third World universities must also emphasise research, both basic and applied, since this will become the necessary ground for the upgrading of the country's productive system. Research must be connected both to the world's scientific networks and to the specific needs and productive structure of the country. This probably requires the existence of specialised organisations that must be part of the university system, organising both connections toward the world and toward the economic structure of the country (information centres, international exchange programmes, bureaus of technology transfer, bureaus of industrial or agricultural extension, university-enterprise networks, etc.).

Institutional reforms of universities, or the creation of new universities, should be undertaken under co-operative agreements between international institutions (such as the United Nations or the World Bank) and national governments of the host country, with the support and participation of private firms interested in the upgrading of the technological basis of countries or world regions. They should simultaneously foster institutional innovation (the setting up of new institutions or the reform of the existing ones to make them able to manage the contradictory requirements of various university functions), and provide the necessary resources for the upgrading of the system. Foremost among the needed resources is the human capital represented by faculty and researchers of top quality, fully integrated in the world's scientific and technological networks. While in the long term the new Third World universities should be able to compete for resources in the open world market, as well as generating their own high-quality academic personnel, in the coming years the sudden improvement in the quality of the universities will probably have to come from a combination of several policies:

- The training or retraining of young faculty and doctoral students in centres of excellence of advanced countries, after taking the necessary measures to provide them with the scientific and professional conditions to receive them in their home countries after their training period.
- The recruitment of nationals of Third World countries established in the universities of advanced societies, offering them equal or better conditions of work than the ones they enjoy in the universities where they are employed. Aid programmes should target specific individuals and provide the necessary support for endowed chairs and research centres in areas of priority.
- The temporary use of visiting foreign faculty in strategic fields of research under strictly planned conditions, conducive to the

formation of a research group in the Third World university, and to the continuation of the linkage between the newly established group and the visiting faculty once they return to the centre of excellence from where they were recruited. In other words, the critical matter here is to use visiting faculty as priming devices for the setting up of linkages between less developed and more developed university centres.
- The use of talent existing in the private firms and public sector of Third World countries, as adjunct professors able to provide their experience and knowledge to a university world that had been generally ignored because of the low social and economic status of the university system.
- The establishment of joint research centres and training programmes between technologically advanced private firms (either national or multinational) and national universities supported by international organisations. These mutually beneficial agreements, of which there are already numerous examples, should be integrated in a broader programme of institution building, instead of being kept, as is generally the case, under the close control of the participant corporation.

Once the two basic elements of a good university are established, that is, a proper institutional setting and high quality faculty, material resources in terms of equipment and physical plant can be provided without being wasted. Only after such infrastructure exists, can recruitment of students begin and the necessary funds for fellowships and tuition be facilitated.

It is obvious that such programmes of multilateral investment in higher education are expensive and will only yield substantial results in the medium term, at the earliest in a ten-year period. It is also true that such is the case for most development programmes investing in infrastructure. The key issue is to understand that the most important infrastructure in the economy of our age is the human brain and the collective capacity of a given society to link up all its brains with the brains of the world.

Still, it is an expensive programme that, given the permanent limit of scarce resources, will have to concentrate in some centres of higher education that operate, at the same time, as models for other systems, and as the providers of informational inputs for entire regions of the world. Some countries are large enough to receive aid directly to their existing national institutions, from which large numbers of people will benefit and major natural and industrial resources will be generated (China, India, Indonesia, Nigeria, Brazil and Mexico).

In other instances, it will probably be advisable to build regional international universities (such as the University of Central America, the South East Asian Institute of Technology, the West African International University) that will concentrate financial, technological and human resources in a few centres of excellence, able to generate world-class research and training in a few years. However, the experience of several international university centres (in some of which this author has been a faculty member) shows the absolute need to anchor international universities in the national universities of the region, instead of bypassing them. It is the essential condition to be truly useful to the economies and institutions of each country, instead of creating a pool of graduates that generally dissolve themselves in the international networks or become marginal in their own countries upon their return. A possible solution to the problems I have mentioned could be the absorption of high-quality faculty members back into the national universities of their own countries, after they have spent a limited time (five years for instance) in joint centres, or regional universities, formed by association between the universities of the countries in the region. Thus, the joint centre could become an element of integration and cross-fertilisation between the various national universities, selecting the best students, and being formed by faculty of the national universities on a rotating basis.

In any case, specific organisational forms can be found if the basic principle is assumed: it is necessary to concentrate international and national resources in a few centres (either in large countries or in regional groupings of countries) that will operate

CHAPTER 3 Castells: Universities as dynamic systems of contradictory functions

in direct connection with the development needs of their societies and economies. International aid (both public and private) should be channelled through these institutions, with strict control over the proper use of the funds in respect of the national sovereignty and cultural identity of the countries involved.

While it is relatively easy to agree on the importance of improving higher education for the development of the Third World, the question arises of who could be interested in supporting such a major undertaking and why countries or firms would be ready to assume the substantial economic cost and political effort required for such a new form of development policy.

At the turn of the millennium, humankind could envisage a bright future after the end of the Cold War and the demise of the Communist threat, counting on the development process that is well engaged in most of Asia, and expecting the current technological revolution to yield its promises, as yet unfulfilled, of a dramatic enhancement in economic productivity. We seem indeed to be on the edge of not the end, but of the beginning of history, if by history we understand the opportunity for the human species to fully develop its biological and cultural capacities.

Yet, at the same time there are substantial pitfalls in our social organisation, if we consider the extent of economic inequality and political oppression at the world level and the lack of harmony between economic growth and ecological conservation. Since most of these evils take root in the context of poverty and underdevelopment prevailing in large areas of what is still called the Third World, it would seem that the construction of a more stable, more promising international order in the aftermath of the Cold War requires the multilateral tackling of the development process on a planetary basis. Advanced countries, and their private firms, cannot thrive in a shrunken planet, concentrating their technology and their resources on a diminishing segment of humankind. And this is for several fundamental reasons:

- Morally, our model of society will be judged by our children

by its capacity to look beyond the immediate self-interest of each one of its individual members.
- Functionally, the growing deterioration of natural resources and collective public health, directly linked to poverty and mass desperation, will affect the whole of humankind: the Peruvian cholera epidemic is only the beginning of what could be a return to the medieval plagues if living conditions are not improved in the sprawling shanty towns of the Third World.
- Politically, widespread misery and functional marginality for countries and regions in the midst of a world marked by economic affluence and technological miracles, transmitted by the electronic media, will feed ideological fundamentalism, fanaticism and terrorism, as forms of negation by the excluded against the exclusionary practices of the dominant countries.
- Economically, the potential gap between the fast rate of technological innovation and the slower growth of markets can only be solved in the long term by including new markets in the world economy – new people with new needs to be satisfied. Both the former Second World and the Third World have to be brought into a unified, dynamic world economy, in which today's aid is in fact the investment for tomorrow, in a process similar to the mutual benefits brought to the United States and Western European economies by the Marshall Plan after World War II. A much broader Marshall Plan, multilaterally financed and controlled on a planetary scale, is necessary to integrate the whole of humankind in the development process, thus ensuring material progress and social stability for decades to come. The development of the Third World is in the economic self-interest of the Organisation for Economic Co-operation and Development (OECD) countries and their corporations. Now, if we take seriously the analyses pointing toward the formation of a new economy, in which the ability to generate and process information is a key to productivity, it will not be possible to integrate Third World countries in a dynamic world economy without creating the necessary infrastructure

in higher education. Because research and education policies take time to bear their splendid fruits, such policies must be placed at the forefront of international aid at the present time, when the seeds of a new world order are being sown.

Notes

This paper formed part of a larger report 'The University System: Engine of development in the new world economy', presented at a World Bank Seminar on Higher Education and Development held in Kuala Lumpur, Malaysia, in 1991 (Castells 1991). The paper as it appears in this volume, was first published in 2001 as 'Universities as Dynamic Systems of Contradictory Functions' in the book *Challenges of Globalisation: South African debates with Manuel Castells* (Muller et al. 2001).

Chapter 4

The role of universities in development, the economy and society

Manuel Castells

If we take seriously the notion that we live in a global knowledge economy and in a society based on processing information – as universities primarily are – then the quality, effectiveness and relevance of the university system will be directly related to the ability of people, society and institutions to develop. In the context of a technological revolution and of a revolution in communication, the university becomes a central actor of scientific and technological change, but also of other dimensions: of the capacity to train a labour force adequate to the new conditions of production and management. Universities also become the critical source of the equalisation of chances and democratisation of society by making possible equal opportunities for people. This is not only a contribution to economic growth, it is a contribution to social equality or, at least, lesser inequality. The university's ability to develop new cultures is an additional factor: that is, to be the source of cultural renewal and cultural innovation linked to the new forms of living we are entering. Finally, the university has also been dramatically affected by technological change itself. As an institution that processes information, its own information and communication technologies are deeply affecting the functioning and the culture of the university, sometimes without the full knowledge of what is happening and without controlling these processes. Yet, in spite of all these challenges, possibilities and opportunities for the university system, in many cases universities continue to be corporatist and bureaucratic, defending their own interests – particularly in terms of the professors – and extremely rigid in their functioning in terms of their administration.

To try to understand the processes of change, I will take a wide perspective of the different types of universities that have appeared throughout history, and that combine in our current experience. It is useful to see the universities as fulfilling different functions which are accentuated in some universities at some moments of history, but that, to some extent, constantly combine and re-combine, and that depend on the emphasis on one or the other function. Hence my notion of the university system – not just universities – because different units serve different functions and the whole system has to combine these different functions.

Historically, universities started largely as producers of values and social legitimation. All the major universities in the world started as schools of theology: Bologna, the first in Europe, and then Cambridge, Oxford, Harvard, Salamanca, the Sorbonne and so on. As theological schools, they were producers of values and social legitimation. Other non-religious universities played a similar role in producing, for instance, imperial values in the case of some major universities, justifying domination and Western superiority in the colonial world.

The second function, and in historical terms equally as important as the production of values, was the selection of the elite and the establishment of a stratification in society, making sure that the elites would go through the selection functions in some of these universities. This function is extremely important both then and now. The Ivy League institutions in the United States, or the *grandes écoles* in France, or Cambridge and Oxford in England, are somewhat better than other universities, but not so much better as to account for the fact that 90% of the elites that govern business and the polity come from these universities. The selection of elites is therefore extremely important, more so than the other functions.

CHAPTER 4 Castells: The role of universities

Then the third function, also in historical sequence, was the training of the labour force. This saw the emergence of the professional university – particularly important were the schools of medicine, law and engineering. Engineering schools were critical for the development of industrialisation. Examples include the School of Lausanne (one of the top engineering schools in Europe), Caltech as a pure engineering university in the US, and Imperial College to some extent in the UK.

There is another type of university which is not among those already mentioned, namely the science university. This is the university in which the primary function and emphasis is on the production of knowledge, of scientific knowledge. This is a very late invention that took root in the German universities of the second half of the 19th century. Humboldt was the first to assume that the role of science production was the primary function of the university. This idea was only taken up in the United States much later. The first university to copy the German model was Johns Hopkins – not Harvard or MIT. In the United States, universities that were the so-called Land Grant public universities also developed as science-based universities but with applications into society; for instance, Berkeley started as an agricultural school and Michigan as a mining university. The fourth function is therefore science – science specifically to develop particular industries that were very important for the country.

Fifth then, in historical sequence, are the 'generalist' universities, universities that came to elevate the education level of the population at large, bringing in to the universities at least 20–25% of the propertied classes. These were the universities that developed in France, Italy, Spain and Latin America after World War II, and then in Africa after their independence. 'Everybody should be able to go to university' was the thinking, and it was important to keep the other functions in relatively separate institutions, so as not to be overwhelmed by mass education. Each country developed systems in which the elite would be formed differently and in which science would be produced differently. In the case of Europe, they separated the research centres from the universities to create national research centres, and so on. This generalist type of university is what I call the mass teaching university: not to provide training but to provide degrees, with degrees granting access to the labour market and allowing graduates to be trained on the job.

The final function is what I call the entrepreneurial universities. These universities focus on innovation and the connection between the world of business and that of science and technology. The classic example of this type is Stanford, which deliberately organised itself to be a great scientific university while at the same time connecting constantly to the business world. MIT also moved decisively in this direction, as have many other universities in the world – in Singapore, most notably. The notion is an interaction, a very close interaction, between excelling in science and technology, and at the same time being able to develop an entrepreneurial system.

All of these functions are combined in different ways throughout the entire university system; one of the key issues is how to articulate these different functions without downplaying one or the other. For instance, it is obvious that not every university can be a research university. But at the same time, all universities have to have access to the research centres that exist in the university system for specific purposes, and they may develop a small nuclei of research that is, on the one hand, linked to the needs of society and the economy and, on the other, fed by the networks of research that can be constructed in the entire university system. Moreover, because we are in a global economy and in a global research system the notion of universities being stand-alone, major research centres is gone. The critical thing is to be in the networks of global production of knowledge, of research and innovation. For that, what you need is not to be the best or even the best in every aspect. You need to have a ticket to enter one of the networks; you have to provide something that is not necessarily the best in the world but is interesting enough that all the other participants in the global research network of one particular field want you to be in the network. For this, of course,

CHAPTER 4 Castells: The role of universities

the internet is crucial. You don't necessarily have to go to other research centres; you can spread your results, connect and work in a global network of research without necessarily having to spend every two years in another country.

In the current condition of the global knowledge economy, knowledge production and technological innovation become the most important productive forces. Therefore, without at least some level of a national research system composed of universities, the private sector and public research centres, no country can really participate in the global knowledge economy.

Resources are not forever. What does endure are people with needs, and if you have and develop talented people, you then have the most important resource in the form of the human mind. There are endless examples of how betting on the human mind has been decisive for the development of countries. The East Asian countries that were extremely poor after World War II, and are now 'tigers', all have one thing in common: a very good education system at all levels that is not only based on the traditional value of education, but also on government investment in the quality and quantity of education, and then later based on investment by companies and private universities. Korea, Taiwan, Singapore and Hong Kong all have great education systems and very good university systems precisely because they prioritised education. There is a direct correlation between the capacity to invest in education and universities at the level of economic growth as well as human development, which is fundamental.

In addition, of course, universities have a major role in producing a quality labour force, not only in knowledge but also in terms of the quality of labour. In our type of economy and society, the key quality of the labour force depends on its education, and the labour force's education depends on the educators; in other words, the quality depends on the educators.

The educators are those who have to be trained by the universities of quality; without that – even if we build schools, even with laptops for every child – if there are no good teachers, there can be no good education. And that requires all kinds of things, including the working conditions of the teachers. We often talk about Finland as an exemplary case. What is the most important thing about Finland? It is the quality of the education system and how well teachers are paid and respected in society.

This factor starts with being well trained at university level. Moreover, the type of training that we need these days is what I call 'learning to learn', which is the constant re-programming of skills in a constantly changing economic, technological and socio-cultural environment. All the information is on the internet – if you know how to look for it and what to do with it. We no longer have to implant knowledge in young people's minds that will quickly become obsolete. Therefore, their ability to constantly recycle knowledge and skills requires two things: first, that education is basically creating what I call the 'self-programmable ability' of everybody to change in many different directions all through their professional lives; and, second, retraining throughout the life cycle which can only be done in one way – via distance education through the internet, which can be of high quality and not necessarily at lower costs because it is expensive to do it well.

Therefore, the role of distance education becomes critical because it allows two things: first, to constantly 'recycle' people all through their professional lives; and, second, to immediately teach the professionals who train the nurses, the rural doctors, the teachers. The notion that we have to teach children so well that, in 25 years' time, we will have a qualified labour force is self-defeating.

Developing countries have to leap-frog dramatically, and you can only leap-frog in education by using virtual education to teach those who are already in their jobs. In this respect, South Africa has great potential because of the University of South Africa (Unisa) and other institutions. However, their internet teaching is not very advanced. Internet teaching is the only way forward; other ways are inefficient and burdensome, and ultimately result in an inferior level of education, and there's no reason why it should be like this.

Another possible function of the university is, in our current context, the production and consolidation of values – ethical and personal values – and the formation of flexible personalities. What is meant by flexible personalities? We live in a constantly changing world, accelerating change. We need to develop pedagogic models that don't give precise instructions on how to behave in life, but instead provide people with the capacity to adeptly reorganise their lives in response to the incessant transformation of the living environment. At the same time, flexible personalities are anchored in certain values so that they don't fall apart. Students need to be trained to have a few, fixed values – don't abuse others, don't be greedy, etc. – not a general civic education system. We have to be the role models and demonstrate values by setting an example. In short, all that is required are a set of values and at the same time flexible personalities – that is the ideal combination. This is a fundamental function of the university which is usually not taken seriously by any university that I know of, although some are starting to think about it – particularly in business schools that have realised that without ethics in business, you end up doing bad business that collapses financial markets.

Universities increasingly emphasise interdisciplinarity. This is a bad word in many academic circles, and yet this is what our economy, our science and our technologies demand these days. Everybody talks about bio-informatics and new materials – disciplines on the borders of traditional disciplines. What makes interdisciplinarity so obvious and yet so difficult? Disciplines are like peace treaties between warring factions, so delicate that departments and disciplines cannot be changed at will. Interdisciplinarity is only practised in some disciplines, for instance, in communications, or in city and regional planning. I always end up in these disciplines simply because I feel freer; I don't have to demonstrate whether I am a sociologist or an economist or a political scientist. But try to recruit a political scientist in a sociology department. It is therefore essential that interdisciplinarity is promoted by the university itself. The University of Southern California has a policy to reward interdisciplinarity: if you are interdisciplinary, you get a higher salary. There is also a special chair for interdisciplinary academics. In other words, interdisciplinarity is another critical concern.

Then there is the notion of public and private universities: experience shows that this is not the most relevant matter responsible for efficiency in the university. There are great public universities in the world – Berkeley, Michigan, Cambridge, Oxford. In Europe all the universities are public; only some strange, marginal universities are private. In the United States there is no real difference in quality. There is Stanford, but there is also Berkeley; there is Harvard, but there is also the University of Michigan; there is Wisconsin – all equally good. The private institutions might be more influential in selecting elites, but they are not better. The difference lies in how bureaucratic a university is, how flexible it is, how managerial it is. Private universities which are bureaucratic, and I will not name names, are in fact not competitive. Public universities that are managed efficiently, as was the case at the University of California at one time, can be extremely competitive. How universities are managed is critical. Furthermore, whether a university in legal terms is public or private is not as essential as the university being geared towards the public interest. Institutions may be private but still operate in the public interest. Universities that don't operate in the public interest are businesses, and pay the price for it, in taxation and many other ways. Universities can be private or public but work towards the public interest, accessing both government and private funds, but on this basis.

Finally, there is the notion of the technological transformation of the university – which has to be tackled seriously. We are already in a hybrid system; we are not in either a face-to-face or a virtual university. Face-to-face universities are partly virtual because of the internet – we email our students, we are constantly connected. But all this is happening without any real policy, with no transformation of the university's pedagogic method. Introducing e-learning – not just distance learning – as a critical element in the learning environment at face-to-face universities is as essential as using it in virtual universities. All this depends on the university's capacity to maintain its autonomy. Universities are the last space of freedom, relatively, in society and it is essential to preserve that space not only for scientific but also for social and political reasons. At the same time, we have to earn this autonomy and this freedom every day and use it in the public interest, not in the defence of our privileges. If we combine these two things, we can continue the tradition that started a thousand years ago. If we don't, pressure from society will destroy the university as a space for reflection and innovation.

Note

This chapter is an edited transcript of a lecture delivered by Manuel Castells at the University of the Western Cape, Cape Town, South Africa, on 7 August 2009.

Chapter 5

Rethinking development in the global information age

Manuel Castells

The topic of my lecture today came about when I was trying to rethink development on the basis of a number of empirical studies, interacting with different conceptions and different approaches to development. I try to cut across the distinction between theory and empirical research in society because I always have in mind what this means in terms of policy, politics and change. This is based, on the one hand, on some reflection informed by theoretical frameworks and, on the other, by observation, and making sure the observation modifies the theory. I do this because my principle is that when theory conflicts with observation, you don't throw away the observation: you throw away the theory. We did in fact 'throw away' a number of theories.

What I am going to present is not the surviving theories but the theoretical approaches and insights we reached after the process of filtering what we were thinking on the basis of observing.

We know that 'development' has multiple meanings. This is important: it's not just a terminological debate. Words matter. The world has been differentiating between 'developed' and 'underdeveloped' and 'developing' for a long time; and no one knows exactly what these terms mean anymore.

Sometimes countries, like Singapore, still argue that they should be considered developing because that would mean United Nations subsidies. In fact, these categories don't work, and certainly don't work in a world in which everything is connected through networks which, as we know, both include and exclude. Everything is connected but much is disconnected. Therefore the 'developing' and 'underdeveloped' and 'developed' depends on where you are: in which neighbourhood, at which time and how and why. That is a completely different notion to the one that created this distinction between what used to be the 'developed', meaning the West, and 'underdeveloped', meaning the rest, the huge majority of the world, with Japan being the exception. People kept saying, 'They are developed, but they are not Western' until someone decided they are actually Western because they use technology. Frankly, intellectually and epistemologically speaking, all these categories have largely been dominated by Eurocentrism and colonialism, justifying domination through the notions of civilised and uncivilised, and so on.

Consequently, we decided to cut through this to see what is actually happening in the world. My analysis here will try to go beyond the usual approaches, which are either descriptive (these are the processes of development), analytical (how this can be understood), normative (that which development should be), or apparently technical (which in fact says, 'No, no, no, we're not doing philosophy or ideology here; we are just technical: economic growth or social development'). In fact, values – fundamental values – are all included in the measures of calculation: they are embedded. Thus the way we calculate already conveys a certain number of values and assumptions.

To start with, I provide my own definition of development, which I posit as ideologically free in the sense that it can be filled in with different ideologies, and therefore it is not my ideology: you all can insert your ideology and it works. It is also open-ended in terms of content. I define development as the self-defined process – self is important – by which humans, as a collective, enhance their well-being by creating the structural conditions for the expanded reproduction of the process of development itself, so enhancing their well-being and, at the same time, creating the structural conditions for this process to go on.

CHAPTER 5 Castells: Rethinking development in the global information age

However, the values that inform such development goals – the Millennium Development Goals, for instance – can be very different. For instance, for some, economic growth and accumulation of material wealth as measured by GDP is the critical thing: Let's simplify life; this is development, and then the rest will follow. What was ultimately implied, when it was not blatantly ideological, were Western values; and these so-called Western values were Anglo-Saxon and northern European, and would certainly not include Italy, Spain or Portugal. So, for some, this is enough: measure development as GDP. But we know that GDP is a completely arbitrary measure that was, historically, a provisional statistical measure that Simon Kuznets developed in 1938 in the United States simply to measure how the economy was doing during the Depression. It was a Prohibition artefact, abandoned later on for more sophisticated measures. But people say, 'We have one way to measure everything all together', without considering the price, the floatation of prices or other forms of value. Since then, GDP has become a political 'god' in the world. Any problem you have, you increase the GDP, then you are okay and the rest is subjective. But is the GDP objective? No. GDP is a statistical measure that is historically situated, which has been refined and reformed many, many times to the point that we now don't know exactly what the definition of GDP is, or on which calculations it is based.

For instance, we were talking earlier with a group of African development scholars about the notion that last year Nigeria suddenly became the largest economy in Africa, overtaking South Africa, because new calculations came out. New calculations from where, by whom and under which conditions? I am sure that there are all kinds of statistical warfare going on about this in terms of national pride, without measuring how much personal, human and ecological disaster is involved in this notion of overtaking South Africa with a new measure of GDP.

For others, human well-being is development. But what is human well-being? This point normally starts the discussion. For yet others, you cannot talk about development without sustainability.

But then, what is sustainability? One counter-argument is, 'Do birds or animals have more rights than poor people, who actually have to eat?' What are the different dimensions of sustainability? Again, it is subjective: it is when people consider, as I do, that the conservation of the liveability of the species on the planet is a fundamental value – more important than economic growth – that sustainable development becomes the most important aspect of development. (By the way, I always say the liveability of the 'human species', not the 'planet'. We are not saving the planet. The planet will be okay without us. It will in fact be much better without us. What we are defending is ourselves *on* the planet, not the actual planet.)

Others directly express the values behind the goals of development, and they just say 'development'. Amartya Sen and others focus on human dignity. Development is human dignity: dignity is development.

I will try to cover each one of these categories and assumptions. My purpose being analytical, I will propose a typology of meanings of development that, together, could shed some light on strategies and policies to improve the well-being of humans and their relationship to our environment, which is the only thing that ultimately really matters.

Let's take economic growth defined, as we said, as GDP. There is a whole history of more refined calculations of GDP: more refined but more difficult because when you start including the issue of productivity and how to measure it, and the issue of value, then how do you start measuring services, and what kind of services do you measure, under what conditions? Do we include the value that global financial markets assign to companies and to production in the value that we create? These values assigned by global financial markets are actually very important because the value of a company depends on that financial valuation. But this financial valuation depends, as Paul Volcker has repeatedly pointed out, on perception. It is not that there is reality and then the perception: perception is the reality.

So, how do we include financial valuation in the calculation

CHAPTER 5 Castells: Rethinking development in the global information age

of GDP? This has a very concrete impact on the amount of wealth that the society generates. For instance, in the financial crisis of 2008, two thirds of the wealth in the world was wiped out; it disappeared. How did it disappear? It disappeared from the financial calculations. But at the same time, the financial calculations were determining the way the economy was performing. So, if you have a company and suddenly you are completely devalued and you cannot borrow against the value of the company, then that is a very real effect. But what happens to the GDP depends on perception, and on the calculation of the GDP. In other words, what appears to be a direct, no-problem approach to defining development – for example, let's just measure material wealth – becomes problematic the moment you actually start doing it, when all kinds of methodological, theoretical and statistical calculations arise as problems.

At one point, some well-intentioned United Nations experts started to say, 'Well, GDP does not really measure a number of other dimensions, such as quality of life, an area that depends on basically public goods like health, education, subsistence services, urban infrastructure, etc.' All these aspects were conceptualised as human development. The Human Development Index was basically constructed to include all these public goods and the provision of these public goods. People then even said, 'Well, why don't we do something even more sophisticated that includes the actual happiness of people, not just their well-being?' Bhutan created the Gross National Happiness Index in 1972. Well, why not? If it is human development, what about human happiness? Is that development or not development? And it sounds terrific, except how is it actually calculated? The Bhutan Happiness Index is actually a survey that asks people everywhere in the country how they feel. Thus it is not too different from public opinion polls on the relationship of poverty to government policies. And then along the way, they added a few other things. I like this idea that you have to measure something else.

The fact remains, however, that the fundamental approach to human development in terms of the Northern development approach depends on measurability. Everything that we can measure in terms of economic growth is regarded as development; and then that which we cannot measure, but which is still important – like education – is human development.

The key element in my perspective is that the terms define some relationship between economic growth and human development, particularly under the conditions in which the economic growth is largely dependent on productivity growth generated by a much more productive aggregate production function (I will come back to this later). This means not only the capacity to introduce information and knowledge into production, but also the capacity to operate a much more effective feedback loop between economic growth and human development. The notion that we are in an information and knowledge economy can be absolutely misleading. Not because information and knowledge are not important: they have always been important. There has been no economy and no society in the world in which wealth and power don't depend on information and knowledge. They have always been absolutely critical factors for wealth generation and power generation. What has changed is something called the information and communication technology (ICT) revolution, meaning microelectronics-based ICTs, with all their consequences: the ability to create organisational forms; the infrastructure and the rapidity of processing information, transforming it into knowledge; and using these transformations into knowledge to make actual changes in the production system. That is the difference.

How one actually processes better information is not just about technology. Technology is what affords the possibility of this type of effective processing. The important thing is that the human mind – where the knowledge is embodied – has to be capable of managing this capacity to process information, generate knowledge and implement it in different dimensions of human activity. Ultimately, all of these goals influence the ability of society not just to generate technology for social productivity, but to generate what people call human capital. I don't like the

CHAPTER 5 Castells: Rethinking development in the global information age

term but let's say it refers to human subjects able to further their understanding and their adaptation of information and knowledge in every domain of human activity. This is ultimately about the quality of human labour in the broadest sense: not only the worker but the entire society. This certainly entails education, but all kinds of education, not just higher education, because if we have people in higher education who are uneducated at the primary and secondary level, we don't really have education. And it isn't just about education but also health, because if we are completely neurotic and sick, we will not be able to process anything even if we are highly educated. Thus higher education requires health: not personal health with your doctor; it is also about the environment. We have epidemics regardless of how good your health is in your individual existence. The issue is how this impacts the overall quality of humans as producers and creators of everything.

However, this is not just about the actual embodiment in human labour of the ability to generate and produce. It is also about the social conditions and the conditions of stability. We use all of this to generate endless wars and terrors between us. The intelligence and the information that we have embodied in our capacity to create becomes at the same time a capacity to destroy. The moment you say that information development is at the source of enhanced productivity, and enhanced productivity comes from the interaction and the feedback loop between actual material production and the conditions of existence that become a key element in the productivity of this material production, the moment you say that, you have to start including all kinds of elements which have a synergistic relationship between material production and the conditions of material production, which are, at the same time, the well-being of society. This is what I call informational development.

This particular connection and this model of information development is the most effective model for generating productivity and competitiveness. This is something that I developed years ago and that we tried to test. It was originally based on my empirical analysis of two very different contexts in South East Asia, which was really about this feedback loop between the public sector that was providing good quality labour and stability, and then an economic sector that was extremely competitive at the global level. My book on the comparative development of Hong Kong and Singapore and my work on Finland, captured in the book I did with Pekka Himanen, entitled *The Information Society and the Welfare State: The Finnish Model*, shows exactly this synergistic relationship.

Then there is a fourth dimension of development: sustainable development, which includes the capacity to make both economic growth and human development compatible with the conservation of the liveability of humans in our only home, planet Earth, at the micro and macro levels.

And then, finally, there is another dimension of development, which is the holistic concept of development. This concept is normative. It says what we consider desirable in terms of values – such as human rights, animal rights, equality, gender, empowerment and gender equality, solidarity and the ability to live in a multicultural world through the reciprocal enrichment of diverse identities without cancelling any of them out – but at the same time moves beyond the exclusive dynamics of identities. Peace and democracy: these are encompassed by this idea of human dignity that includes and presupposes all the other business of development. It actually isn't a different concept: it presupposes all the rest. It's not descriptive and it's not analytical: it's normative. In that sense, it means that development must increase the quality of life, must be sustainable and must not sacrifice human dignity: in fact, economic growth should actually support and make possible human dignity. That is the way the different elements are interconnected.

I will try to look carefully at each one of these key elements and their interactions to see what the conditions are for these processes of development or the possible synergistic relationship between them. I will end by looking in some detail at what for me is the absolutely key element in the whole discussion: the

CHAPTER 5 Castells: Rethinking development in the global information age

process of implementation of any developmental approach and the agency involved in the implementation, because development is as good as the agency that enacts development.

Any empirically grounded theoretical and policy discussion must be specific to the context in which it operates. And in our space/time, this is what we call the global information age. We cannot talk about development in general: we are talking about the specific conditions within which our world operates today. And this is the global information age. The global information age is characterised by the process of globalisation. Globalisation is not internationalisation and it is not the world economy: these have existed for centuries. It is the process by which a given system, be it economic or cultural, but mainly economic, operates as a unit in real time. This process depends on three new conditions:

- First, the technological infrastructure that allowed this to happen. We are a global system because we did not have this technological (or ICT) infrastructure before.
- Second, an organisational form – called networking – that allows greater efficiency and greater capacity to manage everything on a global scale without losing the purpose and the efficiency in the process. In the same way that the Industrial Revolution created large-scale organisations (vertical organisations, big companies, big enterprises), the new forms of technology that manage information and communication allow the creation of a much more versatile, interactive, flexible, adaptable system on the basis of networking.
- And third, an institutional condition: deregulation, involving withdrawal from the rules that were anchored in the nation state (which, contrary to some theories, have not disappeared).

It is the way in which states operate that opens up the connection between different states at the level of the world so that the networks can take over and criss-cross the planet, articulating activities. So, globalisation is simply the network: it's a global network (or global networks) organising every activity in real time on a planetary scale. In that way, the whole planet is interconnected, which means what is valuable for some networks is connected; and what is not is disconnected. Therefore we go not into First World, Second World, Third World; we go into First World, which is everything that is connected everywhere; and Fourth World which has no value and is thus disconnected.

The information age refers basically to informationalism, that is, to the technological paradigm for our time that is based on ICTs. (These technologies are also connected to the biological revolution because they allow the processing of information that enables us to recombine DNA and therefore to start acting as the re-programmers of living matter.)

That is why it is said that information is not what characterises our time. Instead, it is our ability to process and apply and develop information. I like to refer to one particular study published in *Science*, a great scientific journal. Here is the revolution: in 2002, 52% of the information (all types of information: measurement, understanding and everything else) on the planet was digitised. The article calculated that it was 95% in 2007.

The same researcher told me recently, it is now 98%. So the large majority of this information is digitised and is accessible via the internet and other computer networks. That's what the technological revolution means. Not that there is information: it is information that can be recombined, accessed, developed and utilised on a global scale. That is just one measure of the phenomenon.

What are the key elements that redefine empirically, and then conceptually, the five dimensions of development, and under which conditions? And what are the conditions of their articulation? For this, let me employ empirical observation and try to emphasise the fundamental transformations operating in the world in each one of these five dimensions in the last ten to fifteen years.

First of all, let's look at productivity growth (which, of course, characterises the new economy) linked to information development. We have statistical evidence about the relationship,

CHAPTER 5 Castells: Rethinking development in the global information age

strong networking and human resources, conditions that massively increase after a period of productivity, which is the surge of economic growth on the basis of ICTs, diffusing information and applying knowledge. However, at the same time, we also have statistical evidence that the productivity yields have been concentrated in the financial sector. And there has been a shift to a new form of capitalism, which is global informational capitalism, re-utilising capital using precisely these technologies. The same technologies that increase productivity in the economy also make possible the re-utilisation of capital in every aspect: derivatives, options, futures, etc. This ultimately created the major financial crisis that exploded in 2008–2010. (That financial crisis was complicated and I cannot summarise it here. For those who are not satisfied with this summary, I refer you to the book published last year by Oxford University Press under my leadership entitled *Aftermath: The cultures of the economic crisis*, in which we show the mechanism and then argue that it is the way we conceive the economy that led to the virtualisation of capital that then led to the financial crash.)

At the same time that this crisis emerged – linked to the new interaction between productivity, financial capitalism and new technology/other uses of technology – other economic dynamics took place in most of the world. That is why I always refer to this crisis that we are theoretically living in (in Europe and the United States) as the 'non-global', global crisis. Because at exactly the same time – between 2008 and 2012 – most of the world grew more than ever on a sustained scale. There was a little bump in 2009 because external markets had to be corrected through domestic spending. But fundamentally, all the crises in Europe and the United States over all these years, have witnessed the emergence of the so-called 'newly industrialising' or newly developing countries. No one knows what these terms mean. But they refer to China, India, Brazil and Indonesia. To a large extent, it means most of the world: Latin America has been growing very fast; Russia, on the basis of energy and raw materials, has been growing; both East and South East Asia have been growing.

What are the key factors beneath these new development processes that have transformed the notion between periphery and the network?

Technology is there. There is a perception that China is cheap labour. Not at all. China is high technology and relatively cheap labour, which is increasing in price. The most valuable company in the world now in terms of capitalisation value is a company called Alibaba, an e-commerce company in China. It is one of the few very large Chinese companies that is not owned by the government. Another giant is Huawei, which is multi-sectoral and invests in everything (but is a government company). The largest computer maker in the world is Lenovo. Among other things, they acquired IBM just a year ago. IBM does not manufacture computers: we know this. IBM provides services. Most of the actual computer makers have disappeared from the Western world: their whole value evaporated but we still need computers. We need computers in order to sell everything online. And to sell everything online, Alibaba has actually started to control eBay.

What are the factors for this growth that includes countries previously considered unlikely to be sources of it? Imagine Bolivia as being a miracle in the global economy. Bolivia has lithium, which is crucial in much of modern microelectronic production as well as in medical applications such as antidepressants, which are a growing market. Ecuador and Chile are the biggest sources of lithium. Again, what are the key elements that have led to the emergence of a completely new world, in which the economic growth process has been redefined in the last ten years?

First, macro-economic destabilisation. This is not simply about controlling public spending. In most of the countries I have mentioned – in Latin America, in Asia – public spending has increased. It has decreased in Europe and the United States, but in Latin America, even social spending has increased. Macro-economic destabilisation lies in fact in the regulation of capital flows: the disruptive effects of free capital flows. Is China globalised? Yes and no. It is globalised in terms of the export markets but in terms of financial capital, it isn't. There is a border – China is in

CHAPTER 5 Castells: Rethinking development in the global information age

the global financial market but the global financial market is not in China, and the Chinese have been insulated from the impact of the global financial crisis. Consider virtually any country. Brazil, for example, manages exchange rates very tightly. After their crisis they had in 1999, they decided it would not happen again. And most of the Latin American countries have maintained very tight financial regulation.

Second, knowledge and information has been important. Most of these countries have incorporated the new technological systems into their production, not necessarily by *having* high-tech industries but by *using* high-tech in their industries, and particularly in their use of science- and technology-based informational tourism, informational agriculture and informational fish farming. Take Chile, which is now the economic miracle in Latin America. This miracle is not related to the Pinochet free market approach, but to the Chilean government's democratic approach in terms of state-led competitiveness in a free, open global market. Here are some examples. Chile has constitutionally made provision that 2% of its copper exports – copper is Chile's most important export – goes into a reserve fund that no one can touch. This reserve fund invests in science and R&D, with one exception: if there is an earthquake, they can use it for reconstruction. However, the fund is mainly a kind of saving fund for the future. What is Chile's main export after copper? Most people would say wine, which is a major export, but not the main one. This particular export has three times more value (not volume) – salmon. There were no salmon in Chile when I started working there 40 years ago. Perhaps there were a few in the mountains, but not in real quantities. The Chileans went to Norway to study how salmon farming was done, and then created a much more efficient, cheaper fresh-salmon exporting industry that has overtaken Norway in both the United States market, which is the important one, and the Latin American market. In Latin America, you eat salmon everywhere, as we do everywhere in the world. This salmon, however, is certainly not from Norway; it is from Chile.

Besides the companies I have cited, Indian and Indonesian

companies have been investing in structured industries practically everywhere. I mentioned Chile and salmon, but there are large areas of Argentina and Brazil being developed to produce soya for the Asian market, using a new business model that they call network business. It allows major agricultural producers who don't have land to rent the land, hire workers on a temporary basis, and use technology under licence. This all comes together when there is an order from China, for example, for a big soya consignment. Then they put together all the elements of this expertise; they act as the experts; and then they dissolve the network. After that, they recreate the network on the basis of another order for export. All this is about technology. All this is about communication, but it is not communication to produce chips: they produce chips to create communication to do their business as they do.

Structured industries have a key role in this new development. Structured industries are more important for the new growth in the world today than high-tech industries. They are, of course much more important than the old production processes, like automobile production. I am not even counting the dynamic economy, which is the economy of drug trafficking and other illegal activities. According to the calculations of the United Nations Centre for Crime Prevention, money laundering alone – just money laundering within the criminal economy, not even its production – makes up about 7% of the world's GDP, which is more than the total earnings of the world's automobile and electronic industries combined. This is now where the big money is going.

As we have seen, the old industrial production system is really going downhill from just producing automobiles. Eventually, they will unleash the capacity to produce electric cars. China has been the key market for the South, but so have India and Indonesia. What is happening now is that, on the basis of the extraordinary economic dynamism of these new giant economies, the rest of the South is developing. This is certainly the case in both Latin America and Africa. As you know, China has created a new model of growth (let's not call it development), in which the need to absorb the huge amount of energy and raw materials coming from

CHAPTER 5 Castells: Rethinking development in the global information age

this economic growth of between 10–12% per year (already over the past 15 years) is pumping up the structured exports everywhere on the planet. Because of this, all the other countries in the world are exporting to China, while at the same time China is investing in their countries. As an example, Bolivia has signed a major strategic agreement to sell China all its lithium production over the next 20 years; however, it has not yet even started to extract the lithium from the mines. As South Africans, you will know about all the strategic agreements between China and Mozambique, Angola, South Africa (to some extent), and so on.

Higher education and R&D continue to be the central factors of production. This is critical; but the need here is not for something that has to be in unison everywhere. These countries are all tapping into global networks. If they can, they develop primary and secondary education but without great quality. They proceed with what I call warehousing of children rather than the education of children. Their university systems are expanding dramatically but not necessarily with great quality. What they have is enough knowledge, enough research, to connect to the global networks of research and to send students to study in overseas institutions, who come back to the country through a different model. AnnaLee Saxenian, a colleague at Berkeley, calls this model not 'brain drain' but 'brain circulation'. A student goes to Stanford from India, Taiwan or Israel, gets a degree and then starts a company, and after a few years, has a healthy business. In Silicon Valley, 40% of companies now have a CEO who is a foreigner, particularly Chinese or Indian. The human capital of the world goes to Silicon Valley. But they do not just stay in Silicon Valley, but go back to China and set up a company; and then they move between China and Silicon Valley, and this sustains the network. Then other people come along and do the same thing. Thus, this network of high-tech production is not necessarily only concentrated in the main centres but is extended throughout the networked planet. Basic research is more and more concentrated, but the uses of this research depends on entrepreneurs and globally distributed innovation.

Of course the dark spot in this flexible model continues to be Africa because it is very difficult to set up minimum levels of innovation and technological research in most African countries. But in Asia and Latin America, it is already happening. However, because this network process is as described, the wealth being generated is increasingly concentrated in global networks, reproducing and enlarging the process of accumulation, but at the same time expanding social inequality (measured in income and assets).

It is interesting that the most successful book on Amazon in the United States has recently been Thomas Piketty's *Capital in the Twentieth Century*. This shows statistically that this particular model is highly dynamic. It is not going to collapse by itself. It is increasing wealth at an unprecedented level, but not recycling the wealth into the economy, but rather into caches of asset control that ultimately creates oligarchs who do not need to do anything except accumulate and keep accumulating.

Consequently, we have, on the one hand, a decline in spite of the traditional supremacy of the Cold War, and a massive expansion of wealth and markets in a large majority of countries (about 75%): not wealth for the people, but for the countries that control the people. Simultaneously, there is an increasing concentration of social and economic problems. Overall, in quantitative terms, human development has improved, whether we measure it with general education indicators, or with health indicators such as infant mortality, mortality, life expectancy, etc. This improvement is in spite of recent, well-documented epidemics. But in the world, and particularly in the so-called 'newly developing' countries, has there been a substantial improvement in education, health, basic service delivery infrastructure, sewerage, water? Yes. Housing is not good, but it is much better in terms of the rate of growth. Is there less poverty? Interestingly, there is huge inequality but less poverty, when poverty is defined in bureaucratic terms to mean a certain level of income according to whichever statistical agency is measuring it.

It should be remembered that this is also culturally determined.

CHAPTER 5 Castells: Rethinking development in the global information age

Fernando Chirino tells me there is no word in Quechuan for poverty. The equivalent word, *pasha*, does not mean a lack of money but a lack of family and friends. This is real *pasha*, and you are really in trouble. But having no money is sometimes good, sometimes bad. And he reminded me of an anecdote from one of his fieldwork studies when he was in Bolivia at the time of the Argentinean crisis. He asked a poor Bolivian in the street: 'So what do you think about the world?' 'Oh bad, the world is going very bad, particularly for Argentina.' 'Wait a second, you are much poorer than any Argentinean.' 'Yes, but they are not used to being poor.' So, the point really is how you perceive poverty, and not whether the bureaucrat says, 'You are poor' or 'You are not poor'.

But, with all these provisos, there is still the idea that statistically defined poverty has diminished in most areas of the world. In 1990, taking Latin America as a whole, not just the star countries, 48.4% of the population lived below the poverty line. In 2013, it was 27.9% – a 20 percentage point decline, which occurred at the same time as massive demographic growth.

I am not biased towards communication because I am a communications professor. I became a communications professor because I considered it to be important. It's not that I forgot about sociology and went into communication. I go after the problems rather than finding out how problems come to me. Of course, communication is absolutely essential. Every survey in the world – our study on communication in Latin America, in Africa or in China – showed that communication today is absolutely fundamental for people. It is the most important item in poor people's budgets. The data show that, with 7.6 billion people on the planet, there are seven billion mobile phone numbers. Not devices. Numbers. And numbers mean subscribers. Everybody is connected regardless of precisely how – whether good or bad.

There may be bad quality connections, but, of this seven billion, three billion are smart phones. Certainly, some Swedes have three smart phones and know how to use them. But in Argentina, the rate of mobile phone penetration is 120%. In Bogota, it is 95%.

The point is that there is massive access to communication. We have shown statistically and demographically in Latin America that it is directly correlated to economic growth, but also to poverty reduction. However, all this communication doesn't do anything to improve inequality. On the contrary, it increases inequality in society – the more you communicate, the more unequal you become. However, poverty is reduced.

Increasingly, there is synergistic feedback between human development and growth in productivity. And again, it is not just education per se, but the ability to connect educational institutions, and to advance the production of goods and services throughout the world.

A most interesting case is Costa Rica, a small country of 4.5 million people which has had democracy since World War II. Costa Rica country has been growing steadily, not spectacularly, but with one of the steadiest growth rates over the years in Latin America. So what are their exports, and based on their exports, what is Costa Rica's export industry? Unless you have direct knowledge of this little country, you wouldn't know that 43% of their exports is microelectronics. After that, it is ecotourism, yet another informational industry. Ecotourism requires a very serious environmental policy. As it happens, 25% of Costa Rican territory is national parks, which is a huge value-add to tourism in Costa Rica.

How has this success been possible? First, through pacifism (see the chapter by Isadora Chachon [2014] entitled 'Pacifism, Human Development, and the Information Model'). Costa Rica took the decision in 1948 to permanently eliminate all armed forces, and is the only country in the world with no armed forces, despite being situated in one of the most violent regions in the world. Costa Rica specialises in diplomacy, and has a whole army of diplomats, who are sent everywhere – although it is usually only the Nicaraguans who bother them. This has come about through a constitutional amendment that decreed that the amount they were spending on the military – approximately between 8% and 10% – should be directed towards education and/or health instead.

CHAPTER 5 Castells: Rethinking development in the global information age

Thus they created a welfare state, and destroyed the welfare state at the same time. They did not have a military coup. (You need a military to have a military coup.) Therefore they have stability. All the international institutions have a presence in Costa Rica, as does every major corporation that wants to do something in Central America or the northern part of Latin America. It's a nice country, with peace and stability.

The second reason for their success is human development. They created a welfare state with full health coverage and a skilled technical labour force that attended universities and technological institutes. This fact resulted in microelectronic giant, Intel, locating there, establishing the high-tech sector in Costa Rica. Many other companies started to arrive in the country and make use of local labour, trained at the country's universities.

The third observation is, 'be careful not to be too smart'. Intel is leaving Costa Rica for China for this very reason. As pleasant as it is to live in Costa Rica, the prospect of being in the middle of the Chinese market is more attractive. It remains to be seen if Costa Rica – having been able to do the smart thing and attract Intel, create clusters of qualified technical labour – can survive when Intel goes to China. Being married to a multinational is not such a good thing when it moves with the global market. It is a clever strategy to enable a process of synergy and development in which the basis for technological development is created. But the jury is still out on the matter of Costa Rica.

As discussed earlier, human development is working, as shown by quantitative indicators. But indicators of quality of life in most countries show a massive decline in what I would call the subjective conditions of life: violence; fear; metropolitan areas that are destructive in terms of health, transportation, pollution, etc. If we measure human development with traditional indicators, things look wonderful. However, if we measure what people do and think about their actual living conditions, we see a different situation. Take Brazil. They had a progressive government with a distribution policy that halved poverty and drove economic growth. They are doing well in terms of economic growth. All the indicators we have mentioned are positive. But the Brazilians, starting last year and continuing to this day, protest more and more, specifically against their urban conditions – against the fear, violence, the housing, transportation, pollution, the aggravated respiratory diseases, and so on. My one-line summary is that we are improving human development, but moving towards inhuman development, which is all these other conditions.

Let me briefly consider the other dimensions, starting with sustainable development. The usual indicators are not relevant if we take development to mean sustainable development.

Most indicators around the globe are deteriorating. Global issues are not being tackled because of disagreements between nations. And we always knew that the bottom line for environmentalists was whether the whole world followed the same development model as the United States. If they did so with the same intensity and with the same growth, then the whole world, including the States, would grow, and this would be totally unsustainable. We are there already. The rest of the world is using the same model that the United States traditionally used, and is growing three to four times faster. Antarctica is melting.

It was first forecast, and now it is happening. Some people say, 'Who cares about the penguins?' But we will have to pay the consequences: everybody will experience the consequences. Science and technology are absolutely capable of controlling this process, knowing exactly what is happening and why, and measuring and establishing a number of indicators. But given the state of global governments, what indicators do science and technology apply to environmental degradation? Basically, scientific knowledge tells us exactly and precisely how we will die, and not how we will be saved, because it is not science and technology that can save us: it is policies, it is countries, it is people. And in this, we are way behind.

Next, one must consider dignity. On the one hand, there has been a rise in global consciousness of the basic dimensions of human existence. Take gender equality. In spite of everything, there has still been a major improvement in gender equality because of women's current state of awareness, which is the most important thing. It is not the law, it is how women think about themselves.

The protection of children, dealing with a dignified ageing process – these are both positive trends. Animal rights: these are still contested, but the concept that we are as good as the way we treat our animals (or the animals that are not ours) is well established. This is a major indicator. Banning torture and illegal imprisonment. Although it still happens all the time, in principle it shouldn't, which again is another transformation.

On the other hand, we still have oppressive racial discrimination; we still have slavery. Political rights are formalised but not enforced; freedom of expression is free until it's not. Peace abounds but we have multiple wars all the time. The banning of the arms trade has never happened because the world's most important powers are its biggest arms dealers. Global organised crime is rampant and controls entire countries through its institutions; and we know exactly where they are and when there are attempts to deal with them. And then, we have observed a major rise in racism and xenophobia all over the world, particularly in Europe. At this point, depending on the country, between 15 and 25% of Europe's population have explicit racist and xenophobic tendencies, and are ready to translate them into mainstream politics.

If we measure by these standards, where is dignity? We are going backwards. The principles of dignity are now enshrined in all laws, even international laws. The practice of dignity is only enforced when people, particularly women, are able to resist the trends in society. But the trends in society go against what has been achieved in terms of consciousness and in terms of the law. We do have some elements which are linked to people's capacity to inform and mobilise themselves and alert public opinion. And that largely depends on internet freedom and people's global capacity to communicate with one another, which is, incidentally, not a small minority – three billion people in the world now have access to the internet, and seven billion people are connected via mobile phones. We have a global communication network that can mobilise and construct what I call the spaces of autonomy from which societies change themselves. But, because of that, there are increasing threats to internet freedom. The internet is being used more and more for surveillance and is being targeted as such by most governments in the world.

The final key issue is that none of the debates on development, and none of the policies we design, can work unless there is a transformation of agency. This means a transformation of the institutions, organisations and human constructions that ultimately manage development, assign goals and implement them. Starting empirically, the recent processes of economic growth and human development have been enacted fundamentally by the state – by governments, not by markets.

This is extremely important to understand. Latin America in the 1990s decided that deregulation – free markets – was the route to development. The region collapsed economically due to several kinds of crisis, and it collapsed socially and politically as well. And throughout the continent, either populist or democratic governments were elected, but with a different orientation that established a new development model in most of Latin America.

An exception is Columbia. Columbia is a special and different case because it has had a very serious civil war that it is still trying to end. However, by and large, a new model has started: a so-called neo-developmentalism in the Latin American countries where the state takes the lead.

This was exactly the process that took place in East Asia. Remember that famous World Bank report about 12 years ago that said markets were key to development. Markets were seen as key to opening up the global economy, and therefore increasing global competitiveness because domestic markets were too small and too poor for major development. But the actual key actor in East Asia and South Asia, according to the World Bank and according to my own empirical observations, was the state. It was government. We now have the same thing being repeated in Latin America. After all, there is this wonderful paradox that the so-called miracle, the economic miracle of our time that has saved capitalism from deeper crisis in terms of market function,

CHAPTER 5 Castells: Rethinking development in the global information age

is China, that is, a communist state. China is a state that remains communist and a state, controlling everything politically and bureaucratically, mainly through large government-owned companies and with a prescribed strategy throughout.

Interestingly, the same thing is happening in Indonesia, to a large extent, with military production; and in India, this was what ultimately led to Bangalore becoming a government hub that stimulated technological development.

In Latin America, it is absolutely clear that this has been the case. There are some bad examples – Venezuela has destroyed the economy through a patrimonial state. But in other cases – Brazil particularly, but also Chile – it has not been the market; rather it has been different levels of state initiatives and state policy.

However, if the state is the actor of the new process of development, it requires major transformation, since most states are inefficient, bureaucratic, corrupt – certainly corrupt – and in some cases more than that. They require organisational transformation. They require what we call the 'welfare state 2.0'. We can show empirically that the European welfare states are going downhill, not because of economic factors, but because of the increasing costs and bureaucratisation of the welfare state.

We also observe massive corruption of the state, which makes the key agency of development unable to perform in the long term, particularly in such places as Africa. I would say the most important development problem in Africa is that the key actor for development in the world now is the state. And the African state is the weakest, most corrupt, most inefficient, most predatory of all states. Let's put South Africa to one side: still corrupt and inefficient, but not predatory; not yet. But if we take state by state in Africa, the main problem is that the states are instruments, not only for oppression – that's normal – but of predation on their societies. And predatory doesn't just mean corrupt: it means it organises the economy of the country to sell the structured economy – the resources of the country – to whoever and then puts the wealth into the pockets of individuals or their families, in a Swiss bank, or (increasingly) in a Bahamas bank (which is safer), or in a Russian bank. This is currently happening. Thus, the predatory state is a fundamental problem in Africa.

At the level of the world at large, the issue is that there is an increasing disconnection between citizens and their governments, even in democratic countries. The data show that two thirds of citizens in the world don't recognise their governments as democratic, including in the United States and Europe. In the United States, money controls politics; and then money controls America. This is what people feel, but they don't have answers. So they vote for whichever party; or they develop new social movements.

The United Nations is not an international, independent institution; it is a co-governmental institution. I know this personally because in 2000, Fernando Henrique Cardoso was appointed by Kofi Annan to organise what they call a panel of high-level personalities in which there were all kinds of prominent people, and one academic – me. For two years we worked on the relationship between the United Nations and the global society, looking at how we could establish a non-governmental connection. We presented the report and Kofi Annan liked it very much; and then it had to be presented to the General Assembly. The General Assembly took 20 minutes to return the report to Kofi Annan and tell him, 'Who do you think you are? We are the representatives of the people of the world and we pay your salary, by the way. So, shelve this report and don't ever come back with such an idea.' It is in the minutes of the UN General Assembly.

Non-governmental organisations (NGOs) are sometimes a partial answer in terms of legitimacy: they are more legitimate than any other institutions in the world. I call them *neo*-governmental organisations, not *non*-governmental because, in most cases, they are directly or indirectly subsidised by some kind of government.

The consequence of all this analysis, on the one hand, is that if we consider that development is the process by which empowered and informed people define their own goals (not the Millennium Development Goals, but their daily goals) and try to implement them, there is a fundamental problem. More serious than the models of development or the conceptions of development, is the

CHAPTER 5 Castells: Rethinking development in the global information age

disconnection between people's capacity to determine their lives and the nature of the institutions that are supposed to implement all these programmes. This is ultimately the most important problem of development. In fact, in the interests of the developmental state, what is required at this point is the development of society, with people taking development into their own hands. And they are doing it, but not yet through institutions. We are in the process of a historical transition, caught in a very special moment in which the existing economy is highly dynamic. Human development – measured by traditional forms of indicators – is improving and increasing, but the actual perception of this as well as people's living conditions are deteriorating. The main reasons for this are violence, fear, institutional crisis, the predatory state, corruption, and an inability to feel safe because those who are in charge of making you safe are themselves the most unsafe institutions.

Under such conditions we are entering a period of historical transition in which people resort to the oldest forms of social change in humankind's history. We take it into our own hands: we confront the institutions; we try to solve the problem by ourselves. We don't know how, but eventually we will do it. And this happens with all sorts of consequences, good and bad. I'm not normative in that sense: people can do horrible things, but they will do them by themselves, and they are doing them by themselves. That is what is behind the wave of social movements I have been studying for a few years, in which hundreds of millions of people in over one hundred countries and in over five thousand cities in the world have been protesting, camping, marching, organising on the internet against the institutions, with only a little negotiation because people don't trust them.

In my view, frankly, there is one interesting thing in all these developments and that is what is happening in Brazil these days. I was there this time last year when the movement had started a year ago. They wanted me to go again, but I could not. I had to be in South Africa. They said, 'But we have the World Cup.' I said, 'But at this point, there are other problems in Brazil.' They answered, 'No, you will see, it will be a very fun World Cup.' Could we have ever imagined that Brazilians would be totally opposed to the World Cup and protest against it so massively, even though they are very proud of their team, who they want to win the Cup? They are against the World Cup because of the corruption in FIFA, because of the corruption of local authorities that have given in to the interests of the construction companies taking over cities and destroying much of the environment. This notion was expressed very well in one of the major demonstrations recently: 'We exchange one hospital for ten stadiums.' If the Brazilians can do that, the whole world can.

Note

This chapter is an edited transcript of a public lecture delivered by Manuel Castells at the Stellenbosch Institute for Advanced Study (STIAS) in Stellenbosch, South Africa, on 5 June 2014.

Section 3: Putting Castells to work in Africa

Chapter 6

Roles of universities and the African context

Nico Cloete & Peter Maassen

While the first of CHET's 'Castells books', *Challenges of Globalisation: South African debates with Manuel Castells* (Muller et al. 2001), was primarily about the challenges that South Africa and its universities were facing during rapid globalisation, the second and third books, *Universities and Economic Development in Africa* (Cloete et al. 2011) and *Knowledge Production and Contradictory Functions in African Higher Education* (Cloete et al. 2015), concerned themselves more directly with the developmental roles of the university in Africa in relation to the knowledge economy.

In his lecture at the University of the Western Cape in 2009 (see Chapter 4), Castells provided a typically encompassing, but interlinked view of higher education in society (Chapter 4: 57):

> If we take seriously the notion that we live in a global knowledge economy and in a society based on processing information – as universities primarily are – then the quality, effectiveness and relevance of the university system will be directly related to the ability of people, society and institutions to develop. In the context of a technological revolution and of a revolution in communication, the university becomes a central actor of scientific and technological change, but also of other dimensions: of the capacity to train a labour force adequate to the new conditions of production and management. Universities also become the

critical source of the equalisation of chances and democratisation of society by making possible equal opportunities for people. This is not only a contribution to economic growth, it is a contribution to social equality or, at least, lesser inequality.

Castells is referring here to the core functions of the university. He echoes in this the work of many great thinkers on the ideas underlying the university including Alexander von Humboldt, Cardinal Newman and, more recently, Clark Kerr. The latter emphasised that research universities cannot be single-purpose institutions, but rather must be pluralistic in the sense of combining various functions. In his work, Kerr has argued that it is far too simple to claim that the three main university functions are teaching, research and service (see, for example, Kerr 1991: 47–67).

Drawing on Kerr and Castells, the four key roles of higher education can be summarised as follows. Firstly, historically, universities played a major role as ideological apparatuses; that is, as producers of values and social legitimation. These institutions were rooted in the European tradition of church-based theology schools (Bologna, Cambridge, Oxford, Harvard and Salamanca). Other non-religious universities played a similar role in producing, for instance, imperial values in the case of some major universities, and of justifying domination and Western superiority in the colonial world. But, as times changed, a key task of these institutions became the shaping of civic values and 'flexible personalities' in the development of prospective (re-centring) identities, which uses future-oriented narratives to construct a new basis for social belonging and citizenship (Cross et al. 1999). To this day, the formation and diffusion of ideology is still a fundamental role of universities, despite claims to the contrary (Cross et al. 1999).

The second role – historically as important as the production of values – was the selection of the dominant elites. The selection of the elites is accompanied by a socialisation process that includes the formation of networks for their social cohesion, and the establishment of codes of distinction between them and the rest of society (Castells 2001). Values and elite selection became closely connected through networks exemplified by, for example, the Ivy League institutions in the United States, the *grandes écoles* in France, or Cambridge and Oxford in England. But, as demand for access to higher education grew, universities differentiated. And while for some institutions elite selection and formation remained their primary role, large numbers of generalist universities emerged which increased higher education participation rates dramatically. Martin Trow (2007) referred to this as the shift from elite (15% participation rate) via mass (15–40%) to universal (over 40%) higher education; or in Peter Scott's (1995) terms, the massification of higher education. Scott's important contribution was to show that massification is not just a linear expansion of participation; it is also an integral part of modernisation, with associated socio-economic, cultural and science and technology changes. In addition, Scott (1995: 1) added that a characteristic of massified systems is that they are 'endlessly open, radically reflexive with considerable ambiguity and radical discontinuities'. Castells has warned against the dangers attending the strategy of 'endlessly open', as we have seen above.

In these massified systems, the notion of 'elite' has changed dramatically – from the university selecting students belonging to a political and/or socio-economic elite class, to the university being an institution for selecting academic talents; that is, ideally at least, an academic elite, independent of (or at least much less dependent on) class or background. John Shaplin, reviewing Thomas Pikkety's work on university endowments, education and social mobility, reports that research shows that the proportion of college degrees earned by children whose parents belong to the bottom two quartiles of the income hierarchy stagnated at 10–20% during the period 1970 to 2010 (Shaplin 2014). By contrast, the proportion of college degrees earned by children whose parents are in the top quartile increased from 40% to 80% – meaning 'parental income is an almost perfect predictor of university access' (Shaplin 2014). Massification is thus a mixed blessing, as Castells has warned.

The third role for universities was the training of the labour force. The professional university has always had this basic function, ever since it started specialising in the training of church bureaucrats. Both the Napoleonic model (with its introduction of *grandes écoles*) and the Chinese Imperial systems used specific institutions to select and prepare the state bureaucracy (Castells 2001). However, this role extended to other emerging professions – the schools of medicine, law and engineering were critical as training institutions for industrialisation development. In due course, 'training' changed from being the reproduction or transmission of 'accepted' knowledge to 'learning to learn' or to become 'self-programmable' workers, which refers to the ability to change and adapt to many different occupations and new technologies all through one's professional life (Castells 2001).

The fourth role for universities is associated with the relatively late invention of the German research university model that emerged in the second half of the 18th century. This saw the development of a different type of university that could be called a 'science university', in which the primary focus is on the production of scientific knowledge. While the science-orientation seems to be the most obvious function of a university (implying the generation of new knowledge), the true research-intensive university forms a minority institution in higher education systems, and particularly so in developing countries (Altbach 2013).

The popularity of the research-orientated university came from the success of the German universities which, by 1933, had trained and employed twice as many Nobel prize winners as the then US and UK universities combined (Watson 2010). After the Second World War, this dominance was taken over by the US university system. In certain respects, the US system combined the classic German research university model with the so-called 'Land-Grant' university model, which had a specific focus on science with application into society.[1] Originally, the

---

1   The Land-Grant universities were established via the Morrill Act of 1862 (which was amended in 1890). Interestingly, both the Massachusetts Institute of Technology

role of these Land-Grant universities was to develop and apply knowledge for improving the productivity of US agriculture; to contribute to solving specific problems resulting from the rapid urbanisation of the US (Gornitzka & Maassen 2007); and to support the development of specific industries that had regional or national importance. Other key functions of the Land-Grant universities that are seldom mentioned included the requirement of the provision of extension services (especially in the area of agriculture), as well as the stated intention to provide greater access to higher education throughout the US (Douglass 2007).

As emphasised by Kerr, and indeed by Castells, a challenge for universities is that they cannot specialise in only one function; in fact, many try to fulfil all four roles at the same time. Therefore, a critical element in the structure and dynamics of university systems is to combine and make compatible various contradictory functions. For example, ideological apparatuses are not purely reproductive machines, as Pierre Bourdieu sometimes implied.[2] Both conservative and radical ideologies are not only in the system but in individual universities as well. And often, the more the socio-political rule of society relies on coercion rather than on consensus, the more universities become centres of challenge to the political system. In such cases, universities are still predominately ideological apparatuses, although they work for social change rather than for social conservatism (Kerr 1991).

Another tension arose when the developmental potential of universities became apparent and many countries tried to build 'research universities', 'technology institutes' and 'university–industry partnerships'. After centuries of using universities as ideological apparatuses and training institutions, the university rather quickly came under pressure to be a productive force – implying that universities had to be connected simultaneously to the informational economy and to the socio-cultural changes the society was undergoing (Gornitzka & Maassen 2007). Here, the

---

and the University of California, Berkeley, started as Land Grant universities.
2   See, for example, Bourdieu and Passeron (1990).

issue is not to have universities as societal transformers, or to isolate the universities from the social into secluded laboratories or the boardrooms of multinational firms, but to develop institutions which are solid and dynamic enough to withstand the tensions triggered by the simultaneous performance of contradictory functions. As Castells (Chapter 3: 42–43) put it:

> The ability to manage such contradictions while emphasizing the universities' role in generating knowledge and training labour in the context of the new requirements of the development process will to a large extent determine the capacity of countries and regions to become part of the new world economy.

Finally, in the current conditions of the global knowledge economy, knowledge production and technological innovation become the most important productive forces. This requires that every country has at least some level of a national research system (comprising universities and other types of higher education institutions, private sector and public research centres, and private sector research and development) in order to be able to participate in the global knowledge economy (see Castells, Chapter 4 above). There has been a growing policy focus on the university's contributions to innovation and economic development – the main assumption being that more complex and competitive economic and technological global environments require rapid adaptation to shifting opportunities and constraints. As such, the university is expected to play a central role in this adaptation since, as the main knowledge institution in any society, it is assumed to link research and education effectively to innovation.

This expectation has been the underlying rationale for reforms aimed at stimulating universities to develop more determined institutional strategies to enhance research opportunities and a strong, unitary and professional leadership and management capacity. Furthermore, higher education policies have become increasingly coordinated with other policy areas, such as innovation and technology, as part of national (and supranational) knowledge and innovation policies (Braun 2008: 234). At the same time, there is a growing insight into the simplicity and relative one-sidedness of these policies. As is argued by Mazzucato (2013: 52), in her seminal book *The Entrepreneurial State*, it is crucial to separate the role of the university in the production of knowledge from the role of industry in innovation through the development of early stage technologies: 'Getting universities to do both runs, amongst other things, the risk of generating technologies unfit for the market.'

Both the British government, following the Asquith Commission (1945), and the French, following the Brazzaville meeting (1944), saw the university in the colonies as extensions of the British and French university systems, and assumed that the best students would study in the metropolis (Sherman 1990). The model was not Oxbridge or *grande écoles*. According to Castells (2001), the recruitment of social elites – first for the colonial administration and later for the new political regimes – became the fundamental function of universities in the 'Third World' – not only in Africa, but also in Latin America and East Asia. Mamdani (2008) concurs with this by stating that the purpose of Makerere University in Uganda was to train a tiny elite on full scholarships (which included tuition, board, health insurance, transport and even a 'boom' to cover personal needs). From the point of view of the students, this was an extraordinary opportunity; from the point of view of the society, an extraordinary privilege (Mamdani 2008).

Higher education in Africa is still an elite system, although the private sector has increased access to mainly small, low quality institutions which, in the majority of cases, should not be called universities.[3] The higher education participation rate in sub-Saharan Africa is still much lower than in the rest of the world, averaging between 5–10%. In the HERANA group of countries specifically (see Chapter 7 below), only Mauritius and Botswana had a participation rate above 20% by 2012 (World Economic

---

3   One of the most bizarre examples of this is Mauritius where, with a population of less than 1.5million, there are more than 60 'universities'.

Forum 2012). There has been a common misconception that a major problem in African higher education is that it has massified without resources. In reality, nowhere on the continent is there a differentiated and massified system; there are simply overcrowded elite systems (i.e. they massified without resources).

However, when it came to the ideological apparatus function, things unravelled very quickly owing to the instability of the conflicting and competing political elites – the universities were cauldrons of conflicting values, ranging from conservative-reformist to revolutionary ideologies. The contradictions between academic freedom and political militancy, and between the drive for modernisation and the preservation of cultural identity, were detrimental to the educational and scientific tasks of the university. These new universities could not merge the formation of new elites with the ideological task of forging new values and the legitimation of the state (Castells 2001).

This analysis of Castells does not mean that there was not an intention for or a discourse about the university contributing to professional training and, more broadly, to development. A basic assumption following independence was that universities in Africa[4] were expected to be key contributors to the human resource needs of their countries; in particular, the development of human resources for the civil service and the (public) professions. This was to address the acute shortages in these areas that were the result of the gross underdevelopment of universities under colonialism, as well as the departure of colonial administrators and professionals following independence.

The training function in Africa has become more important – although not as important as for the 'explosion' in Asian universities, which have increased their enrolment and technical training on an unprecedented scale (Carnoy et al. 2013). African universities have also grown, but much more moderately than

---

4 At the time of independence, the higher education systems in most African countries were mostly limited to a single national university. It is thus not possible to speak of a higher education system as such at that time.

their counterparts in the rest of the world, and mainly at the lower degree or diploma level. Much of the growth in student numbers has taken place in traditional fields such as law, humanities and social sciences, rather than in science, engineering and technology (Bunting et al. 2014; Kapur & Crowley 2008). The scientific function has received far less attention.

Soon after independence, a 'development' discourse emerged and 1960 was heralded as the 'Year of Africa' and the beginning of the so-called 'development decade'. In September 1962, UNESCO hosted a conference on the Development of Higher Education in Africa. A decade later, in July 1972, the Association of African Universities held a workshop in Accra which focused on the role of the university in development (Yesufu 1973). The importance of the university in newly independent African countries was underscored by the now-famous 'Accra declaration' that all universities must be 'development universities' (Yesufu 1973). Controversially, workshop participants agreed that this was such an important task that the university could not be left to academics alone; it was also the responsibility of governments to steer universities in the development direction.[5]

While many nationalist African academics enthusiastically supported the role of the 'development university', seeing it as a plus in their contestations with the expatriate professoriate that dominated institutions, it sat uncomfortably with expatriates and some more 'globally-oriented' African academics. This was at least partly because this 'development discourse' was more along the lines of the land-grant model rather than that of the research-orientated model. It was also partly because this latter group was more comfortable with the traditional model of the university as a self-governing institution (i.e. governed primarily by scholars) that predominated in the UK and the US at the time. This self-governing model was the dominant model during the first two decades following independence and there was considerable

---

5   Arguably, this was the last time, until 2009, that governments in Africa agreed, at least in continental statements, that universities are important for development (MacGregor 2009).

agreement between universities and 'liberation' governments[6] that the role of elite universities was to produce human capital for the new state.

Despite the rhetoric about the 'development university', African governments did little to promote the development role of these institutions. In part this was because many of these governments had not developed a coherent development model, with notions of what the role of the universities would be. Instead, many had become increasingly embroiled in internal power struggles, as well as the external politics of the Cold War and the politics of funding agencies such as the World Bank. Instead, 'not leaving the universities alone' became interference by government, rather than steering (Moja et al. 1996). Furthermore, universities became sites of contestation – partially around the development model of the new state, and partially around the lack of delivery which included inadequate funding for the institutions. The result was that many governments, other stakeholders and academics became sceptical, if not suspicious, of the university's role in national development.

It was during this period that the World Bank in particular, in part based on the infamous 'rate of return to investments in education' study (Psacharopoulos et al. 1986), concluded that development efforts in Africa should be refocused to concentrate on primary education. This is evident in the dramatic decreases in per capita spending on higher education in Africa: 'Public expenditure per tertiary student has fallen from USD 6 800 in 1980, to USD 1 200 in 2002, and recently averaged just USD 981 in 33 low-income SSA [sub-Saharan Africa] countries' (World Bank 2009: xxvii). This is a staggering decrease of 82%. At a meeting with African vice-chancellors in Harare in 1986, the World Bank went so far as to argue that higher education in Africa was a 'luxury' and that most African countries would be better off closing their universities at home and training graduates overseas instead. When the Bank realised this position was unsustainable, they modified it to argue that universities should be trimmed

---

6   Many of the liberation leaders had studied at foreign universities.

down and restructured to train graduates only in the skills that the market required (Mamdani 1993). This was followed by a number of privatisation drives which, in 1997 at Makerere University, led to the creation of part-time and temporary staff, competition between faculties for vocational (income-generating) courses, and later the introduction of private and public students in the same public university. The cumulative effect of this was, according to Mamdani (2008), the commercialisation of the university at the expense of quality and research.

Castells (2001) argued that the major area of underperformance in Africa and, to some extent, Latin America is in the research or 'generation of new knowledge' function. Africa is at the bottom of almost every indicator-based ranking and league table in science and higher education. For instance, in 2002, Africa's share of publication output was 1.6% and of researchers by region/continent was 2.2%. By 2008, Africa's share of publications had risen to 2.5% although the share of researchers declined slightly, from 2.2% to 2.1% (Zeleza 2014).

In his 2000 lecture (see Chapter 3 above), Castells presented a number of structural and institutional reasons which might explain the lack of progress in research. These included low funding levels and 'the cumulative character of the process of uneven scientific development' leading, amongst others, to a lack of centres of excellence that were at the cutting edge of a specific area of specialisation (Castells 2001: 215–217). In other words, the academic environment in African universities is not attractive enough for talented national scholars, who as a consequence move to overseas universities, especially in North America and Europe, which offer more attractive academic environments. In addition, the main institutional reason for a lack of progress is argued to be the difficulties African universities have in managing contradictory functions (i.e. managing the political and ideological functions alongside the academic activities of the university), as well as managing the tension between the social friction – rapid expansion – and the scientific function of research.

However, there was a revitalisation of higher education in

the post-2000 period and a number of the accepted reasons for poor performance did not hold anymore. Over the last 10 to 15 years, universities and university systems have gone through far-reaching quantitative and qualitative changes in many developing countries and emerging economies such as the so-called BRICS countries (Brazil, Russia, India, China and South Africa). In general, however, sub-Saharan universities still appear to be lagging behind. In their book, Altbach and Balán (2007) focus on the transformation of research universities in Asia and Latin America. According to these authors, their analysis did not include Africa because they believed that 'Africa's academic challenges are sufficiently different from those of the nations represented here that comparison would not be appropriate' (Altbach and Balán 2007: vii). Strikingly, the authors did not provide any arguments or data for their claims.

The gloomy analyses of higher education in Africa by Castells and Mamdani presented above were largely based on the four decades from 1960 to the end of the 1990s. During the late 1990s and early 2000s, some influential voices started calling for the 'revitalisation' of the African university and for linking higher education to development (Sawyerr 2004). From this followed a series of revitalisation initiatives and this issue would be revisited again in 2015 at an all-Africa higher education summit in Dakar.

Perhaps a brief reflection on the term 'revitalise' is appropriate. The Collins dictionary defines revitalise as 'breathe new life into, bring back to life, reanimate, refresh, rejuvenate, renew, restore, resurrect'. This raises questions as to what has to have new life breathed into it or to be restored or resurrected. Mamdani provided an evocative reflection during the 1990 symposium on academic freedom held in Kampala and organised by the Council for the Development of Social Research in Africa (CODESRIA), which suggests that the revitalisation needed had to do with 'relevance' (Mamdani 1993: 11):

> We discovered local communities, communities which we had hitherto viewed simply as so many natural settings. Forced to

address these communities, we were compelled to look at ourselves from the stand-point of these communities. We came to realise that universities have little relevance to the communities around us. To them, we must appear like potted plants in greenhouses – of questionable aesthetic value – or more anthropological oddities with curious habits and strange dresses, practitioners of some modern witchcraft. To academics accustomed to seeing ourselves as leaders-in-waiting or students accustomed to be cajoled as the leaders of tomorrow, these were indeed harsh realities. We were forced to understand the question of relevance, not simply narrowly from the point of view of the development logic of the state, or even narrower market logic of the International Monetary Fund (IMF) and the World Bank, but broadly from the point of view of the needs of surrounding communities. But we had always resisted any demand for a broad relevance in the name of maintaining quality. Faced with popular pressures for democracy in education, universities and independent states were determined, not only to preserve intact those universities inherited from colonial mentors but also to reproduce replicas several times over to maintain standards.

From another perspective, is the university that needs to be revitalised the 'commercialised' Makerere University referred to earlier? Mamdani (2008) described this commercialisation as reform that devalued higher education into a form of low-level training that lacked a meaningful research component. And, while Makerere is a case study of market-based reform at a single university, it raises larger issues about neo-liberal reform of public universities globally (Mamdani 2008: vii). Or, does revitalisation mean that new life must be breathed into university systems where the 'generation of new knowledge' function is the major area of underperformance (Castells 2001)?

Interestingly, most of the revitalisation reports were produced in preparation for major donor-driven events. Both the Sawyerr (2004) publication and the African Union/NEPAD (2005) workshop report, *Renewal of Higher Education in Africa,* contributed to the

Gleneagles G8 summit. Similarly, the United Nations University project report (2009), *Revitalizing Higher Education in Sub-Saharan Africa*, but particularly the Pityana (2009) paper, 'Revitalisation of Higher Education: Access, equity and quality', were prepared for and delivered as proposals to the 2009 UNESCO World Conference on Higher Education.

No systematic assessment of the outcomes of these pleas for revitalisation has been done. However, in an overview of the public donor dimension in Africa, Maassen and Cloete (2009) wrote that while the G8 summit certainly created a momentum for a new focus in Africa, the G8's renewed commitment to Africa was far from uncontroversial: not only did part of the British government react negatively, but agencies such as the United Nations Envoy for HIV/Aids and even the IMF responded critically to the debt-relief proposals.

Regarding higher education in particular, two of the most important documents to be released following the G8 summit were the *Africa Action Plan* and the *Report of the Commission for Africa*. The Africa Action Plan focused broadly on developing research and higher education capacity as well as information and communication technologies. The Commission for Africa report identified four priorities in the sector, namely: professional skills, physical infrastructure, human resources and research capacity. It specifically called for a fund of USD 500 million to be created for revitalising African institutions of higher education and a fund of USD 3 billion for strengthening science, engineering and technological capacity.[7] Of the call for USD 500 million, only the USD 10 million allocated by the UK Department for International Development (DFID) to the Association of African Universities during 2006 could be seen as a direct outcome of the G8 meeting. However, what did change was that DFID, in responding to the Millennium Goals and the UK Prime Minister's enthusiasm during the G8, finally abandoned their rather slavish

---

7   It has to be noted that the Commission charged with making recommendations to the G8 did not directly represent the G8.

support for the outdated World Bank policy to not support higher education – long after the World Bank itself had abandoned this position (Maassen & Cloete 2010).

As for the UNESCO World Conference, the most positive outcome was the unanimous expression of support for the importance of higher education by a group of 16 African ministers of education at a preparatory meeting in Dakar entitled *New Dynamics on Higher Education and Research: Strategies for change and development*.[8] In particular, the ministers 'called for improved financing of universities and a support fund to strengthen training and research in key areas' (MacGregor 2009). Perhaps more importantly, MacGregor reported that there had been considerable awareness about the role that should be played by knowledge as the driving force of development with an emphasis on reforming higher education systems (MacGregor 2009). Ironically, however, soon after committing to an increased emphasis on strengthening higher education at the World Conference, UNESCO itself then devalued the status of higher education by merging the higher education division with the general education division within its own structures. Since then, not much has emerged from this structure – which, in 2014, was without a director.

Concurrent to the revitalisation discourse, other voices arose to support higher education in Africa. The World Bank itself, influenced by Castells's (1991) 'engine of development' paper, started to embrace the idea of the role of higher education in the knowledge economy and for development in the developing world. In 2002, the World Bank report *Constructing Knowledge Societies: New challenges for tertiary education* described how tertiary education contributes to building a country's capacity for participation in an increasingly knowledge-based world economy, and investigated policy options for tertiary education that had the potential to enhance economic growth and reduce poverty (Salmi 2002). This amounted to a 360-degree turnaround from the Bank's earlier notion of higher education as a 'luxury'.

---

8   This title is arguably a considerable improvement on 'revitalisation'.

However, in personal communications, Salmi admitted that the Bank had neither the political will nor the capacity to implement a programme to build capacity in African countries to participate in the knowledge economy. To its credit the World Bank did sponsor studies such as Bloom et al. (2006), which empirically demonstrated a relationship between investment in higher education and an improvement in gross domestic product in Africa. Additional evidence has been generated by subsequent studies by the African Development Bank (Kamara & Nyende 2007) and the World Bank (2009).

A much stronger political voice came from Kofi Annan, the then Secretary General of the United Nations, who strongly promoted the importance of universities for development in Africa (quoted in Bloom et al. 2006: 2):

> The university must become a primary tool for Africa's development in the new century. Universities can help develop African expertise; they can enhance the analysis of African problems; strengthen domestic institutions; serve as a model environment for the practice of good governance, conflict resolution and respect for human rights, and enable African academics to play an active part in the global community of scholars.

While the above statements clearly demonstrate support for the role of higher education in development, they do little to clarify what this role is. There seem to be two different notions hidden within the idea of a 'development tool' – a direct instrumentalist or 'service' role and an 'engine of development' role that is based on strengthening knowledge production and the role of universities in innovation processes.

The instrumentalist role is arguably the more dominant of the two notions in Africa and indeed has been so since the 1960s. For instance, the demands for university revitalisation by, especially, foreign donors and multilateral agencies such as the United Nations and UNESCO are, in many cases, underpinned by the assumption that universities are 'repositories of expertise' which should be applied to solving pressing development issues, such as poverty reduction and education for all. This thinking of 'university as service provider' in Africa is also strongly present within academia itself, and particularly in certain post-colonial contexts. *University World News* reported that at the Association of Commonwealth Universities conference (April 2010) it was stated that: 'Universities must be "citadels not silos", defending communities around them rather than being inward-looking, if they are to actively advance global development goals' (MacGregor & Makoni 2010), and that universities must 'orientate their activities more directly towards supporting UN Millennium Development Goals' (MacGregor 2010). The chief executive officer of the Southern African Regional Universities Association, Piyushi Kotecha, argued that in recent decades, higher education had assumed growing importance for both personal development and for driving social and economic development: 'Now more than ever before, higher education in developing nations is being expected to take on the mantle of responsibility for growth and development, where often governments fail' (MacGregor 2010). This 'direct' instrumentalist notion assumes that universities have a concentration (surplus) of expertise, and presumably spare time, that must be applied directly, or in partnership, to pressing socio-economic issues such as poverty, disease, governance and the competitiveness of private firms or companies.

The second role for higher education embedded in Annan's 'development tool' is Castells's 'engine of development' notion which, as highlighted earlier, has much more recently become the dominant discourse for many developed countries. The underlying vision of this notion is the need to create a university that is dynamic and responsive to socio-economic agendas and that gives priority to innovation, entrepreneurship and competitiveness. Supporting Annan (perhaps on the other end), the high-profile African scientist at Harvard University, Calestous Juma, has promoted the role of higher education in science-led development through, amongst others, the UN Millennium Project Task Force on Science, Technology and Innovation (Juma & Yee-Cheong

2005). In addition, the African Ministerial Council on Science and Technology, established in November 2003 under the auspices of the African Union and NEPAD, created a high-level platform for developing policies and setting priorities on science, technology, research and innovation for development in Africa.

In conclusion, in developing countries, and especially in sub-Saharan Africa, there are different forces and policy arguments driving university dynamics. Here the university is positioned in a development cooperation policy arena where the dominant actors are operating in policy frameworks co-determined by ministries of foreign affairs and development cooperation agencies. The development mission of the university is primarily linked to poverty reduction and community support, rather than economic competitiveness, entrepreneurship and innovation. This raises two key questions: What are the consequences of these different policy frameworks for African universities? And, how do they affect the circumstances under which African universities are expected to contribute to economic development?

While Castells's analyses of the functions of universities outlined above provide an innovative, sociologically based framework for discussing the development of universities around the world, in the case of Africa, these analyses were not informed by strong empirical evidence. Many negative stories are told about African universities when it comes to their facilities, research output, overcrowded lecture halls, weak leadership and so on. But are these stories all there is to tell? What is required is research that does not take these factors as a given, but instead conducts detailed empirical analyses of the dynamics of a number of African flagship universities and their socio-economic and political contexts, while acknowledging Castells's thesis on the contradictory functions in contemporary universities.

Chapter 7

Universities and economic development in Africa

Nico Cloete, Tracy Bailey, Pundy Pillay, Ian Bunting & Peter Maassen

During the post-independence period, every African country has struggled with the problematic of the role of higher education in development. Until the mid-1990s, the role of higher education in development programmes and policies in Africa was somewhat of an anomaly, with most education development projects focusing on primary school education. International donors and partners regarded universities, for the most part, as institutional enclaves without deep penetration into the development needs of African communities. As such, higher education was seen as a non-focal sector and even as a 'luxury ancillary', a view that was for many years promoted by the World Bank (Brock-Utne 2002; Hayward 2008; Maassen et al. 2007; Mamdani 2008; Psacharopoulos et al. 1986; Sawyerr 2004).

Dramatic declines in expenditure on higher education were associated with these policies: spending per student fell from USD 6 800 in 1980, to USD 1 200 in 2002, and later to just USD 981 in 33 low-income sub-Saharan African countries. Lack of investment in higher education delinked universities from development, led to development policies that had negative consequences for African nations, and caused the decline, and in some cases closure, of institutions and areas of higher education that are critical to development (Hayward 2008).

During the 1990s and early 2000s some influential voices (including the World Bank 1999, 2007, 2009) started calling for the revitalisation of African universities and for linking higher education to development. At a World Bank seminar in Kuala Lumpur in 1991, Manuel Castells argued that in an information or knowledge economy, the knowledge institution (university) will be 'the engine of development' (Castells 1991: see Chapter 3 above). This paper had, according to Jamil Salmi, contributed substantially to the recognition at the World Bank about the importance of knowledge, as their subsequent series of publications show: *Knowledge for Development* (1999); *Constructing Knowledge Societies: New challenges for tertiary education* (Salmi 2002); *The Knowledge Economy* (2007) and *Accelerating Catch-up: Tertiary education for growth in Sub-Saharan Africa* (2009).

Research during the last decade has suggested a strong association between higher education participation rates and levels of development, and considerable theoretical and empirical evidence has emerged about the importance of the university in producing high levels of what Castellls calls 'self-programmable' skilled workers, and research and innovation (Carnoy et al. 1993; Castells 2001). However, this notion has also become something of an ideology: the European Commission and the OECD in particular, often beat this drum without empirical evidence and it is the current dominant discourse (Douglass et al. 2009).

Many rapidly developing nations such as Korea, China and India put knowledge and innovation policies, and higher education, at the core of their development strategies, based on the assumption that the ability to absorb, use and modify technology developed mainly in high-income countries will drive more rapid transition to higher levels of development and standards of living (Pillay 2010).

For Africa, the change in direction was clearly signalled when Kofi Annan, then Secretary-General of the United Nations, promoted the importance of universities for development in Africa, stating that: 'The university must become a primary tool for Africa's development in the new century' (quoted in Bloom et al. 2006: 2). This position was endorsed ahead of the UNESCO World Conference on Higher Education in 2009 when a group of African education ministers called for improved financing of universities and a support fund to strengthen training and research in key areas (MacGregor 2009).

The Higher Education Research and Advocacy Network in Africa (HERANA)

The Higher Education Research and Advocacy Network in Africa (HERANA) was established in 2008 with funding support from the US Foundation Partnership (Ford Foundation, Carnegie Corporation of New York, Rockefeller Foundation and Kresge Foundation) and from the Norwegian Agency for Research and Development (NORAD). It was managed by the Centre for Higher Education Trust (CHET) in South Africa.

The HERANA network consisted of eight African universities – the University of Botswana, University of Cape Town, University of Dar es Salaam, Eduardo Mondlane University, University of Ghana, University of Mauritius, Makerere University and the University of Nairobi – and more than 50 participating academics from Africa, Europe and the US.[1] The universities included in the study were selected primarily on the basis of previous collaboration, and because each was regarded as a national or flagship university.

At its inception, the broad aim of the project was to investigate the complex relationships between higher education and economic development in selected African countries with a focus on the contexts in which universities operate, the internal structure and dynamics of the universities, and the interaction between the national and institutional contexts. It

---

1 Nelson Mandela Metropolitan University (NMMU) participated in the first two phases of HERANA and was included because of its comparability in terms of its size and profile to the other African universities. The University of Cape Town was added to the HERANA network at the request of other African universities who wanted to be compared to the flagship university in South Africa (UCT is the highest ranked university in South Africa). NMMU did not participate in the third phase of the HERANA project.

also aimed to identify factors and conditions that facilitate or inhibit universities' ability to make a sustainable contribution to economic development.

The first phase of the HERANA project began with a review of the international literature on the relationship between higher education and economic development This was followed by case studies of three systems that have effectively linked their economic development and higher education policy and planning – Finland, South Korea and North Carolina State in the US (Pillay 2010).

In the second half of phase 1 of the HERANA project, data were collected at both the national and institutional levels in the eight African countries and HERANA universities.

In Phase 2 and 3 HERANA continued its focus on knowledge production, albeit at an institutional level only. Activities in Phases 2 and 3 included the collection of data on the academic core and the institutionalisation of data collection and analysis at the eight participating African universities in order to guide research-informed policy-making in support of creating research-intensive universities.

This chapter provides the findings and insights from Phase 1 of the HERANA project and shows how Castells's model of the four university functions and, in particular, the university function of knowledge production for development, shaped the early work of the HERANA project.

Notions of the role of the African university in development

At a more systemic level, the HERANA project sought to establish how national and institutional stakeholders conceptualise the role of higher education and of the university in development. HERANA was keen to establish whether there was consensus or disjuncture between the national level and the universities included in the project. HERANA's analytical framework for addressing these interests comprised four notions of the relationship between higher education (especially universities) and national development; notions that draw loosely on Castells's proposition that there are four historically determined and contradictory university functions. In particular, the notions of the university as ancillary and of the university as a critical producer of new knowledge that fuels its function as an engine of development, derive from Castells's thinking on the functions of universities, and his conceptualisation of self-programmable labour, innovation and the knowledge economy. The four notions are:

- *The university as ancillary*: When the starting-point for development is predominantly ideological, it is assumed that there is no need for a strong (scientific) knowledge basis for development strategies and policies. Neither is it necessary for the university to play a direct role in development since the emphasis is on investments in basic healthcare, agricultural production and primary education. The role of universities is to produce educated civil servants and professionals (with teaching based on transmitting established knowledge rather than on research), as well as different forms of community service.
- *The university as self-governing institution*: The knowledge produced by the university is considered important for national development – especially for the improvement of healthcare and the strengthening of agricultural production. However, this notion assumes that the most relevant knowledge is produced when academics from the North and the South cooperate in externally funded projects, rather than being steered by the state. This notion portrays the university as playing an important role in developing the national identity, and in producing high-level bureaucrats and scientific knowledge – but not directly related to national development; the university is committed to serving society as a whole rather than specific stakeholders. This notion assumes that the university is most effective when it is left to itself, and can follow institutional priorities, independent of the particularities of a context. It also assumes there is no need to invest additional public funds to increase the relevance of the university.
- *The university as instrument for development agendas*: In this

notion, the university has an important role to play in national development – not through the production of new scientific knowledge, but through expertise exchange and capacity building. The focus of the university's development efforts should be on contributing to reducing poverty and disease, to improving agricultural production, and to supporting small business development – primarily through consultancy activities (especially for government agencies and development aid) and through direct involvement in local communities.

- *The university as engine of development:* This notion assumes that knowledge plays a central role in national development – in relation to improving healthcare and agricultural production, but also in relation to innovations in the private sector, especially in areas such as information and communication technology, biotechnology and engineering. Within this notion, the university is seen as (one of) the core institutions in the national development model. The underlying assumption is that the university is the only institution in society that can provide an adequate foundation for the complexities of the emerging knowledge economy when it comes to producing the relevant skills and competencies of employees in all major sectors, as well as to the production of use-oriented knowledge.

These four notions are situated in the interaction between the following scenarios: (1) Whether or not a role is foreseen for new knowledge in the national development strategy; and (2) Whether or not universities, as knowledge institutions, have a role in the national development strategy.

Drawing on data gathered via interviews with national and university stakeholders, several insights emerged with regard to the envisaged or projected role of the university as knowledge producer in development.

At the national level, three main observations are made based on the data collected. Firstly, the instrumental notion was the strongest, followed by engine of development and self-governing. Secondly, the engine of development notion was to be found

CHAPTER 7 Cloete et al.: Universities and economic development in Africa

mainly in science and technology policies and in national vision statements, but seldom in ministries of education – with the exceptions of Botswana and Mauritius. The references to the knowledge economy, and its importance in vision statements, seem to draw considerably from 'policy-borrowing', particularly from World Bank and OECD sources and websites. Thirdly, in the case of the instrumental notion, most national government officials felt that universities were not doing enough, but there were no policies that spelt out, or incentivised, this instrumental role.

Regarding the institutionally located notions, the following observations could be made. Firstly, self-governance and the instrumental roles were strongest, which reflect the traditional debates about autonomy and community engagement, respectively. Secondly, only within the universities of Ghana and Dar es Salaam was there still a traditional notion of the university producing human capital for the nation, and of the university 'knowing best what is required'. Interestingly, the leadership of neither of these two institutions expressed a knowledge economy discourse. Thirdly, Mauritius was the only institution with the engine of development as the dominant discourse, and it corresponded with the view of government. At Makerere there was considerable agreement between government and the university, except that there was an increasing awareness at the university about the knowledge economy and the engine of development notion. Finally, at NMMU, which is an institution where a former 'traditional' university was merged with a technikon (polytechnic), all four notions were present and in contestation.

In terms of notions of the role of the university in development, at both national and institutional levels, the most obvious unresolved tension was between the self-governance and instrumental roles. This reflects the well-known tension between institutional autonomy, on the one hand, and engagement or responsiveness, on the other.

At the national level in most of the countries, the dominant expectation for higher education was an instrumental one, with a constant refrain that the university was not doing enough to contribute to development – but often referring to social problems, and not economic growth. The engine of development notion was stronger amongst government stakeholders than within the universities, but it could be that government saw knowledge as a narrow instrumental, rather than an engine of development notion. It is nevertheless surprising that amongst university leadership the support for a knowledge economy approach was weak.

The academic core of eight African universities

The university's unique contribution to development is via knowledge – transmitting knowledge to individuals who will go out into the labour market and contribute to society in a variety of ways (teaching), and producing and disseminating knowledge that can lead to innovation or be applied to the problems of society and economy (research, engagement). Part of what impacts on a university's ability to make a sustainable contribution to development therefore focuses on the nature and strength of its knowledge activities, or in Castells's terms, its education and scientific functions.

According to Burton Clark (1998), when an enterprising university evolves a stronger steering core and develops an outreach structure, its heartland is still in the traditional academic departments, formed around disciplines and some interdisciplinary fields. The heartland is where traditional academic values and activities such as teaching, research and training of the next generation of academics occur. Instead of 'heartland', this study used the concept 'academic core' – it is this core that needs to be strong and relevant if flagship universities – such as those included in this study – as key knowledge institutions, are to contribute to development.

While most universities also engage in knowledge activities in the area of community service or outreach,[2] a key assumption is

---

2   See Chapter 9 of this volume for a more detailed account of the HERANA project's empirical work on university–community engagement, including outreach and

that the backbone or the foundation of the university's business is its academic core – that is, the basic handling of knowledge through teaching via academic degree programmes, research output, and the production of doctorates (those who, in the future, will be responsible for carrying out the core knowledge activities).

The eight participating HERANA universities are the leading knowledge-producing institutions expected to contribute to research and development in their respective countries. This is well expressed in the University of Botswana research strategy (2008: 3):

> The university has the largest concentration of research-qualified staff and research facilities in the country and has an obligation to develop the full potential of these resources. By doing so, it can play a central part in the multiple strategies for promoting research, development and innovation that are now on the national agenda.

A review of the vision and mission statements of the eight universities reveals a number of common aims relating to both the nature and strength of their academic cores, as well as their contribution to development. These aims can be summarised as follows:

- To have high academic ratings, making them leading or premier universities – not only in their respective countries but also in Africa;
- To be centres of academic excellence which are engaged in high-quality research and scholarship; and
- To contribute to sustainable national and regional social and economic development.

The question HERANA poses is: Does the evidence support these ambitious aims for academic excellence? In other words, is there evidence that these universities have strong academic cores or, at the very least, are moving in that direction?

---

community service, on the academic core of the university.

Data on the academic core in African flagship universities

CHET started to compile data on a group of African universities in 2007 as part of a project titled 'Cross-National Higher Education Performance (Efficiency) Indicators'.[3] The data collected was discussed at a workshop in March 2009 where it emerged that although a basic data set had been compiled from institutional representatives and planners, most of the universities had experienced difficulties in completing the 2007 data templates. The first finding about the academic core was clear: there is a need to improve and strengthen the definition of key performance indicators, as well as the systematic, institution-wide capturing and processing (institutionalisation) of key data.

To evaluate empirically the strength of the academic core of the HERANA universities, eight indicators were identified, all of which refer to characteristics or activities that reflect the production of high-quality scholarship which, in turn, forms the basis of each university's potential contribution to development. The eight indicators, and the rationale for their inclusion, are outlined below. They are divided into five input and three output indicators. Some of these indicators are based on traditional notions of the role of flagship universities (e.g. the production of new knowledge and the next generation of academics) while others (e.g. science, engineering and technology enrolments and student–staff ratios) are pertinent to the African context.

The five input indicators are as follows:

1. *Increased enrolments in science, engineering and technology (SET)*: In African governments and foreign development agencies alike, there is a strong emphasis on SET as important drivers of development (Juma & Yee-Cheong 2005). Included in SET are

---

3   See http://www.chet.org.za/programmes/indicators/

the agricultural sciences, architecture and urban and regional planning, computer and information science, health sciences and veterinary sciences, life sciences and physical sciences.
2. *Increased postgraduate enrolments*: The knowledge economy and universities are demanding increasing numbers of people with postgraduate qualifications.
3. *A favourable academic staff to student ratio*: The academic workload should allow for the possibility of research and PhD supervision.
4. *A high proportion of academic staff with doctoral degrees*: Research (CHET 2010) shows that there is a high correlation between staff with doctorates, on the one hand, and research output and the training of PhD students, on the other.
5. *Adequate research funding per academic*: Research requires government and institutional funding and 'third-stream' funding from external sources such as industry and foreign donors.

The three output indicators are as follows:

1. *High graduation rates in SET fields*: Not only is it important to increase SET enrolments, it is crucial that universities achieve high graduation rates in order to respond to the skills shortages in the African labour market in these fields.
2. *Increased knowledge production in the form of doctoral graduates*: There is a need for an increase in doctoral graduates for two reasons. Firstly, doctoral graduates form the backbone of academia and are therefore critical for the future reproduction of the academic core. Secondly, there is growing demand for people with doctoral degrees outside of academia (e.g. in research organisations and other organisations such as financial institutions).
3. *Knowledge production in the form of research publications in Web of Science journals*: Academics need to be producing peer-reviewed research publications in order for the university to participate in the global knowledge community and to contribute to new knowledge and innovation.

The strength of, and changes in, the academic core

The data indicate that, apart from NMMU and Ghana, each of the universities had at least one 'strong' rating (see Table 2 in Appendix 1) across the eight indicators. Cape Town was rated 'strong' for all eight indicators, Mauritius for four of the eight, Dar es Salaam and Nairobi for three of the eight, and Botswana, Eduardo and Makerere for two of the eight indicators.

A large number of 'weak' ratings appear in the scores of different universities. Eduardo was rated as 'weak' on six of the eight indicators; Botswana and Ghana on five of the eight indicators. Makerere and Nairobi were rated as 'weak' on four of the eight indicators, and Mauritius on three of the eight indicators. NMMU had two 'weak' ratings and Cape Town none.

On the input side, Cape Town's overall rating was 'strong', and those of Dar es Salaam, Mauritius and Nairobi were about midway between 'strong' and 'medium'. Two universities, Makerere and NMMU, had overall input ratings which were close to the average 'medium' rating. Three universities – Botswana, Eduardo and Ghana – had overall input ratings mid-way between 'weak' and 'medium'. On the output side, Cape Town's average rating was 'strong', and no other university had output ratings of above 'medium', except NMMU had a 'medium' rating. The remaining seven universities had overall output ratings below the 'medium' rating.

From these scores the institutions can be broadly categorised into the following groups:

- Group 1: University of Cape Town, the only university which was 'strong' on all input and output ratings.
- Group 2: University of Mauritius, Makerere University and NMMU which had 'medium' or 'strong' ratings on both the input and the output sides.
- Group 3: The universities of Dar es Salaam, Nairobi and Botswana which had overall 'medium' and 'strong' ratings on the input side, but were 'weak' on the output side.

- Group 4: University of Ghana and Eduardo Mondlane which had 'weak' ratings on both the input and the output side.

The data indicate that, with the exception of Cape Town, the other universities do not have academic cores that live up to the high expectations contained in their mission statements. However, the data show considerable variance amongst the institutions in terms of input indicators, and some convergence regarding output indicators, again with the exception of Cape Town.

Two input indicators with considerable variation are student–staff ratios and permanent academics with doctorates. With regard to student–staff ratios, two institutions managed to decrease the instruction loads of their academic staff (Mauritius: ratio of 24:1 in 2001 to 16:1 in 2007; NMMU: 31:1 down to 28:1) (see Table 2 in Appendix 1). The student–staff ratio at Ghana increased substantially from 12:1 in 2001 to 31:1 in 2007, as did that of Botswana from 14:1 in 2001 to 27:1 in 2007. The ratios at other institutions increased, but not dramatically.

These ratios do not support the stereotype of 'mass overcrowding' in African higher education; certainly not at the flagship universities. While one institution (Ghana) had a ratio of over 30:1, six institutions were under 20:1. These gross figures do, however, obscure substantial variations within the fields of study offered by institutions. For example, at Nairobi, the student–staff ratio in 2007 in SET was 8:1 while it was 42:1 in business. More unfavourable examples are Ghana where the 2007 SET ratio was 9:1 and the business ratio was 68:1, and Makerere where the 2007 SET ratio was 11:1 and the business ratio 96:1. More 'normal' variations were observed at Cape Town which, in 2007, had a 22:1 ratio for SET and 42:1 for business, and Dar es Salaam which had 14:1 for SET and 22:1 for business.

A study by CHET (2010) on higher education differentiation showed that in South Africa there is a highly significant correlation of 0.82 between the proportion of the academic staff of a university that has a doctorate as their highest qualification and the research publications produced at that university. This implies that it is only in exceptional cases that academics without a doctorate publish in internationally recognised peer-reviewed journals or books.

The data show that in 2007 three universities had proportions of permanent academics with doctorates of 50% or higher. They were Nairobi (71%), Cape Town (58%) and Dar es Salaam (50%). This is very strong capacity – in South Africa, only 3 of 23 universities in 2007 had a proportion of 50% or higher of permanent academic staff with doctorates. Ghana, Makerere, Mauritius and NMMU had, in 2007, proportions of permanent academic staff with doctorates in the band 30% to 49%. No trend data are available for this indicator to comment on whether the percentages of staff with doctorates are increasing or decreasing.

The three output indicators are SET graduation rates, doctoral graduates and publications in ISI-recognised journals. For SET graduation rates, an average annual ratio of 25% SET graduates to SET enrolments is roughly equivalent to a cohort graduation rate of 75%, a ratio of 20% is equivalent to a cohort graduation rate of 60%, and a ratio of 15% is equivalent to a cohort graduation rate of 45%. The SET graduation rates show that Botswana, Makerere, Mauritius and Cape Town all have rates of at least 60% of the cohort of students graduating, while Dar es Salaam's is just under 60%. The rest are under 50%. Eduardo Mondlane, which had the highest proportion of enrolments in SET (54% of its enrolments during 2001–2007), had the poorest graduation rate.

Doctoral output is very low. Five of the universities (Botswana, Dar es Salaam, Ghana, Mauritius and Eduardo) produced 20 or fewer doctorates in 2007, while three universities (Makerere, Nairobi and NMMU) produced between 20 and 40, and Cape Town over 100. Most worrisome is that amongst all the institutions, the growth in doctoral graduations is below 10%, with the exceptions of Ghana, Dar es Salaam and Makerere, which grew from a very low base. At the University of Nairobi, doctoral enrolments declined by 17%.

The slow growth in doctoral enrolments is in sharp contrast to the 'explosion' of masters enrolments. At Dar es Salaam, enrolment of masters increased by 23.5% (from 609 in 2001 to 2 165 in 2007). Three other universities (Mauritius, Makerere and Botswana) had average annual increases of higher than 10% between 2001 and 2007. At the other universities growth was below 10%, with Cape Town growing less than 1%.

As was indicated above, the fast growth in masters enrolments was not matched by a commensurate expansion in doctoral studies. For example, at Nairobi, masters enrolments between 2001 and 2007 grew at an average annual rate of 7.7% while doctoral enrolments declined. At Makerere, masters enrolments grew at an annual rate of 15.5% while doctoral enrolments grew at only 2.3%. The continuation rates from masters to doctoral studies seem absurdly low in certain cases. An ideal ratio of masters to doctoral enrolments should be at least 5:1, which is an indication that masters graduates flow into doctoral research programmes. In 2007, Cape Town, Mauritius and NMMU all had ratios of masters to doctoral students below 4:1. Botswana, Dar es Salaam and Ghana all had ratios between 10:1 to 23:1, while the other three – Eduardo Mondlane, Makerere and Nairobi – had ratios above 50:1.

Regarding research publications, it is assumed that a flagship knowledge producer must produce research-based academic articles that can be published in internationally peer-reviewed journals and/or books. The target for permanent academics was set at one research article in a Web of Science indexed journal to be published every two years, which translates into an annual ratio of 0.50 research publications per academic. In our sample, which deals with average ratios for the period 2001–2007, only Cape Town (with an average of 0.95) met this requirement. With the exceptions of NMMU (0.31) and Mauritius (0.13), the ratios of the other universities imply that on average each of their permanent academics is likely to publish only one research article every ten or more years.

From the above it is evident that particularly the output variables of the universities are not strong enough to make a sustainable knowledge production contribution to development. Nevertheless, there are some positive trends. The majority of universities have strong input performance in academics with doctorates, student–staff ratios, and an increase in enrolments at the masters level. On the output side, the graduation rate of SET is quite strong for most of the institutions. There is also an increase in research output, albeit from a very low base. However, it should also be noted that even though the research productivity in terms of academic articles produced is increasing at the universities in the study, since the productivity in the rest of the world is increasing much faster, the relative position of Africa as knowledge producer is decreasing gradually. Sub-Saharan Africa contributes around 0.7% to world scientific output, and this figure has decreased over the last 15 to 20 years (French Academy of Sciences 2006).

Capacity and productivity

There is a long-held common-sense view that the lack of research output in African universities is simply a lack of capacity and resources. However, a closer inspection of the input and output indicators raises some interesting questions about this assumption. In order to explore this further, we selected Cape Town from Group 1, Dar es Salaam from Group 3 and Ghana from Group 4 as representatives of these groups and plotted a comparative graph based on standardised scores (see Figure 1).

The data show that there are surprising similarities between Dar es Salaam and Cape Town in terms of input indicators such as SET enrolments (Cape Town 41%, Dar es Salaam 40%), student–staff ratio (Cape Town 13:1, Dar es Salaam 14:1) and academics with PhDs (Cape Town 58%, Dar es Salaam 50%). Ghana, on the other hand, is only similar to the other two in terms of staff qualifications. On the input side, the big difference between Cape Town, on the one hand, and Dar es Salaam and Ghana on the other, is in percentage of postgraduate students (Cape Town 19% versus Dar es Salaam 9% and Ghana 7%) and research income per permanent staff member (Cape Town USD 47 700 versus Dar es Salaam USD 6 400 and Ghana USD 3 400).

CHAPTER 7 Cloete et al.: Universities and economic development in Africa

Figure 1: Academic core indicators (standardised data) for three selected African universities, 2007

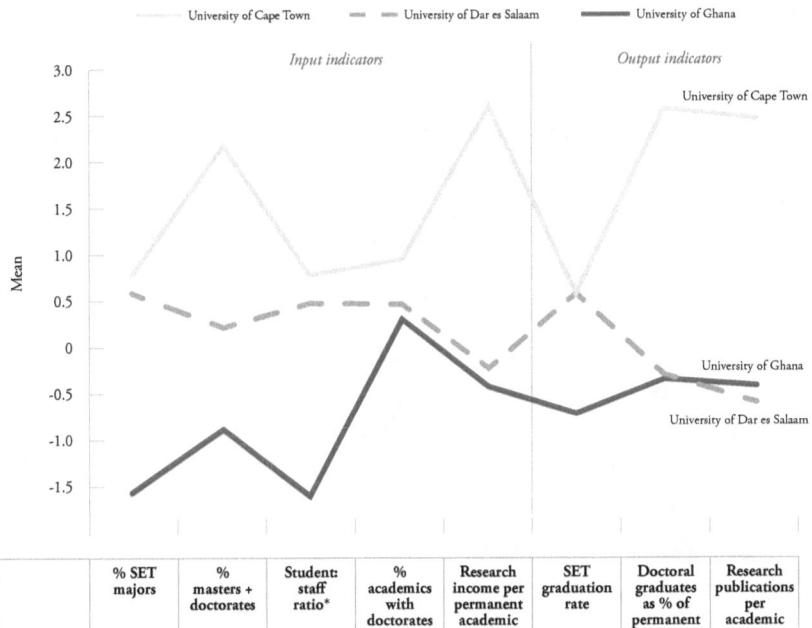

University	% SET majors	% masters + doctorates	Student: staff ratio*	% academics with doctorates	Research income per permanent academic ppp$	SET graduation rate	Doctoral graduates as % of permanent academics	Research publications per academic
Cape Town	41%	19%	13	58%	47 700	21%	15.00%	0.95
Dar es Salaam	40%	9%	14	50%	6 400	19%	2.18%	0.08
Ghana	19%	7%	22	47%	3 400	16%	0.17%	0.11

* In the data table the student:staff ratio is given, whilst the inverse of the student:staff ratio has been used in the graph representing the results of the k-means clustering. This was done because a high student:staff value is unfavourable and should thus reflect a low value in the k-means clustering. The University of Ghana has a high value for student:staff value in the table but the inverse shows a low value in the graph of the means for the clustering.

With regard to output indicators, Cape Town and Dar es Salaam have similar SET graduation rates (21% and 19%, respectively). The dramatic difference is in doctoral graduates (average for 2001–2007): Cape Town 15% of academic staff, and Dar es Salaam and Ghana less than 3% per academic staff member; and publications (2007): Cape Town 1 017, Ghana 61 and Dar es Salaam 70.

These data pose some intriguing issues for higher education in Africa. Cape Town and Dar es Salaam have remarkably similar profiles in terms of SET (input and output), student–staff ratios, and staff with doctorates, but are not comparable regarding the production of doctorates and publications. What distinguishes Cape Town from the other institutions is much higher proportions of postgraduates, research income and knowledge production outputs.

In terms of input capacity, Cape Town and Dar es Salaam are surprisingly similar, with the exception of research income (resources). Does this mean that research income is the only factor that prevents Dar es Salaam from achieving the same level of outputs as Cape Town?

During interviews with senior academics, three factors emerged that raise questions and warrant further research. The first is the problem of research funding. Not only is there very limited research funding, but the cumbersome application procedures and the restrictions on what the research funds can be used for makes consultancy money much more attractive; in other words, consultancy money directly supplements academics' income, and the researchers also have much more discretion about how it is used. The negative side of consultancy funds is that there is no pressure or expectation to publish, nor to train postgraduate students. It thus affects negatively both aspects of knowledge production, that is, postgraduate training and publishing.

Incentives to publish, as is the case in many countries, are a problem. After obtaining the professorship, publishing in international journals is not directly rewarded, but is rather a matter of prestige or 'institutional culture'. In order to incentivise this activity, universities in Africa might have to start exploring incentive systems. In South Africa, the national government subsidises each institution to the tune of about USD 45 000 per PhD graduate and USD 15 000 per accredited publication. But this is not a simple correlation. Two of the universities with the highest publication rates per permanent academic (Cape Town and Rhodes) do not pass a portion of the subsidy directly to the academic or the department, but put it in a pool which funds common research infrastructure, or where everybody can compete for it.

Another dimension that certainly warrants further exploration is the relationship between research and consultancy. A PhD study by Langa (2010) suggests that having a strong academic network link, with publications, is an entry for getting consultancies. So, it is not that academics choose research or consultancy; some do a balancing act between research and consultancy, while others seem to 'drift off' into consultancy and foreign aid networks.

A second problem that is affecting the production of doctorates, and associated research training and publication, is the huge increase in taught masters courses which do not lead to doctoral study. For example, the University of Cape Town had 2 906 masters enrolments and 1 002 doctoral enrolments in 2007. In contrast, in 2007 Dar es Salaam had 2 165 masters students and only 190 doctoral enrolments (see Table 3 in Appendix 1). This means that there is a serious 'pipeline' problem at universities like Dar es Salaam. This could be because the masters degree does not inspire sufficient confidence in students to enrol for the PhD, or because there are no incentives to do so, or because individuals are pursuing their PhD degrees abroad. Whatever the reason, the effect is a serious curtailing of PhD numbers and hence of an essential ingredient in the knowledge production process.

According to the discussions with interview respondents, the third factor that distracts academics from knowledge production is supplementary teaching. The new method of raising third-stream income – namely, the innovation of private and public students in the same institution, with additional remuneration for teaching the private students – has the result that within the university, academics are teaching more to supplement their incomes. In addition, the proliferation of private higher education institutions, some literally within walking distance of public institutions, means that large numbers of senior academics are 'double' or 'triple teaching'.

PhD supervision, in a context where the candidate in all likelihood does not have funds for full-time study and where there are no extrinsic (only intrinsic) institutional rewards, is a poor competitor for the time of the triple-teaching academic. The same applies to rigorous research required for international peer-reviewed publication: it is much easier and far more rewarding to triple teach and do consultancies.

The implication of the above is that the lack of knowledge production at Africa's flagship universities is not a simple lack of capacity and resources, but a complex set of capacities and contradictory rewards within a resource-scarce environment.

Conclusions

The main conclusion from the HERANA Phase 1 research is that the knowledge production output variables of the academic cores do not reflect the lofty ambitions expressed in their mission statements. With the exception of the University of Cape Town, none of the universities in the HERANA group seem to be moving significantly from their traditional undergraduate teaching role to a strong academic core that can contribute to new knowledge production and, by implication, to development.

Amongst the universities there is considerable diversity regarding input variables. The weakest indicators are the low proportion of postgraduate enrolments and the inadequate research funds for permanent staff, with the strongest input indicators in manageable student–staff ratios and well-qualified staff.

On the output side, SET graduation rates are generally positive. But there is a convergence around low knowledge production, particularly doctoral graduation rates and ISI-cited publications. The most serious challenges to strengthening the academic core seem to be the lack of research funds and low knowledge production (PhD graduates and peer-reviewed publications). The study also suggests that the low knowledge production cannot be blamed solely on low capacity and resources; the problematic incentive structures at these universities require further study.

These findings should be interpreted in a context that, according to the system-level analysis done by the HERANA project in Phase 1, there is inconsistency within and between African nations insofar as articulating the role of the university in development and infrequent acknowledgement of the contribution of the university as a producer of knowledge to national economic development.

In terms of further research, there is a clearly identified need to improve and strengthen institution-wide capturing and processing (institutionalisation) of key performance indicator data and to focus more on key performance indicators more directly related to knowledge production.

For Castells, the education function, if injudiciously expanded, 'suffocates' the scientific research function. The market also offers competing rewards. Between teaching and the allures of consultancy, we can surmise that Castells's stern warning about balancing the functions for universities in developing countries is not heeded – and research consequently languishes.

Chapter 8

Research universities in Africa?

Nico Cloete, Ian Bunting & François van Schalkwyk

The main findings of the second phase of the HERANA project provided empirical support for Castells's assertion that the focus of African universities had historically been on elite formation and training, and that 'research production at seven of the eight (UCT excluded) was not strong enough to enable them to build on their traditional undergraduate teaching roles to make a sustainable, comprehensive contribution to development via new knowledge production' (Cloete et al. 2011: 165). HERANA Phase 2 also concluded that in none of the countries was there a coordinated effort between government, external stakeholders and the universities to systematically strengthen the contribution that higher education can make to development (Cloete et al. 2011).

This chapter continues the thread from HERANA Phase 2 but focuses more specifically on findings from the third phase of the HERANA project, specifically on knowledge *production* and the ambitions of African universities to become research-intensive universities.

The need for research universities in Africa

Internationally, there is growing consensus among national policy-makers and other central socio-economic actors that the university is a driver for economic growth and development. This has to do with the role of the university in producing a highly skilled and competent labour force, as well as in producing new knowledge. Both contributions are essential to the creation of innovation and development of a national economy that is globally competitive. This position is well summed up by Olsson and Cooke in an OECD/IHERD report:

> Top research universities in industrialised countries [...] usually dominate the global ranking tables. In contrast, their counterparts in middle and low-income countries have, if anything, more important missions because they are the engines of local and regional knowledge development and natural leaders of their own evolving academic systems. As these systems become increasingly complex and the need to nurture knowledge networks for research grows ever more essential, the success of these institutions becomes even more crucial for national development policy. (2013: 18)

Echoing the above sentiments, Altbach (2013) states that, while research universities in the developing world have not yet achieved the top levels of global rankings, they are extraordinarily important in their countries and regions, and are steadily improving their reputations and competitiveness on the international stage. A key point is that research universities around the world are part of an active community of institutions which share values, foci and missions.

But not all universities are research universities. Research universities are a relatively small percentage of the higher education sector. In America, the proportion of research-intensive universities is about 5% (220 research universities in a system of more than 4 000 post-secondary institutions: see Chapter 3: 39 above), in the UK 25% (25 research universities among 100 universities) and in China 3% (100 research universities out of more than 3 000 institutions countrywide). In many smaller developing countries, there is often only one research university and many countries have none (Altbach 2013).

A clearly differentiated academic system is needed for research universities to flourish. For that, developing countries need to differentiate the missions of institutions in the post-secondary system, and to organise institutions in a rational way. But according to Altbach:

> The fact is that few if any developing countries have a differentiated academic system in place; and this central organisational requirement remains a key task [...] These institutions must be clearly identified and supported. There must be arrangements so that the number of research universities will be sufficiently limited so that funding is available for them and that other resources, such as well-qualified academics, are not spread too thinly. (2013: 328)

The reluctance of governments in Africa to support differentiated research universities is a major stumbling block towards developing a research university.

Does Africa have research universities?

Altbach and Balán (2007) did not include Africa in their book *World Class Worldwide* that deals with the transformation of research universities in Asia and Latin America. They justify the exclusion of Africa on the grounds that the continent's academic challenges are sufficiently different from those of Latin America and Asia (Altbach & Balán 2007: vii). They provide no empirical evidence for the exclusion of Africa. Nevertheless, in the current context of world class and rankings, an inevitable starting point is considering how Africa is doing in the global rankings, and it is obvious that African universities do not fare well.

Times Higher Education's (2017) ranking of universities in BRICS and Emerging Economies scoring has a heavy bias towards research, with half of the score made up of 'direct' research components: 30% of the score for 'Research (volume, income and reputation)' and 20% for 'Citations (research influence)'.

Other components could be described as being comprised of 'indirect' research such as 'Doctorates awarded to academic staff' at 6% (academic staff with doctorates reflect an institutional commitment to producing the next generation of academics and the awarding of PhDs is an indicator of new research capacity), 'International collaboration' at 3.34% (often predicated on research collaboration), and 'Industry income' at 10% (in which case the university must have produced knowledge or have the expertise to apply to transfer existing cutting-edge knowledge to industries eager for innovation and invention).

Times Higher Education's (2017) ranking of universities in BRICS and Emerging Economies[1] reveals that in the Top 20 there are two universities from Africa, both from South Africa (University of Cape Town, 4th; University of the Witwatersrand, 8th). Only ten other sub-Saharan African universities appear in the ranking of 300 universities, and only three of these are outside of South Africa: University of Ghana, University of Nairobi and University of Ibadan.[2] In comparison, Russia has three universities in the Top 20 while Brazil and India each have one university in the Top 20. China and Taiwan lead the way with seven and three universities respectively in the Top 20.

Evidence about Africa's performance on the global research and science stage is not encouraging. Zeleza, in a broad-ranging review of Africa's performance in science, technology, engineering, and mathematics (STEM), shows that Africa remains at the bottom of the global science, technology and innovation league tables and lags behind on key indicators, such as the gross domestic expenditure on research and development,

---

1   The BRICS & Emerging Economies Rankings use the same 13 calibrated performance indicators as for the World University Rankings, but the weightings are specially recalibrated to reflect the characteristics of emerging economy universities. Universities are excluded from the BRICS & Emerging Economies Rankings if they do not teach undergraduates or if their research output amounted to fewer than 200 papers a year between 2010 and 2014.

2   Makerere University is not listed in the BRICS and Emerging Economies Rankings because Uganda is not eligible for inclusion. It is ranked in the 401–500 band of the World University Rankings 2016–2017 of 980 universities.

number of researchers and share of scientific publications and patents (Zeleza 2014: 1).

While Africa is at the bottom of every indicator, a positive feature is the growth in the publication of journal articles in Africa. According to Elsevier (Schemm 2013), from 1996 to 2012, the number of research papers published in scientific journals with at least one African author more than quadrupled from about 12 500 to over 52 000. During the same time the share of the world's articles with African authors almost doubled from 1.2% to around 2.3%, although admittedly from a low base.

A more favourable picture also emerges from the latest assessment of the state of science in the African Union. Using the Scopus database for peer reviewed publications, the African Observatory for Science, Technology and Innovation (2013) reports that, over the period 2008 to 2010, African Union publication output grew by 43% compared to the world average of 18%. If the African Union were considered a country, it would, in the BRICS context, be just behind India, China and Brazil, but ahead of Russia in publication output.

Zeleza argues that there is a considerable literature, by both national and international agencies and scholars, on the capacity constraints and challenges facing African countries in building robust research systems. Four key issues are highlighted:

1. Basing science policy on the technological and industrial needs of the particular society and integrating it into national development plans, with adequate and stable funding for implementation;
2. Massively expanding the size and support for the higher education sector;
3. Incentivising the business sector to invest in research and development by itself and through industry–university collaborations; and
4. Promoting scientific literacy as a critical means of popularising science, technology and innovation in society. (Zeleza 2014: 7)

However, the underlying assumption of Zeleza's synthesis is 'more for everybody' because in Africa no government or university sector wants to openly promote differentiation; at the same time, in all the countries there are national, first post-independence universities which are much better resourced and have much higher status than most other public and private universities. Research by CHET shows that, in South Africa, the sector is differentiated into clearly distinguishable clusters or groups in terms of a wide range of performance indicators (Bunting 2013). This differentiation occurred due to a combination of historical factors and performance-based funding in the post-1994 higher education system.

Castells (2001: 215–217) presents a number of structural and institutional reasons which might explain this lack of progress. The structural reasons include low levels of funding and 'the cumulative character of the process of uneven scientific development' leading, amongst other things, to a lack of centres of excellence that are at cutting edge of a specific area of specialisation. In other words, the academic environment in African universities is not attractive enough for talented national scholars who relocate to overseas universities as a consequence, especially in North America and Europe, which offer more attractive academic environments. The main institutional reason for a lack of progress is that African universities battle to manage the contradictory functions described by Castells; that is, African universities are unable to manage successfully the political and ideological functions alongside the academic teaching activities of the university.

An empirical overview of research at seven African universities

In its analyses of research outputs at African universities from 2001 to 2014,[3] the HERANA project, in collaboration with the

---

3 To achieve consistency in the data reporting, all dates have been converted to calendar years. If for example a university reports its academic year as 2013/14, then its data for that year will be reported as simply 2014. Seven of the original eight HERANA universities submitted data covering the full 14-year period. The

Centre for Research on Evaluation, Science and Technology at Stellenbosch University, extracted from the Web of Science[4] all papers which contained at least one author whose address was that of one of the eight flagship universities. If the authors of a research publication recorded on a citation index were employed by different universities, then full publication units were assigned to each of the universities concerned (Bunting et al. 2015).

To ensure maximum accuracy, the data that had been collected, systematised and analysed were returned to each institution's planning department in three stages for verification. The publication emerging from this research, *An Empirical Overview of Eight Flagship Universities in Africa* (Bunting et al. 2015), was also reviewed by each of the participating institutions before finalisation. A dataset which is unique to the African context was developed during this process, and contains 11 years of comparable data across these eight flagship universities.[5]

In its analyses of performance indicators, the HERANA project followed the OECD guidelines in taking the primary high-level knowledge inputs of universities to be doctoral enrolments and academic staff, and their high-level knowledge outputs to be doctoral graduates and research publications. For the purposes of these analyses, staff members were defined as persons who were on the payroll of a university in either a full-time or part-time capacity. They were classified as permanent if they held a full-time contract of more than three years, and as temporary if they did not have such a contract. The staff employed by universities were placed into three broad categories: academic (more than 50% of time on research or instruction); administrative (including executive management, deans and other senior administrative positions spending less than 50% of their time on teaching/research); and service (mainly lower-skilled, such as cleaning and gardening employees).

University of Dar es Salaam was not able to meet the data requirements for the HERANA Phase 3 of 2011/12 to 2013/14 (but has subsequently done so).

4   Web of Science: http://thomsonreuters.com/thomson-reuters-web-of-science/
5   See http://www.chet.org.za/data/african-he-opendata

A key component in the analyses of performance was the link between knowledge outputs and high-level academic staff inputs of universities, which were taken to include their permanent academic staff with doctoral qualifications, and their senior academic staff who hold ranks of full professor or associate professor. These two sets of permanent academics do not necessarily overlap: some staff with doctorates may hold the rank of lecturer or senior lecturer, while some professors and associate professors may not have doctoral qualifications. The key issue is that a university's permanent academic staff in the two groupings should be its research leaders.

The data shows substantial enrolment growth over the 14-year period (see Table 1 in Appendix 2). Total enrolments increased by 147 000 (or 162%) in 2014 compared to 2001. Undergraduate enrolments increased by 123 000 (or 155%) and postgraduate enrolments by 24 000 (or 212%). The average annual growth rate in total enrolments was a very high 7.7% over this period. The patterns of growth differed widely across the seven universities (see Figure 1 in Appendix 2). Three universities (Nairobi, Ghana and Eduardo Mondlane) accounted for 111 000 (or 76%) of the total growth of 147 000. Their average annual growth rates ranged from 10.2% to 12.8%, compared to the growth rates of between 3.0% and 4.1% for the other four universities. The most striking is Nairobi which increased by almost 53 000 students (average annual growth rate of 11.9%).

The average annual enrolment growth rate in enrolments of 7.7% between 2001 to 2014 was more than double the average annual growth rate of 3.4% in permanent academics. The most striking data are those for Nairobi which reported an average annual increase of 11.9% in student enrolments and an average annual increase of only 0.1% in permanent academics (see Figure 1 in Appendix 2). Figure 1 illustrates the relationship between growth in student enrolments and academic staff. It shows that UCT, Botswana and Makerere maintained a 'balance' between staff and student growth and Nairobi grew too fast in terms of student growth while Eduardo Mondlane grew fast in both.

Figure 1: Percentage growth in enrolments and academic staff at eight African universities, 2001–2014

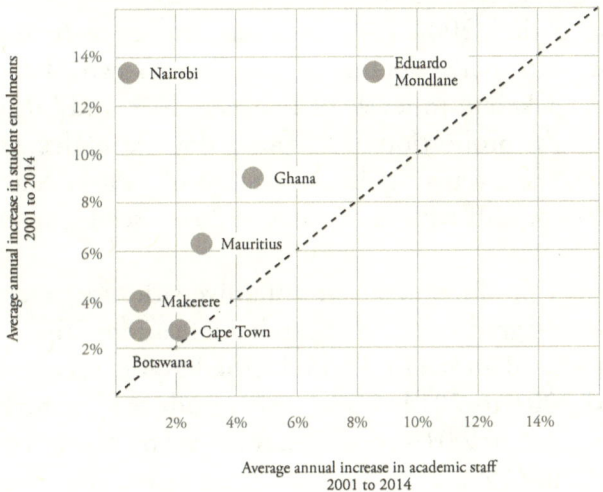

In terms of producing more doctorates and research publications, the proportion between postgraduate and undergraduate student numbers is important (Cloete et al. 2015). The data show that with the exception of Cape Town, the other six universities were mainly undergraduate institutions in 2014 with four having an undergraduate proportion of more than 90%. It is clearly difficult for African universities to change the mix between undergraduate and postgraduate students: during the period 2001 to 2014 the decrease in the proportion of undergraduates was only 2 percentage points (see Figure 2 in Appendix 2).

A university which is well equipped for the production of high-level knowledge should be one which has a high proportion of senior academic staff and a high proportion of academic staff with doctorates. The 2014 data for the proportion of permanent academics in the senior ranks to the proportion of those with doctorates as their highest formal qualifications show that Cape Town and Botswana were the only universities with more than

50% of academic staff in the senior ranks, and Botswana, Ghana and Cape Town were the only universities with more than 60% of staff with doctorates (see Figure 3 in Appendix 2).

During the period 2001 to 2014 there was growth in the percentage of staff with doctorates at Cape Town, Ghana, Mauritius and Makerere to levels of between 40% and 70% in 2014. However, the proportion of staff with doctorates decreased at Botswana and there was a significant decline of 21% at Nairobi to just over 20% of staff with doctorates in 2014 (see Figure 4 in Appendix 2).

The knowledge production outputs of universities are generally taken to be doctoral graduates and research publications. The seven universities produced a total of 3 538 doctoral graduates over the 14-year period 2001 to 2014. Cape Town produced the highest total and proportion of 2 013 and 57%, followed by Nairobi with a total of 539 and 15% of the doctoral aggregate. The overall trend is an increase in output (see Figure 5 in Appendix 2). For example, Nairobi's doctoral graduate total increased from 26 in 2001 to 100 in 2014, and Makerere's total increased from 10 in 2001 to 54 in 2014. Nairobi, with the largest increase in student enrolments, and the biggest decrease in staff with doctorates also shows an increase in doctoral output. The only decline is at Mauritius, and the lack of doctoral graduates at Eduardo Mondlane is attributable to the fact that their doctoral students are registered in Sweden as part of Swedish SIDA grants. From 2016 this will change with doctoral students registered at Eduardo Mondlane and participating in joint doctoral programmes with Swedish and South African universities.

The research publication data show that the seven universities produced a total of 32 371 research publications over the 14-year period 2001 to 2014. Cape Town was assigned 23 055 whole units (or 63%) of the total for this period, followed by Makerere with a whole unit total of 4 012 or 12% of the total. Figure 2 shows that there was an increase in output at all the universities, with Makerere and Ghana showing the strongest growth.

CHAPTER 8 Cloete et al.: Research universities in Africa

Figure 2: Journal articles indexed in the Web of Science for eight African universities, 2001–2014

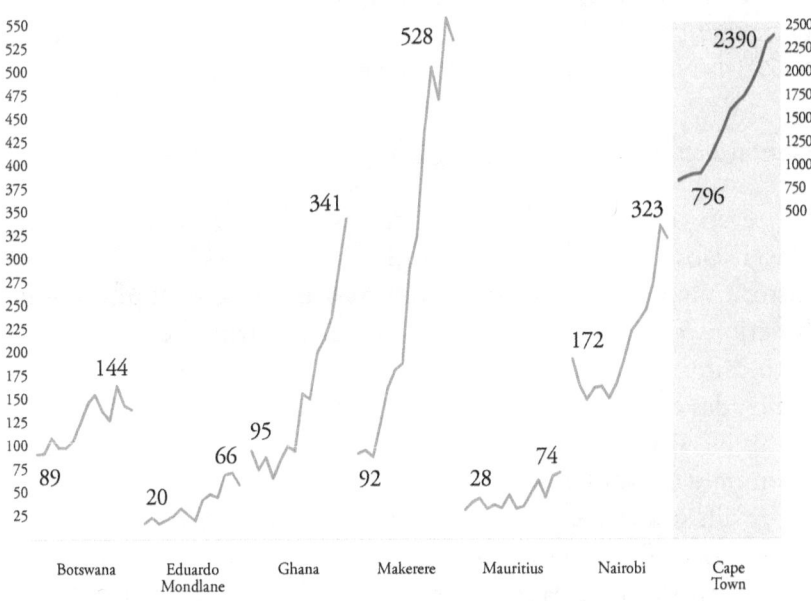

Table 1: Ratios of total publication units to total permanent academic staff at eight African universities, 2001–2014

	2000/01	2004/05	2007/08	2010/11	2013/14
Botswana	0.13	0.13	0.19	0.18	0.20
Cape Town	1.18	1.24	1.76	2.02	2.19
Eduardo Mondlane	0.04	0.04	0.03	0.04	0.04
Ghana	0.14	0.10	0.20	0.20	0.27
Makerere	0.09	0.15	0.24	0.41	0.38
Mauritius	0.14	0.16	0.13	0.22	0.25
Nairobi	0.14	0.11	0.13	0.17	0.26

Table 1 expresses the research publication units allocated to the seven universities as ratios of their permanent academic staff totals. The resulting ratios are related to a HERANA performance target of 1.0 research publication units per permanent academic staff member per annum. The data in the table show that only Cape Town exceeded the target. Its ratio of research publications to permanent academic staff members rose from 1.18 in 2001 to 2.19 in 2014. None of the other six universities exceeded a ratio of 0.5.

Contradictory functions

In terms of the different functions of universities, Castells (1991) observed that 'because universities are social systems and historically produced institutions', they undertake all of the four functions simultaneously within the same structure – although with different emphases at different historical moments. Castells concludes that the 'critical element in the structure and dynamics of university systems is to combine and make compatible seemingly contradictory functions'.

To illustrate these possible 'contradictions', three case studies were chosen from the group of HERANA universities. These case studies appear in a paper entitled 'Data Trends and Institutional Performance: An overview of seven HERANA universities', which was presented at a meeting in Cape Town in November 2015 (Bunting & Cloete 2015).

The University of Mauritius was selected because it is located in the only African country studied that had a pact about the role of higher education and explicit knowledge economy policies. The universities of Nairobi and Makerere were included because they are both large, well-known African universities that have intentions and policies to become research-led, but are grappling with trading off enrolment expansion with a focus on doctoral training and research, albeit with somewhat different outcomes.

Mauritius
Mauritius is the only country in the HERANA group that has a very explicit role for higher education in development, as articulated in national policy documents such as 'Developing Mauritius into a Knowledge Hub and a Centre of Higher Learning', and

is currently rated the most competitive economy in Africa by the World Economic Forum.

However, the assessment of the University of Mauritius as a flagship institution showed that it met only 3 of 13 flagship targets – those relating to its proportion of students in science, engineering and technology (SET), and to its throughput rates of masters and doctoral graduates. Furthermore, the institution exhibited a number of weaknesses in relation to knowledge production, for instance:

- Mauritius remained primarily an undergraduate institution over the 14-year period 2001 to 2014, with more than 90% of students enrolled in undergraduate programmes. As a consequence, Mauritius' proportions of masters and doctoral enrolments remained low, and below the flagship targets as well as the averages for the other HERANA universities.
- Mauritius's total of tenured academics grew at only half the average annual rate of its total student enrolment growth over the period 2001 to 2014: 3.3% compared to 6.6%. Student to academic staff ratios nevertheless remained favourable, and the capacity of Mauritius' academic staff to supervise doctoral students and produce research outputs improved. By 2014, 47% of tenured academics held doctoral degrees, but doctoral enrolments in that year totalled only 20. There were therefore seven academics with doctorates available per doctoral student requiring supervision.
- The research outputs of Mauritius were low throughout the 14-year period. In 2014, the university had 295 tenured academics, and they produced a total of only 144 research articles. Its average annual article output per academic staff member has been about 0.5, which is below both the flagship target of 1.0 and the output averages of other HERANA universities.

In summary, the assessment of the University of Mauritius shows that despite Mauritius being the only country in the HERANA project that had a pact of policies and strategies to be a leader in the knowledge economy, without a policy of differentiation in the higher education system, the University of Mauritius has not been able to make a trade-off between being a largely undergraduate teaching institution and a research-led flagship university. In other words, the contradictory functions of training for the labour market and producing (and applying) scientific knowledge have not been managed in a way that allows the university to assume a role as a producer of new knowledge. As previous HERANA-related research has shown, there is clearly misalignment between system-level aspirations and the University of Mauritius's ability to fulfil those aspirations (Van Schalkwyk 2011).

Nairobi
The University of Nairobi has taken some steps towards its ambition of being a research-intensive university, such as establishing an office for a deputy vice-chancellor for research, appointing a director of research, increasing research funding, introducing recognition and incentives for outstanding researchers, and strengthening support for postgraduate research.

The assessment of the University of Nairobi as a flagship university shows that by 2014 the university met only 3 of HERANA's 13 flagship targets. It had a high proportion of enrolments in masters programmes, a favourable ratio of full-time equivalent students to academic-staff in science and technology programmes, and a high throughput rate of masters graduates.

The assessment also highlights the areas in which the university appears to be facing serious challenges, including the following:

- Nairobi had substantial increases in masters students between 2001 and 2014. The total of masters enrolments increased from 1 700 in 2001 to 11 800 in 2014; an average annual increase of 10.8%. In 2014, 17% of Nairobi's students were enrolled for masters degrees, which implied that it could not be termed a 'primarily undergraduate' university. But despite this increase in masters students, the number of doctoral

enrolments remained low and reached only 700 in 2014. The proportion of Nairobi's students in doctoral programmes reached only 1% in 2014, which was well below the HERANA flagship target of 3%.
- Nairobi's total undergraduate plus postgraduate student enrolment grew at an average annual rate of 11.9% between 2001 and 2014. In marked contrast, its total of tenured academics increased at an average annual rate of only 0.1% over the period. Its student to academic staff ratios for fields of study in business and management, education, and social science and humanities became increasingly unsatisfactory over the period.
- The numbers of Nairobi's academic staff who had doctoral degrees and who could be expected to supervise research students dropped by half over the five-year period 2010 to 2014. In 2010, 600 or 45% of the university's permanent academics held doctoral degrees, compared to the 2014 total of 302 or 24%.
- Nairobi increased its research outputs in the form of doctoral graduates and research articles over the 14-year period 2001 to 2014. Its doctoral graduate total increased from 26 in 2001 to 100 in 2014, and its research article total from 172 to 314 in 2014. Its publication output relative to the number of academics employed was however only 0.26 in 2014, compared to the flagship target of 1.0.

In summary, Nairobi is an interesting example of a university that is trying to resolve the tensions of enrolment expansion (earning more income) and developing a stronger research postgraduate function, but without a supporting government policy framework. However, from the research and doctoral output figures, it is clear that the staff complement cannot cope with the contradictory pressures.

Makerere

Makerere's strategic plan has three pillars: becoming a research-led university, transitioning from a teacher-centred to a learner-centred institution, and making a paradigm shift from outreach to knowledge transfer.

In order to move towards a research-led institution, Makerere instituted a number of strategies and structures, including the establishment of a directorate of research and graduate training, strengthening institutional planning, developing a framework for research management, and developing a research monitoring framework.

The assessment of Makerere shows that the institution met 3 of the 13 flagship targets. These relate to its favourable ratio of full-time equivalent students to academic staff in science and technology programmes, as well as the throughput rate of total graduates and of masters graduates. The assessment also showed that over the period 2001 to 2014, Makerere had faced specific challenges, including the following:

- The proportions of masters students and of doctoral students were below the flagship targets, below the average for the HERANA universities. In 2014, 6% of Makerere's enrolments were in masters programmes and 1.4% in doctoral programmes, compared to the targets of 12% and 3%. Nevertheless, between 2001 and 2014, masters enrolments doubled from 1 100 in 2001 to 2 200, while doctoral enrolments grew phenomenally from 32 to 563 (an average annual rate of 22.7%).
- Of particular concern for Makerere's ambition to become a research university is that it has remained a predominantly undergraduate university: in 2001, 94% of the student body was at the undergraduate level and this proportion had only dropped to 90% by 2014 – compared, for instance, to 65% at the University of Cape Town.
- Makerere's proportion of tenured academics with doctoral degrees improved to 44% in 2014, which was close to the flagship target of 50%. Its proportion of senior academics who could be research leaders was however problematic, being only 30%, which was half of the flagship target of 60%.

These proportions, and in particular the low proportion of senior academics, raise concerns about Makerere's research leadership capacity.

- Makerere's research publication output went from 92 in 2001 to 528 in 2014, an average annual increase of 14.4%, which was substantially higher than the average annual increase of 8.8% for the HERANA universities. But the publication totals were still low relative to the number of tenured academic staff. In 2014, Makerere's ratio of research publications to tenured academics was 0.38, which was well below the flagship target of 1.0.
- Makerere's research output in the form of doctoral graduates increased from 10 in 2001 to 54 in 2014. The output per tenured academic was however well below the flagship target: 0.04 compared to the target ratio of 0.15.

While Makerere's overall research outputs are low in international terms, the improvements in doctoral enrolments and graduation, and in research productivity, do represent substantial increases from the low starting base. These improvements also show that institutions with determined strategies and structural changes – such as capping undergraduate growth and increasing doctoral enrolments while curbing masters-level growth – can bring about change, even under adverse conditions.

Managing contradictory functions

Two important ideas put forward by Manuel Castells were the importance of a university system and the challenges associated with managing contradictory functions. The challenge, then, is to develop institutions that will be strong and dynamic enough to withstand the tensions inherent in these contradictory functions, while at the same time be able to respond to what they see as their specific 'mission' or task in a particular moment in the history of the system. In Castells's formulation, the challenge is not to do with the endless rhetorical calls to shift the university from the so-called ivory tower to the community, or the diametrically opposite demand of shifting the university from the public arena to secluded laboratories or capitalist boardrooms. Rather, for Castells (1991: 14; see also Chapter 3: 42–43 above):

> The ability to manage the contradictions while emphasizing the universities' role in generating knowledge and training labour in the context of the new requirements of the development process will to a large extent determine the capacity of countries and regions to become part of the new world economy.

While it is important that different institutions fulfil different functions, which might be accentuated at different moments of history, universities need the capacity to constantly combine and re-combine their functions and emphases. Furthermore, this has to happen both within a university and also within a higher education *system* because all the contradictory functions of a system cannot be resolved within a single university (Castells 1991). That is why system differentiation is so critical. Ideally, these various functions of the university need to be distributed throughout a system with particular institutional types undertaking different combinations of functions. Yet it is in determining these combinations that prevailing debates and contestations arise.

While there are national factors (such as the lack of a coherent research policy framework) and institutional factors (such as incentives for teaching privately sponsored students) that mitigate against strengthening an institutional research culture, a major structural obstacle is the lack of differentiation in the national system.

Differentiation

Van Vught (2007: 5-6) has argued that differentiation has the following positive effects for higher education systems:

- It improves access for students with different educational backgrounds and achievements;
- It enables social mobility by offering different modes of entry into higher education, multiple forms of transfer, and upward as well as 'honourable downward' mobility;
- It can meet the needs of the labour market by creating a growing variety of specialisations that are needed for economic and social development;
- It serves the needs of interest groups by allowing many to develop their own identity and political legitimisation; and
- It permits the crucial combination of elite and mass higher education: this combination is more diversified than elite systems on their own as they absorb a heterogeneous clientele and try to respond to a range of demands from the labour market.

Van Vught (2007) concluded that despite these obvious advantages, in recent decades, tertiary systems around the world have been becoming less diverse and differentiated. He attributed this to a combination of uniform (one-size-fits-all) government policies which tend to drive towards homogenisation, and the ability of powerful academic communities to defend their norms and aspirations (Van Vught 2007).

Njuguna Ng'ethe from the University of Nairobi reported on one of the first (and only) systematic studies focusing on differentiation in Africa (see Ng'ethe et al. 2008). This World Bank-sponsored investigation covered higher education systems in 12 African countries and, for comparative purposes, Korea, Singapore, Chile, the United Kingdom and France. Significantly, Ng'ethe observed that the expansion of higher education in Africa had not been accompanied by differentiation; instead, there was evidence of institutional isomorphism whereby newly established institutions strove to replicate the dominant 'mother' university (MacGregor 2008). In other words, the impulse was for universities to become more and more alike, rather than to develop diverse missions.

Ng'ethe highlighted four aspects which contribute to the trend towards institutional homogenisation in Africa (see MacGregor 2008).[6] Firstly, in most African countries, higher education funding is based on total student enrolments. Thus, even if an institution starts out with the intention of specialising in a particular area, in a context of low regulation, institutions are free to add other academic programmes, which are often money-spinners (meaning cheaper but popular). This can have the effect of undermining the potential for differentiation. Secondly, the uniform approach to institutional governance, in which institutions are established in the same way, under similar laws, does not allow for differentiation in governance mechanisms. If this is added to the undifferentiated government funding mechanism, then there is a great homogenising pressure. Thirdly, a phenomenon in African higher education is that of off-shore (private) providers. While these institutions do introduce some level of differentiation by offering degrees from other countries, they also offer popular courses in commercial areas (e.g. business administration or information and communication technology). In this regard, Ng'ethe concluded that 'overseas universities are not driving a high level of differentiation' (MacGregor 2008).

Finally, even when it appears that there are different types of institutions as reflected in different nomenclature (such as 'universities of technology'), more often than not, the curricula are not very different across these apparently different institutional types. The same can be said of academic programmes where different course titles belie otherwise very similar content.

Manuel Castells (see Chapter 4 above) emphasised the importance of the relative quality of a university system and observed that 'the quality, effectiveness and relevance of the university system will be directly related to the ability of people, society and institutions to develop' (Chapter 4: 95). The case

---

6 Ng'ethe's focus on the issue of differentiation in the African context was mainly on size and shape (programme/curriculum) differences, with little attention to differentiation in terms of knowledge production (doctoral education and research output), which is the core focus of the HERANA project.

studies of the three African flagship universities discussed above illustrate that neither a university alone, nor a government on its own, can bring about a differentiated system that creates the conditions favourable for research-intensive institutions to thrive.

An important question is whether differentiated systems are more likely to be created by a strong, regulating government, or by autonomous institutions operating in market-like settings. As the studies referred to earlier show, the situation in Africa is not different from elsewhere; that is, autonomous higher education institutions do not attempt to develop a profile which is different from all other higher education institutions. Instead of looking for a fitting niche, each institution is driven by income- and status-maximisation. As a consequence, higher education institutions are naturally inclined to mimic other successful institutions, thereby effectively limiting system-level differentiation.

This change dynamic can only be moved in a differentiation-enhancing direction through effective government-led policies, incentives and regulations. Unfortunately, as the HERANA data show, the current situation in Africa deviates from this emerging understanding of the factors that stimulate system differentiation in higher education. First, government policies aimed at increasing the capacity of the higher education system by establishing new universities have in general used one basic university model, resulting in new universities becoming 'clones' of existing universities in the same system. Second, public and private institutions that enjoyed the level of institutional autonomy that allowed them to develop unique profiles have, in general, combined mimicking and budget-maximising behaviour (e.g. recruiting large numbers of fee-paying 'private' students).

As part of the broader HERANA project, Bailey (2015) concluded from the study of higher education councils in Africa that there was evidence of a shift from a state control approach to a state supervision model of higher education governance in all eight countries. This is a very significant and positive development in sub-Saharan Africa. A state supervisory system is characterised by 'multi-level multi-actor' governance which includes the redistribution of decision-making powers, responsibilities and accountability among external and internal stakeholders. The governance architecture in such systems consists of a parent ministry (and its relevant department or unit) with overall responsibility for policy-making, strategic planning and ensuring compliance; semi-autonomous agencies responsible for, amongst others, policy implementation, distributing and monitoring public funds, external quality assurance and regulation (including setting norms and standards), monitoring and analysing, and providing expert advice; as well as informal national-level forums, comprising different levels of institutional leadership, which can make proposals to the parent ministry regarding the development of the sector.

A strong indicator of the move towards a state supervisory approach to governance is the emergence of specialised, semi-autonomous government agencies in what is often referred to as a process of 'agencification'. Here, the main motives for the establishment of such agencies include demands on governments for greater efficiency, responsiveness, transparency and accountability; decreased political interference in governance matters; and enhanced technical expertise and the specialisation of functions.

The study on higher education councils (Bailey 2015) concluded that factors that were inhibiting the ability of the national councils/commissions to carry out their governance roles more effectively related to a lack of capacity and appropriate expertise; the lack of comprehensive and up-to-date data; a lack of system-level coordination; and the absence of the necessary leverage to compel institutions to meet their targets or the absence of a pact to guide the work of the councils/commissions within the overall system. Key policy issues identified were the need for a more detailed national plan for the tertiary/higher education system in each country; a review of governance roles and coordination at the system level; capacity-building and identification of expertise; the location (government or agency), development and maintenance of higher education management information systems; and greater clarity regarding autonomy and political independence – that is, a better understanding and acceptance of the need for governments' higher education agencies to have an adequate degree of operational autonomy (Braun 2008).

A concurrent study by CREST (Mouton et al. 2015) of science (research) granting councils in Africa concluded, amongst others, that the relatively low investment in R&D in many sub-Saharan African countries, which has a direct impact on the science funding models, points to different 'inscriptions' of science in different countries and different values accorded to science. On the one hand, some governments clearly recognise the value and importance of science and hence invest in science funding and in the establishment of a national funding agency. On the other hand, many governments have not – at least until very recently – judged science to be of sufficient value and importance to invest in the establishment of a relatively autonomous agency to disburse state funds for research and development. But the fact that there has been a surge of interest in the recent past in reformulating existing science policies as well as in the establishment of a separate ministry of science, may be indicative of a change even amongst the latter category of countries. Both the Mouton et al. (2015) and Bailey (2015) studies conclude that there is an urgent need for greater investment in science and the restructuring and strengthening of the research systems in the countries studied.

In conclusion, while the universities seem to be committed to strengthening the knowledge production function, Mauritius shows that even with government policies on the role of the university in the knowledge economy in place, if there is not a deliberate commitment to differentiation at both the national and institutional levels, the function of undergraduate training will continue to dominate. And, despite strong institutional commitments to strengthening research at both Nairobi and Makerere, without national support that can curtail the strong pressure for fundraising by means of expanding undergraduate enrolments, African universities will not be able to manage the contradictory functions of undergraduate training and knowledge production.

Chapter 9

*African universities and connectedness
in the information age*

François van Schalkwyk

In China Miéville's *The City and The City*, the cities of Besźel and Ul Qoma co-exist in the same geographical space and in the same time continuum. In both cities, the citizens' complicit but voluntary perception of separateness sustains their cleavage. Citizens are socially programmed to 'unsee' the inhabitants, buildings, machines and urban furniture of the other city, and to cross over without sanction is to 'breach', invoking punishment meted out by the eponymous oversight authority that is a law unto itself. Movement from one city to another is permitted, but is subject to authorisation, and entry is controlled via a shared border-crossing at The Copula Hall. The Copula is a switch of sorts, allowing passage from one social order to another across a shared physical space.

Manuel Castells postulates the 'discovery of a new social structure in the making, [...] conceptualised as the network society because it is made of networks in all the key dimensions of social organisation and social practice' (Castells 2010: xviii). In Castells's network society, structurally different from previous networks because of the advent of digital information and communication technologies, space and time collapse to create a new space of flows while, simultaneously, citizens search for meaning in their local realities. In such a society, and particularly for those global citizens who occupy key social institutions, universities included, switching between networks can be both complex and contradictory.

While previous chapters in this collection have paid attention to the role of the university in Africa, and placed particular emphasis on their aspirations to become research intensive within a quadrant of competing historical functions described by Castells, this chapter explores with reference to Castells's narrative of the network society how universities are connecting in an increasingly digitally networked world to meet their objective of producing new knowledge while simultaneously meeting the expectations of their relevance to society.

This chapter is therefore a modest attempt to extend Castells's theory of the network society by exploring the possibility of different types of connectedness in university networks. It does so by examining the connections university academics make in different networks, proposing a particular type of connectedness in operation at universities, and by showing that the directionality of connections between nodes matters for development. The focus is on two African universities as key social institutions in the production and dissemination of new knowledge in a globalised world.

On networks in the Information Age

Networks as a form of organisation is neither new nor disruptive; it is the advent of digital networking technologies in the information age that gives rise to the network society, a society whose social structure is determined by networks activated by digital information and communication technologies (Castells 2009). Digital networks are therefore the axis on which the reorganisation of society's constitutive processes turn, shifting from hierarchical flows of information to the processing of flows of information that are global, horizontal, reflexive and indifferent to historical notions of communications across time and space.

From the global digital network emerges a new form of spatiality, the space of flows: 'the material support of simultaneous social practices communicated at a distance. This involves the production, transmission and processing of flows of information. It also relies on the development of localities as nodes of these communication networks, and the connectivity of activities located in these nodes by fast transportation networks operated by information flows' (Castells 2010: xxxii). While the network is therefore global, the nodal 'localities' retain their importance as geographically defined sites for the location of local, place-specific, face-to-face micro-networks. Castells emphasises the inherent contradiction between the space of flows and the space of places. In the network society, cultural and social meaning is defined in place terms, while functionality, wealth and power are defined in terms of flows.

In the Castellian conception of the network society two separate but interacting processes prevail: the mode of production and the mode of development. The mode of production constitutes the production of goods and services in specific social relationships, driven historically by capitalism. The mode of development is constituted by those technological arrangements through which labour acts on matter to generate products and evolves according to its own logic, which is predominantly predicated on the interaction between scientific and technological discovery (see also Chapter 2: 24–25 above). According to Castells, economic development and technological development are necessarily separate processes because technological development is also driven by non-economic considerations such as invention and experimentation. The outcomes of inventiveness and experimentation may or may not be taken up by society.

It is not only the modes of production and development that are distinct in the network society; multiple, distinctive networks exist, each with their own geography and their own logic: 'the most strategically important observation for an analysis in terms of spatial networks is that these global networks do not have the same geography; they usually do not share the same nodes. [...] Political agencies, nationally and internationally, build their own spatial sites and networks of power. The global network of scientific research does not overlap with the networks of technological innovation' (Castells 2010: xxxviii). Each network is defined by a programme, formulated by social actors, that assigns to a network its goals and its rules of performance (Castells 2009: 20).

Distinctive networks may compete with one another but they may also cooperate. Cooperation depends on the connectedness between networks and is made possible by introducing interoperability via shared protocols and languages/code, or by the presence of switches (connecting points).

On the African university in the Information Age

The trajectory of the African university as a social institution in terms of its historically-determined functions and its relationship with society has already been described (see Chapter 6). What is clear is that the contemporary African university must grapple with competing demands, both exogenous and self-imposed.

According to Castells, African universities must take seriously their scientific function of knowledge production: they 'must also emphasise research, both basic and applied, since this will become the necessary ground for upgrading the country's productive system' (Chapter 3: 49) and '[w]ithout the self-determination of the scientific community in the pursuit of the goals of scientific research, there will be no discovery' (Chapter 3: 47–48). However, in a world where trust between society and its public institutions is waning (a point made by Castells in Chapter 5 above), academics are increasingly expected to engage with those beyond their ramparts and, in doing so, they are expected to become relevant and responsive to the needs of society. Castells is attuned to the social pressures that universities face: 'But universities as organisations are also submitted to the pressures of society, beyond the explicit roles they have been asked to assume, and the overall process results in a complex and contradictory reality' (Chapter 3: 41).

Responding to the needs of society is often framed under the banner of 'university–community engagement' or of its 'third mission'. Typically, the notion of 'engagement' (or 'third mission')

CHAPTER 9 Van Schalkwyk: African universities and connectedness

is used to denote the university's closer relationship with the market and/or society in order to meet the needs of society; a relationship imposed on the university by society as it expects the academy to find solutions to the challenges it faces.

Such engagement is normative, an activity to be undertaken by academics that is inherently good for society. But proponents of engagement rarely consider the academic dividends for the university, that is, the scientific returns from its engagement with society (other than, from a scientific point of view, the relatively lower returns of higher levels of transparency and accountability to external stakeholders). And the engagement literature fails to acknowledge that these returns to the university are not necessarily (narrowly) self-serving – it is the academic dividends that accrue to the university that place the university in a stronger position to contribute to social and economic development.

Key then to the relationship between higher education and development is the establishment of a productive interaction between the university's knowledge enterprise and its engagement activities. An overemphasis on the basic knowledge activities of teaching and research – in other words, a predominantly inward orientation – risks the university becoming disconnected from the needs of society. However, an overemphasis on connecting to those external to the university potentially leaves the university with little new knowledge to foster innovation and fuel development. The challenge for universities is to manage this inherent tension between 'buffering' (protecting) the core technologies of the institution and 'bridging' (linking) those with external actors (W. Scott 2001: 199–211). In the words of Castells (Chapter 3: 42):

> The real issue is not so much to shift universities from the public arena to secluded laboratories or to capitalist board meetings, as to create institutions solid enough and dynamic enough to withstand the tensions that will necessarily trigger the simultaneous performance of contradictory functions. The ability to manage such contradictions, while emphasising the role of universities in the generation of knowledge and the

training of labour in the context of the new requirements of the development process, will condition to a large extent the capacity of new countries and regions to become part of the dynamic system of the new world economy.

There are network dynamics at play here. On the one hand, the university is required to be part of the global network of science if it is to participate in and add value to the flows of network-specific information that will advance knowledge and yield new discoveries:

> [B]ecause we are in a global economy and in a global research system the notion of universities being stand-alone, major research centres is gone. The critical thing is to be in the networks of global production of knowledge, of research and innovation. […] You need to have a ticket to enter one of the networks; you have to provide something that is not necessarily the best in the world but is interesting enough that all the other participants in the global research network of one particular field want you to be in the network. (Chapter 4: 60)

In this sense, it is less about participation than about universities in Africa being included or excluded because the university as a key institutional component of science (in turn, one of the dominant functions in the network society) is organised around the space of flows.

On the other hand, the university must negotiate entry into and foster links in new socially relevant and representative networks. This requires the university to position itself in place-based local networks that first, are distinct from the global network of science and second, are of different kinds (of industry, entrepreneurs, law-makers, neighbourhood communities, and so on). Noting the challenges at the system and organisational levels of managing these contradictions effectively, for academics at African universities who have historically been on the margins of global knowledge production and who are increasingly expected to contribute to national development, engaging with those external to the university in such a manner so as to ensure the creation of knowledge valued by the global scientific community is equally challenging. They must both cultivate the non-scientific networks that will allow them to engage, and maintain their position in global scientific networks by ensuring that they have something of value to offer.

In sub-Saharan Africa, in a context of relatively underpaid and poorly incentivised permanent academic staff, engaged research – that is, research of the kind that situates itself in stakeholder networks rather than exclusively in scientific networks – is often synonymous with consulting work. And there are those who warn of the dangers of such engaged research becoming dislocated from the academy and from home-grown development prerogatives and strategies as researchers bend to the research prerogatives of government and international funding agencies (Cloete et al. 2011; Mamdani 2016; Mkandawire 2011).

***

The above brutal truncation of the network society and the position of the African university, brings to the fore a least two lacunae. The first is that Castells is not specific when it comes to the variety of types of connections made between networks. Shared protocols, code and switches make interoperability possible, but what does cooperation between human networks look like? Being engaged requires academics to connect between two or more different networks: each with distinctive geographies, mega-nodes and logics. For universities, at least two types of networks emerge in the information society: networks that are global and predominantly focused on making connections within the science community to support knowledge production; and networks that are predominantly more local and focused on the provision of solutions in response to the needs and demands of local communities. In other words, there are, for universities, specialised and non-specialised connections to be made – specialised connections between academics, within a globalised academy; and non-specialised connections between academics and predominantly local stakeholders external to the academy.

The second lacuna is that while Castells acknowledges that networks, particularly global digital networks, accelerate infinitely the speed at which information is exchanged, he offers little by way of the velocity, that is, the speed at which information travels in a given direction. In other words, his networks are not specific about the direction of information flows, nor are they specific about the direction in which value travels between nodes in networks.

It is these creases within the grand narrative that this chapter explores. The empirical basis for the explorations is a study by Van Schalkwyk (2015) that sought to examine more closely the impact of university–community engagement projects at two African universities; specifically, the contribution that university–community engagement made to strengthening the core functions of knowledge production (research) and teaching (knowledge transfer) at those universities. Whether the engagement activities of university academics were strengthening the academic core was taken as a proxy for the extent to which those academics are able to manage the tension between supporting the core functions of the university and the pressure for their academic activities to be relevant and responsive to society. Where necessary, the discussion is supplemented by data from additional sources.

The two universities included in the study were Nelson Mandela Metropolitan University (NMMU) located in Port Elizabeth, South Africa, and Makerere University located in Kampala, Uganda. Makerere University is positioning itself as a research university and there is evidence of early successes in moving in that direction if the number of research articles published is used as a proxy for research output (Bunting et al. 2014), while NMMU is a comprehensive university which, in South African terms, implies a mix of both research and teaching in its strategic focus. Makerere relies largely on funding from donor agencies to fund its research (Makerere University 2013) while NMMU has a history of close links with the automotive and other regionally-located industries. These variances were deemed to make each university a potentially informative case to explore how academics are navigating the tension inherent in university–community engagement.

Spaces

Castells points to the contradiction between the space of flows and the space of places in the network society. He also recognises the presence of multiple networks, each with its own geography and value logic. The study of university–community engagement, with its dual interest in the connections university academics make to the academic core of the university (where the university is a potential node in the globalised network of science programmed around the production of knowledge and discovery), and to the communities external to the university (where the university is a potential node in local networks programmed around solving the problems faced by specific communities), provides empirical evidence to explore how academics are pivoting around the university as a switching node in multiple networks.

An examination of the location of university–community engagement projects at NMMU,[1] in other words, their sites of implementation, shows that the execution of projects is almost exclusively local, that is, within either the city, region or country in which the university is located. Data on the location-specificity of 76 university–community engagement projects at NMMU show that 12 (16%) projects indicated South Africa as the site of implementation; 10 (13%) the Eastern Cape Province; 20 (26%) Nelson Mandela Bay Metropolitan Municipality; 7 (9%) a specific precinct or suburb within the Metro; and 2 (3%) indicated that the university campus was the site of implementation.[2] Only 4 (5%) projects indicated that project implementation was at the international level, which is not to suggest that these projects are any less place-based than those with a more local site of

---

1   The analysis in this instance is limited to NMMU because of its larger sample size.
2   The remainder of the projects (18%) provided no site of implementation.

implementation. The obvious point here is that these engagement activities undertaken by academics at NMMU are place-based, and that this requires academics to enter into local, micro-networks in order to connect to relevant actors in the community in a quest for relevance.

At the same time, academics are required to participate in and contribute to the flow of information in the global network of science. Figure 1, using data on the co-authorship of journal articles indexed in Scopus between 2008 and 2012 to create connections between the cities in which authors are located (Beauchesne 2014), reveals three insights. The first is the existence of mega-nodes in the globalised scientific network (highlighted in Figure 2 by adjusting the contrast of Figure 1), determined by the presence of what Castells would term 'powerful' universities on the US East Coast, in the UK, in Northern Europe and in Japan, and, to a lesser extent in Brazil and India. The second is that the connections between mega-nodes on either side of the Atlantic are most prominent. In the cases of Brazil, India, Japan and China, connections are between authors in the same country – partly, but not only, because of co-authors publishing in a language other than English. The third insight is the relatively insignificant contribution by NMMU, notably in relation to the relatively more central nodes of Cape Town and Gauteng in the same country. At face value, it would therefore appear that academics at NMMU are connected both to local networks as a requisite for engaging with local actors and to the globalised network of science, but only marginally so in the latter instance. According to Castells: 'the more organizations depend, ultimately, upon flows and networks, the less they are influenced by the social context associated with the places of their location. From this follows a growing independence of the organizational logic from the societal logic' (Castells 1989: 169–170). It would appear that such an organisational transition is yet to materialise at NMMU, and most likely also at other African universities, including Makerere University, attempting to manage the tension between national development priorities (relevance) and participation in global science.

CHAPTER 9 Van Schalkwyk: African universities and connectedness

A deeper understanding of these dual network connections and how academics at two African universities pivot around these shared nodes, is explored in the section that follows on interconnectedness.

Figure 1: Global collaboration between researchers (2005–2009)

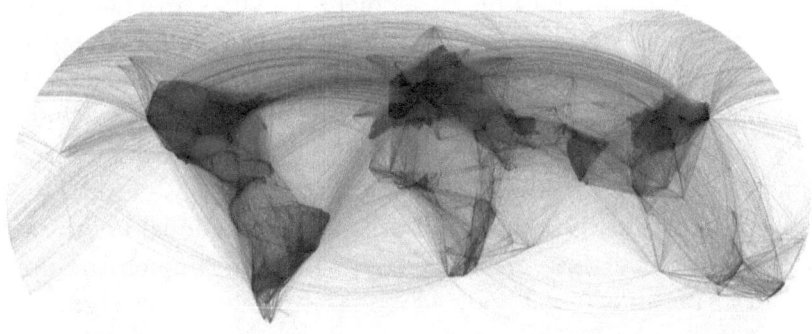

Figure 2: Mega-nodes in science based on global scientific collaboration

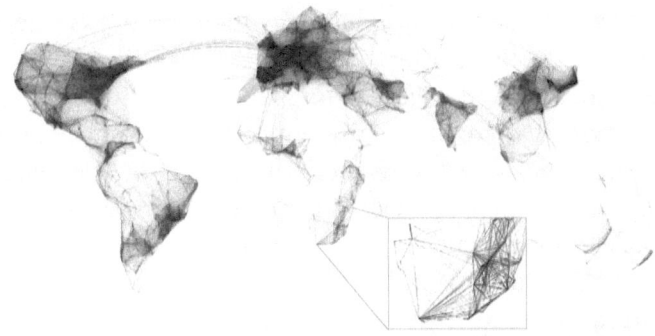

(Inter)connectedness

The study by Van Schalkwyk (2015) operationalised university–community engagement (and the management of the inherent tension) as 'interconnectedness'. Framing university engagement as interconnectedness makes possible the exploration of a particular type of connectedness in the network society. The study defined interconnectedness as 'the relationship (in tension) of academics engaging with those outside of the university while simultaneously linking back to the university' (Van Schalkwyk 2015: 205).

Interconnectedness was operationalised along two dimensions. The first dimension is 'articulation', which has a number of characteristics. First, articulation includes the extent to which the aims and outcomes of engagement activities articulate with the university's strategic objectives. Second, articulation factors in the degree to which projects were self-determined or steered by the interests of external stakeholders. Third, articulation includes the linkages that engagement activities have with external stakeholders such as government, industry, small businesses, non-governmental organisations and others. An additional link is the extent to which there are connections with an 'implementation agency' (i.e. an external body which takes up the knowledge and/or its products generated or applied through research or training). Fourth, articulation takes into account linkages generated through sources of funding in three respects: whether the engagement activity has obtained external funding; the number of funding sources secured; and the extent to which the project developed a relationship with its funders over time.

Seen as a type of connectedness, the articulation indicators are all of a type that are *inside-out* connections. Given that the project as an organised set of activities is the unit of analysis, engagement takes place within the university as a complex organisation with both vertical arrangements (university management and the faculties or schools below it) and horizontal arrangements (the number of autonomous disciplines arranged into faculties or schools) (Clark 1983). Articulation therefore not only includes inside-out connections between the project and those communities outside of the university but also inside-out connections from the project to the host university's structural and symbolic components (the strategic objectives formulated by management and the academic imperatives formulated by peers).

The second dimension of interconnectedness incorporates the extent to which engagement activities serve to strengthen the academic core of the university. According to Clark (1998), when an enterprising university develops an outreach structure, its academic departments, formed around disciplines and some interdisciplinary fields, remain the heartland of the university; the heartland being where traditional academic values and the day-to-day activities such as teaching and research take place. Instead of 'heartland', Van Schalkwyk (2015) used the concept 'academic core' developed by Cloete et al. (2011; see also Chapter 7 above). In Castellian terms, the academic core consists of the mutually dependent education and scientific functions of the university (see Chapters 2 and 3 above). The university as a service provider to the community risks restricting its contribution to the application of existing knowledge in lieu of the production of new knowledge and is, consequently, likely to make only a marginal, short-term contribution to development.

Academic core indicators include the extent to which the engagement activity generates new knowledge (versus applying existing knowledge) using publications and patents as proxies; feeds into teaching or curriculum development; is linked to the formal training of students; enables academics to disseminate their research; and is linked to international academic networks. These indicators are all of an *outside-in* type of connection.

The various aspects relating to 'articulation' and 'strengthening the academic core' were converted into a set of eight indicators which could then be applied to an analysis of the engagement activities included in the study. Four indicators were developed for each of the dimensions to ensure an equal weighting between the articulation and the academic core indicators (see Table 1 in Appendix 3). On the basis of the indicator score totals for articulation and for the academic core, the projects were plotted on a graph depicting the intersection between 'articulation' and 'strengthening the academic core' in order to provide a graphic representation of each project's interconnectedness. Interconnectedness is represented on a third axis, which bisects the articulation and academic core quadrants, and which ranges from disconnected (-9) to interconnected (9).

The articulation, academic core and interconnectedness scores for each of the two African universities in the study are presented in Figures 3 and 4.

Projects at both universities scored higher on the articulation indicators than on the academic core indicators. A closer examination of the articulation scores reveals that projects at both universities scored well in terms of the project initiation and agenda-setting indicators. However, on average, projects scored relatively poorly when it came to the other articulation indicators.

Engagement project scores were low at both universities in terms of their links to specific institutional strategic objectives, as expressed in each university's mission and vision statements. At NMMU, the data show that projects mostly linked to between one and three of the institutional objectives, most often to NMMU's commitment to regional development. By contrast, the data show that NMMU's strategic objective of contributing to both African and global development was consistently absent from the objectives of the university's engagement projects. An analysis of funding sources shows that firms located in the region, as well as funding from the province and the city, made up the bulk of the project funds at NMMU. It would appear, therefore, that for project leaders the local reality in which a project operates trumps the continental and global aspirations of the university.

In the case of Makerere University, the data show that, on average, projects linked to at least two of the university's strategic objectives. As in the case of NMMU, responsiveness to global challenges was rarely cited as a project objective at Makerere University, and most projects indicated an aspiration to respond to national needs (rather than regional needs, as was found to be the case at NMMU). Unlike NMMU, projects at Makerere University relied more heavily on funds from foreign donors, with limited funding from government or industry. Perhaps the finding that NMMU's engagement activities are regionally focused while Makerere University's are nationally focused, is unsurprising given Makerere's position as a national flagship university, while

CHAPTER 9 Van Schalkwyk: African universities and connectedness

Figure 3: Interconnectedness at Makerere University (n=22)

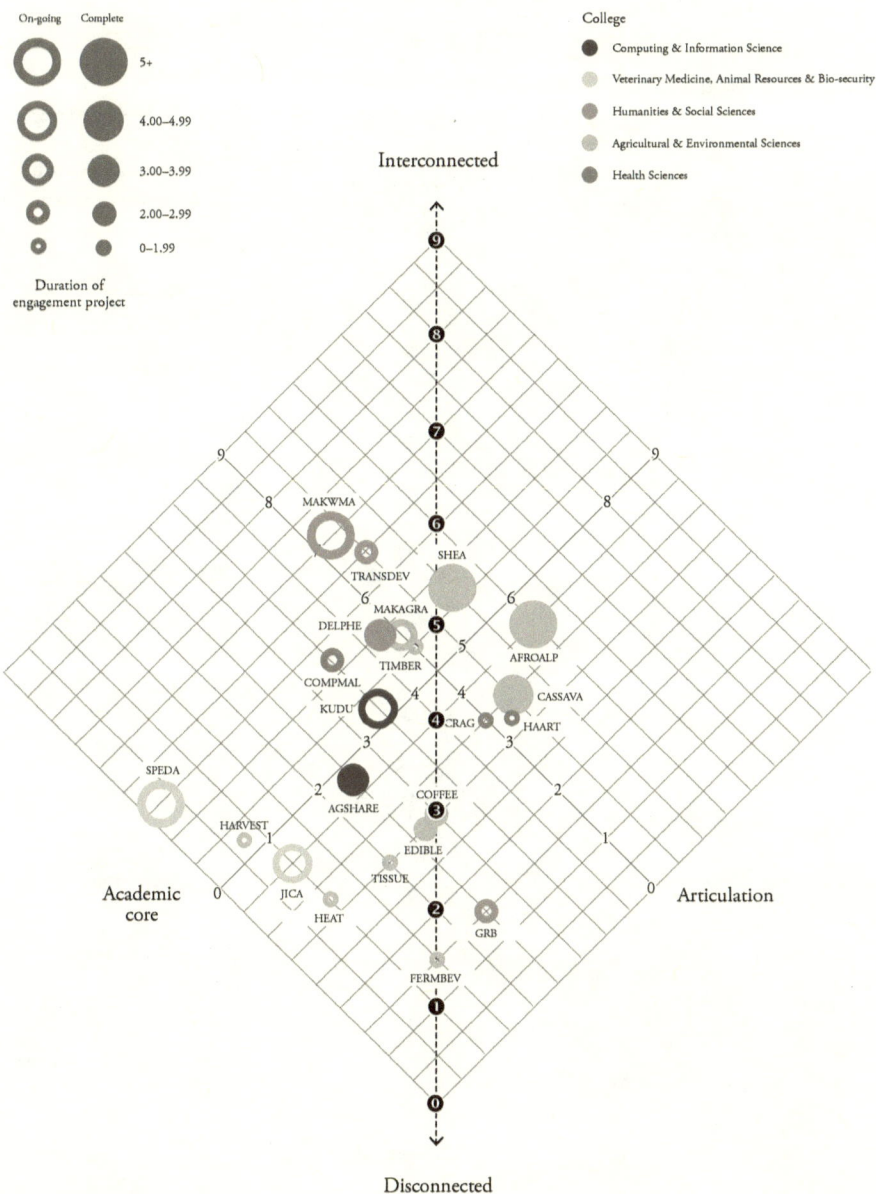

Figure 4: Interconnectedness Nelson Mandela Metropolitan University (n=77)

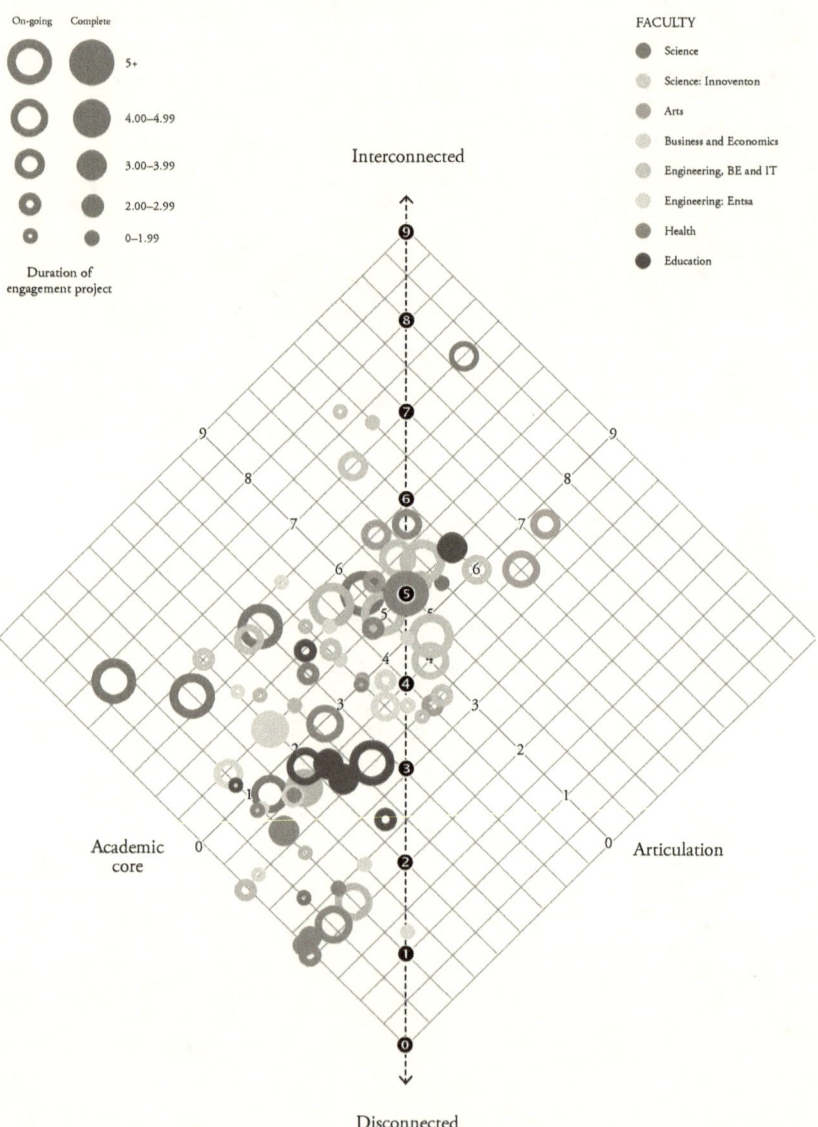

NMMU fulfils a more regional developmental role within its national higher education system.

In the case of external linkages, the scores indicate that, on average, projects at both universities linked to only one external constituent other than the project's funders. This would appear to indicate a tendency to focus engagement activities on a single constituency, in so doing creating a binary relationship between the university and the external constituent, rather than a more networked approach to engagement activities in which multiple stakeholders are active. However, it could also indicate that academics are connecting to a central node in a specific network. The centrality of the node negates the need to connect with other nodes. The specificity of the network points to the location of value in one network that may be absent in other non-scientific networks.

The academic core indicators reveal which projects are high producers in terms of the production, transfer and dissemination of *new* knowledge. From a different vantage point, the academic core indicators also reveal which projects are not linking the knowledge created (assuming such knowledge has indeed been created) to the academic core, even if they are engaging successfully with those external to the university.

At Makerere University, projects scored relatively well in terms of knowledge creation, the availability of knowledge in the public domain and linking to PhD programmes. Projects at Makerere University scored less well in terms of how they linked to teaching and learning activities at the university. Of concern at NMMU is the fact that, on average, projects did not generate new knowledge. Weighing down NMMU's scores to some extent is the fact that much of the knowledge created by its community engagement projects was not publicly available. In particular, many projects at NMMU (24%) received funding from industry, with embargoes being placed on the dissemination of proprietary knowledge. This restricts the flow of information to private networks, and while these networks may nevertheless be global, the flow of information is more likely to be vertical rather than horizontal as would be the case if the information were to be made publicly available. Makerere University, in contrast, scores much better on the public availability of knowledge. Given that in the case of Makerere University, project funding came predominantly (78%) from foreign donors who value and even contractually require the openness and accessibility of the knowledge produced, public access is to be expected. The study did not go so far as to determine the quality of the knowledge produced (using, for example, citations as a proxy for quality). Without a quality indicator, it is not possible to speculate about the value of the publicly available knowledge produced and, consequently, whether such publicly available knowledge would propel Makerere University's position in global scientific networks.

With some exceptions, projects that scored lower on the academic core indicators tended to be projects that were ongoing rather than complete. Certainly, in the case of Makerere University, it is evident that completed projects scored better on the connectedness axis than did ongoing projects. In fact, the samples at both universities tended to have a preponderance of ongoing projects. Given that many of the engagement activities in the sample were still in the early phases and given the time-lag in the academic publishing process, these ongoing projects retain the potential to score more highly on the academic core indicators as they mature. This highlights the importance of not only producing snapshots of university engagement activities at a particular moment in time, but also of tracking engagement activities over a longer period in order to observe possible improvements in linking engagement projects to the core functions of the university.

Disciplinary valency

In the field of chemistry, the valency of an element measures its ability to combine with other elements. Following Clark's (1983) conception of the independence of scientific disciplines from one another for their survival, it is conceivable that engagement may prevail and thrive within one discipline without any impact on another discipline. In other words, projects in different disciplines

CHAPTER 9 Van Schalkwyk: African universities and connectedness

within the same university can be more or less interconnected, and the disciplinary 'charge' of a project may have a bearing on its valency, that is, its ability to combine with external 'elements' to create (inter)connections between scientific and non-scientific networks.

Mindful of this possibility, the study by Van Schalkwyk (2015) included a disciplinary dimension in the data collected in order to capture the disciplinary convergences and variances of the engagement projects studied. In the case of disciplines that claim to be unsuitable for the engagement enterprise, the intention of adding a dimension for discipline or field of study was not to expose those disciplines that are failing to engage, but rather to identify what can be learnt from projects that appear to be doing so successfully regardless of their perceived disciplinary engagement encumbrances. Moreover, a differentiated picture of university–community engagement by discipline would be a first step towards defining different engagement criteria for projects and their respective academic units across the university.

Figure 3 shows that engagement projects at Makerere University are evenly spread across the middle of the interconnectedness spectrum. However, projects in the sample from the College of the Humanities and Social Sciences, and from the College of Agricultural and Environmental Sciences, appear to be the most successful in mediating the tension between linking both externally and with the academy. Projects from the College of Veterinary Medicine, Animal Resources and Bio-security and, to a lesser extent, from the College of Computing and Information Science, appear to be struggling to link their engagement with external communities to the core functions of the university.

At NMMU, Figure 4 shows that the Faculties of the Arts and of Engineering appear more capable than other faculties at the university in managing the tension between engaging externally and strengthening the core. While the Faculty of Health has some projects that score between 4 and 6 on the interconnectedness axis, it also houses several projects (mainly from the Department of Nursing) that populate the disconnected end of the spectrum, mainly owing to poor academic core ratings. This may point to different valencies within a specific faculty – some faculty units may have a more developed academic core while others (such as Nursing) may have a less well-developed academic core, and struggle to conceptualise connections to the core in the design and execution of their university–community engagement projects.

The findings confirm the relevance of discipline as a determining factor of interconnectedness. However, they also show that disciplines that are frequently cited as being at a disadvantage when it comes to making connections to external communities, such as the Faculty of Arts at NMMU and the College of Humanities and Social Sciences at Makerere University, are able to interconnect. This may point to the relevant but lesser contribution of the disciplinary valency of an engagement project when compared to the ability of project leaders to connect between different networks regardless of their disciplinary background.

Differentiating the core

While it seems important to distinguish between projects charged with distinctive disciplinary properties, it is also possible to differentiate at the project-level between the two core functions of research and teaching that make up the academic core. In other words, some projects may link exclusively to either the knowledge transfer function or the knowledge production function.

While very few projects at either university scored well on the academic core indicators, it is possible that some projects chose to focus exclusively on research while others elect to focus exclusively on teaching and learning. An argument could be put forward that research (i.e. the production of new knowledge) is the only imperative for any university and that everything else, including teaching, follows. This stance challenges the inclusion of teaching and learning as an equally weighted contributor to the academic core. The knowledge creation imperative is not disputed; however, conceiving of the knowledge creation and transfer process as one that is unitary is contested. In a differentiated arrangement either within or between institutions in a single national system, it is conceivable that specialisation occurs, with different actors playing different roles at various stages in the knowledge creation and transfer process. Knowledge creation remains a critical and non-negotiable first step in this process, but it seems possible to conceive of a process in which certain academics specialise in knowledge creation while others specialise in knowledge transfer (including teaching and even application). That those with specialist roles in the knowledge creation and transfer process are linked together across or within universities in a differentiated system is essential in ensuring an uninterrupted flow in the process.

From an organisational perspective, faculties, departments, centres and institutes could take a differentiated approach to how their projects connect to the academic core. If this differentiated approach is one that is coordinated and managed, then it could be that no single project scores well on the interconnectedness axis, but that a centre or faculty as a whole may well do so if it were to be taken as the unit of analysis. In other words, the sum of the parts should be taken into consideration before dismissing a coordinated cluster of projects as being disconnected from the academic core.

Switches

The university–community engagement projects referred to thus far are the temporary structural arrangements around which activity is organised and coordinated. But it is academics who create projects and manage their activities.

The indicators of interconnectedness reveal variance in the university–community engagement activities at both universities. Some engagement activities returned a high score and can therefore be described as interconnected, while others returned a low score and can therefore be described as disconnected. Those projects that are interconnected are proxies for academic project leaders who are seemingly well-equipped or agile enough to connect both to the science community and to those communities located externally to the university. In Castellian terms, these academic project leaders appear to be able to connect successfully between the space of flows and the space of places, acting as network switches. In a networked world, this allows academics to 'exercise control over others' owing to their 'ability to connect and ensure the cooperation of different networks by sharing common goals and combining resources' (Castells 2009: 45).

Castells makes it plain that network switches are not (or at least should not be considered as) individuals who are able to mobilise their own personal ambitions to reprogramme networks: '[swtichers] are not persons, but they are made of persons. They are actors, made of networks of actors engaging in dynamic interfaces that are specifically operated in each process of connection' (Castells 2009: 47). Castells does not provide extensive coverage on the agency of individuals in global networks. This gap evokes similar criticism levelled at neo-institutional theorists who, it is claimed, do not account adequately for individual agency within social arrangements (see, for example, Greenwood & Suddaby 2006; Hardy & Maguire 2008; Swanson & Ramiller 1997, 2004). In the analysis presented here, individual academics are afforded agency in the global scientific network. But their agency as switches depends less on their individual or personal character traits and more on what they have to offer: knowledge. And knowledge due to its cumulative and communal origins does not definitively vest in a single individual. To be sure, names of notable scientists are attributed to the discovery of vaccines, genomes and social theories, but their discoveries and treatises are predicated on the work and incremental contributions of others. In this sense, it is the knowledge produced by science and embodied in particular scientists that makes possible their role as knowledge-network switches. What differentiates them is first and foremost the value of the knowledge they have to offer place-based networks (and potentially to other global networks for which knowledge holds currency) and to a lesser extent their ability to attract the attention of powerful nodes in other networks.

CHAPTER 9 Van Schalkwyk: African universities and connectedness

The stand-out example of a project led by a university academic switching between science and community networks is to be found at NMMU. The Ocean Turtle Task Force Project scored 7.625 on the interconnectedness axis, the highest of all the projects at the two universities. The project brings together representatives from national turtle focal points in the Comoros, France, Kenya, Madagascar, Mozambique, Seychelles, South Africa and the UK. Representatives evaluate sites of potential international importance for the conservation, protection and management of sea turtles. The project aims to identify sites of particular ecological, socio-economic, cultural and educational value. Local conservationists meet annually for capacity-building exercises and for sharing data on the challenging topic of conserving migrating sea turtles.

The project aligned with NMMU's strategy and was one of the few projects bearing on NMMU's aspiration of being an African university. The project was initiated by the United Nations Environment Programme; the project proposal was multi-authored, and deviations to the proposal were permitted. The project had in place an advisory group that convened annually. The project had established links to government, NGOs, industry (regional fishing industry bodies) and to fishing communities. Funding came from three sources, all for two years, and with the option of being renewed.

The project has clearly made several place-based connections to articulate the meaning and relevance of its engagement activities. At the same time, the project connects to the non-material global network of science by offering the novel knowledge that has been produced by the project as the result of its localised connections. The project developed new interventions for the tuna fishing industry to protect the sea turtle population, and technology to record and track turtle migration. The findings of the project were presented at academic conferences and published in academic journals, as well as in the form of articles on the web and in the print media. The project led to the introduction of a new 15-week module on marine biology at the university. Postgraduate students participated in the project as researchers and undergraduates were involved as project interns. The project was one of very few at either NMMU or Makerere University that included a network of international academics.

On the other ends of the spectrum are those projects that returned a low interconnectedness score, and that are disconnected, either from the science community or from those communities outside of the university. Which is not to say that these project leaders are not connected; rather they are exclusively connected to one network to the detriment of being connected to other networks.

Of interest at NMMU is how the engagement projects of two extension units in the Faculties of Science and in Engineering (Innoventon and Entsa, respectively) compare with projects located in the parent faculties. In both cases, the engagement projects at Innoventon and Entsa score lower on the interconnectedness dimension than do projects located in the faculties, although the Entsa projects still score relatively well compared to the broader population of engagement projects at NMMU. This would suggest that these extension units, set up to facilitate interaction between the university and external communities, were less successful in linking their activities to core functions housed in their parent faculties.

Describing 'new Third World universities' (Chapter 3: 50) and their place in the network society, Castells refers to specialised organisations that are part of the university system capable of organising external connections which, in conjunction with an emphasis on research, are needed to elevate a country's productive system (Chapter 3: 49–50). Castells is not specific about the role these specialised organisations are to play in the research process but he seems to suggest that in addition to faculty-based academics acting as switches between networks, certain structural arrangements could be put in place to act as switches between faculties and external communities.

The findings of the interconnectedness study show that the specialised organisations at NMMU responsible for 'extension' are focusing predominantly on organising external connections for the application of existing knowledge, either without consideration of where the required new knowledge will come from as the demands of external actors evolve, or with the assurance that the required new knowledge will be produced by NMMU academics located in the faculty. Using bibliometric data on journal articles published as a proxy for the creation of knowledge, it would be possible to determine whether the parent faculties of these extension units are in fact deserving of the assurance placed in them by their extension units. What is not clear and requires further investigation, is whether, even if the extension units are successful at connecting to external communities and their faculties are independently generating new knowledge, there are effective bi-directional institutional connections between the extension units and their host faculties.

Valves

While Castells recognises that in the space of flows, information possesses directionality (Castells 1989), he provides little by way of evidence on how directionality functions in globalised digitised networks, or how information flows between the dynamic intersection of the space of flows and the space of places.

The method proposed by Van Schalkwyk (2015) to operationalise interconnectedness does not claim to capture nor reflect the impact of engagement activities on those actors with whom academics engage. In this sense, the impact of their engagement activities is only measured in one direction; that is, on the university. It is conceivable that projects that score low in terms of the extent to which they strengthen the academic core may nevertheless have a meaningful and positive impact on a particular community or enterprise. However, such place-based impact does not necessarily add value to the university's position as a node in the globalised network of science. Van Schalkwyk's notion of interconnectedness therefore *assumes* a bi-directional flow, even if it did not operationalise impact in both directions due to its primary concern, that is, the impact of engagement on the university's core functions. This is a critical point often overlooked by the proponents of engagement. A singular focus on the flow of value from the university to a place-based community, ignores the vital return flow of information that places the university in a better position to contribute to the flow of information and, by implication, the creation of the new knowledge needed for development, in globalised scientific networks.

The study of interconnectedness shows that at both NMMU and at Makerere University there appears to be an under-appreciation of the requirement for bi-directional flow of information (and value). Most projects display the properties of valves rather than switches in regulating the flow of information. At the same time, there does appear to be a growing recognition at the system level, in South Africa at least, of the pitfalls of valve-like engagement. The South African Department for Higher Education and Training's *White Paper for Post-School Education and Training* (Department of Higher Education and Training 2013) states that 'it is likely that future funding of such [engagement] initiatives in universities will be restricted to programmes linked directly to the academic programme of universities, and form part of the teaching and research function of these institutions'. It remains to be seen whether such sentiments are leveraged or incentivised in order to render them effective.

Conclusion

Like The Copula Hall that connects the doppelgänger cities of Besźel and Ul Qoma, the university and its academics must connect between different social realities, that of science and that of the communities that lie outside of the university. And it must do so to fulfil its dual mandate of knowledge production and relevance. However, unlike The Copula Hall that makes possible sanctioned connections between two co-located physical spaces, universities must connect between two different types of networks, one that Castells describes as being defined in terms of place and one that is defined in terms of (information) flows.

The overarching objective of this chapter was to make a modest contribution to Castells's 'theory' of the network society by exploring the possibility of different types of connectedness in university networks. It did so by examining the connections university academics make as part of their community engagement activities, proposing that a particular type of connectedness is in operation at universities, and showing that disciplinary valency and the directionality of connections matter.

Situating university–community engagement within Castells's network society allows for the interpretation of engagement as the (inter)connectedness of university academics and their host universities within and between networks. Universities seeking to engage with external communities must navigate between two distinct networks in tension – one which is global, programmed by the logic of science and propelled by the flow of information across a space of flows – and one that is local – programmed by the logic of innovation in a space of places. The capacity of universities and their systems to manage this tension and the dexterity of academics and the value of the knowledge they have at their disposal to connect between networks is crucial for development as it connects new knowledge to entrepreneurs (of both the social and economic kind) and to inventors who spur innovation.

The indicators of connectedness reveal a mixed picture at two African universities (Van Schalkwyk 2015): in both cases, there are engagement activities that can be described as interconnected and there are also activities that are clearly disconnected. 'Articulation' scores at both universities were stronger than the 'strengthening the academic core' scores. In other words, the degree to which university–community engagement activities can be said to be strengthening the African university as a key knowledge-producing institution is uneven and too frequently marginal.

The study of two African universities also shows that there are projects located in university structures (organisational sub-units) that are adept at connecting the university to external communities. However, these structures are not simultaneously connecting to the core university enterprise of knowledge production (research) and transmission (teaching). This is not to say that faculties at these universities are not productive or that they are absent from the global networks of science. In fact, if we use publications as a proxy for scientific productivity, then both universities show a marked improvement since 2000 (Bunting et al. 2014). It is therefore still possible, as suggested by Castells, for bridging agents or intermediaries to facilitate bi-directional flows between faculty and outreach organisations. Further research is required to establish the existence and effectiveness of such structural arrangements.

What is clear from the study is that some academics at the two African universities are able to connect across networks, acting as switches in the flow of information between and across different networks. These networked academics make possible the bi-directional flow of information, in so doing connecting the university to external communities in a manner that at the very least creates value for the university as a node in the global scientific network. This illustrates not only the importance of the direction of flows of information for development (often under-appreciated by advocates of university–community engagement), but also the possibility of African universities strengthening their hand when negotiating their participation in global science networks while remaining relevant to local development needs.

Conclusion

Contradictory functions, unexpected outcomes, new challenges

Johan Muller, Nico Cloete & François van Schalkwyk

After considering the detailed empirical pictures sketched by the data collected in the four African papers, it is sobering to return to the very first paper by Castells in this collection and to realise again how prescient it was, and how many pitfalls it anticipated. It pays to reflect again on the kind of theoretical account he was putting forward. In Chapter 3 of this volume (pp. 35–36), he told us that, in contrast to Bourdieu's functionalist theory, his was a *conflict* theory, following that of Alain Touraine's. The important consequence was that we should always expect conflict when attending to functions: conflict was the normal, not the pathological condition. The four academic functions and one social function of universities he went on to anatomise were thus not to be understood as equivalent boxes that university administrators or policy makers could tick as if signing off on a list. Nor could increases or decreases in relevant indicators only be examined on a linear scale. They were social forces that were in collision with each other, and this collision needed to be understood, mediated and managed. His conclusion bears re-statement:

> the critical element in the structure and dynamics of the university system is their ability to combine and make compatible seemingly contradictory functions which have all constituted the

system historically and are all probably being required at any given moment by the social interests underlying higher education policies. It is probably the most complex analytical element to convey to policy-makers: namely, that because universities are social systems and historically produced institutions, all their functions take place simultaneously within the same structure, although with different emphases. (p. 42)

What the crucial factors conditioning mediation are, is the question. The picture sketched by the empirical data provided in Chapters 6 to 9 helps to dramatise how this clash of functions and social interests play out in African universities still labouring to come out from under the shadow of their colonial parent institutions, trying to shake off the legacy of their subordinate status.

Chapter 6 shows how the genesis and tradition of the colonial-era African university is rooted in a role to serve a primarily ideological and elite socialisation function, though these two functions are not pursued further in the empirical indicators of the HERANA research. Nevertheless, the variable imprint of this legacy is clearly seen in the performance indicators of most African universities today. The chapter details the long road back from this legacy tracked in the changing policy documents accompanying the successive establishment of independence in national rule. The chapter speaks optimistically of 'revitalisation' as a new discourse of 'development' begins to emerge in response to influential voices calling for a re-orientation, Castells's included. The chapter ends by distinguishing between two strands of development discourse, one strand what the chapter calls an 'instrumentalist' sense, the other, what we can call, following Castells, an 'engine of development' sense.

But how did the universities interpret this changing policy environment? Chapter 7 examined the vision and mission statements of the eight universities making up the then-newly established HERANA project and conducted interviews with key informants. Castells had predicted that universities in developing countries may react to the 'new' emerging global informational economy by 'rushing' towards the new mode of production and development – making rhetorical commitments to it – without fully appreciating what far-reaching changes this would imply for the economy and universities alike. HERANA documents a clear move, even if it is not exactly a 'rush', towards an economically instrumental and 'engine of development' view of the university in the public face the universities presented in their vision and mission statements.

This was the aspiration. What was the reality? Defining the 'new' paradigm of 'development' as 'knowledge-led', HERANA posited eight indicators of what they called the 'academic core' of the university – SET and postgraduate enrolment and graduation rates, especially of PhDs; international publications. They then compared the eight institutions across the indicators, using data from 2001 to 2007. Their conclusion was not a happy one:

> With the exception of Cape Town, the other universities (in the HERANA sample) do not have academic cores that live up to the high expectations contained in their mission statements. (p. 125)

This indicated not only a disconnect between aspiration and performance; it also indicated that only one of the institutions in the sample could be considered to be making a knowledge-led contribution to development. True, they were responding to social demand, and had increased their enrolment of undergraduates, in some cases quite dramatically. But they had yet to increase graduation at the postgraduate level, especially at the PhD level.

Chapter 8 continued with the same sample of institutions, now called 'flagship' institutions, and using more granular data, compared them on the knowledge indicators between 2001 and 2014. Though more detail and nuance is displayed, the picture produced does not offer any greater grounds for optimism. As the chapter concludes:

African universities are unable to manage successfully the political and ideological functions alongside the academic teaching activities of the university. (p. 140)

This conclusion can be re-phrased in more Castellian terms. First of all, most African universities have retained their ideological and elite socialisation roles. As we have seen, they have made at least public commitments to increasing their research-based activities. But they have also responded to social demands for greater access by granting greater access at the undergraduate level. In a context where resources were not expanding (in contrast to the educational systems of the Asian Tigers, for example: see Castells 2009: 274 & 276; see also p. 26 above), existing staff were expected to teach more. Castells had predicted that, where universities accede to social demand without the corresponding addition of resources, standards drop, and academic teaching becomes little more than 'warehousing', in his resonant phrase. What we see in this chapter, especially in the case of Nairobi University, is that research-oriented scholars quickly find the teaching-heavy environment inimical to sustained high-level research. To simply add new commitments on to existing commitments is to place the system under intolerable strain, where something has to give. Invariably it is the latest addition to the functional roster - the research function, one which requires dedicated nurturance, that falls by the wayside. This is not how to balance the contradictory functions of higher education in an informational world.

Unlike the Asian Tigers, universities in Africa have been left with vague talk of 'development', but with no clear idea what this might mean for specifying the choices universities might make towards an 'informational' economy. It is true that the lineaments of the informational economy are not yet fully evident in Africa; it is also true that without the resources to develop new areas to the requisite high level, these initiatives will wither. But a clearly enunciated development vision, more particularly practical steps to pursue it, is nowhere evident in either the projections of government, the plans of the universities or the academic activities examined by the HERANA research. African universities have found themselves without effective development signposting, either from a directive developmental state like the ones in East Asia, or a robust market as might be said to exist in Europe and the USA, to signal the high-level needs of the present and future economy and the consequent requirements from universities.

In this context, Gornitzka and others (2007) have developed a middle-order governance concept of the *pact* as an explicit normative agreement between government and universities as to what each is expected to do to translate the high-level notion of the informational mode of development into a device that specifies guidelines that can be monitored in the interests of accountability, or turned into empirical indicators for purposes of research. Chapter 8 above shows that even when something like a pact has been enunciated, as it is in Mauritius (the only institution in the HERANA sample with anything resembling a pact), without concomitant targeted funding and government support, left to itself it will remain stuck in the default model for African universities, dominated by the social and not the scientific function. This radical disconnect from any development path of the economy might, with justification, be called 'blind' development.

At whose door should we lay this failure? It is plausible to suggest that this malaise of 'blind' development is the outcome of a state of paralysis created by a titanic clash of social interests unconstrained and unmediated by an encompassing framework of common purpose about the essential goals the university ought to pursue. The political elites in the society at large, and their representatives in government, seem unable to suspend their interest-based politics and patronage pursuits long enough to forge and agree on a broader common development framework for the country at large. Even when such a framework has been forged, its implementation is stalled by the interest conflicts that consume the energies of the political elite. This is particularly evident in South Africa in 2017; a common plan, the *National Development Plan* (National Planning Commission 2012), has in fact been accepted by the national Parliament, but its implementation has been stalled by unbridled interest conflicts in the ruling party.

Student politics on campus likewise mimics the national scene. With political branches of national parties proliferating on campuses, student politics abandons student concerns and becomes a proxy battleground for national political tensions. The relationship between the student bodies and their leaders is cemented by patron–client relationships between the national parties and student leaders, held in place by what Luescher and Mugume (2014) delicately call 'resource-exchanges'.

As for the professoriate; the picture painted in the chapters above shows them to be riven between rival visions of the university; some cling to a golden age vision of autonomy and independence partly superseded in the home countries from which it was transplanted; others are weighed down with teaching responsibilities and could care less; yet others turn to consultancies as sources of remuneration supplementation (Mkandawire 2011; Wangenge-Ouma et al. 2015). This is paradoxical, to say the least: foreign donors and the state, the main sponsors of consultancies that divert academic energies away from academic publication and supervision, are also the loudest voices decrying the lack of research publications in the universities. In the absence of a common purpose, these activities spiral out as various kinds of individual survival or advancement strategies. As we commented above, this kind of academic milieu is not only unproductive for serious scholars, but is actively abrasive, and those that can, seek greener academic pastures, usually abroad.

A secondary consequence of this unmediated clash of social interests is also becoming apparent. In some institutions, students pursue their political battle not only against local and national opponents, but against science itself, epitomised in the rather chilling rallying cry 'Science must Fall' (Steerpike 2016), a possibility Castells warned against in Chapter 3 above (see also Chapter 2).

The second difference between most African universities and successfully developing university systems has to do with *differentiation*, or rather its lack. With the partial exception of

South Africa, African countries do not have a higher education system. Not infrequently, the colonial powers left behind them a national university with an entrenched ideological/elite-socialisation mandate, and the other universities that have since sprung up, public and increasingly private, have developed rather haphazardly in its wake. Insofar as universities are state-organised at all, they tend to be treated all the same, with the same policy tools and funding formulae. Consequently, when the policy emphasis changes, it triggers a chain reaction of mimicry, where less prestigious institutions try to emulate the more prestigious ones. The result, in the absence of any direction or incentive to do otherwise, is *institutional convergence*. There are signs of this isomorphic mimicry in South Africa where there are at least the basic lineaments of a differentiated system based not on design or direction but on differing historical legacies of colonialism and apartheid.

There is a third feature of African universities that marks it out from the universities of the first world. This is the particular form of evolution of the indigenous elite. The institutions Castells cites as performing the elite-socialising function in France – the *grandes écoles*, or in England – Oxford and Cambridge, are a far cry from the national universities of Africa. Where the former increasingly select and educate a highly skilled elite, capable, as in the French case, of training also for high level positions in the private sector (see p. 37 above), the latter are trained to staff the lower and middle layers of the civil service. We may call this cadre of university graduates a demographic or indigenous elite, one which is still also predominantly male. They can be compared with the educated elite in name only.

The main difference, and the one critical to success in the informational economy, is what Castells has called *self-programmability*. The high-level elite trained in France and England are trained to self-adapt; the skills of the indigenous elite, on the other hand, rarely rise above the generic, produced as they were and are to perform reproductive functions for the colonial and post-colonial state. This form of labour, Castells has repeatedly stressed, is uniquely incapable of driving a developmental project towards the informational mode of production.

It is thus not exactly wrong to refer to students in African universities as an elite. In Trow's (1973) terms, they are still part of an elite system that has yet to be massified, even though the increased enrolments and lack of adequate resource allocation leads to overcrowding. We may call these universities 'overcrowded elite institutions'. In Mamdani's terms, these students are still considered indubitably privileged. But unlike Bourdieu's (1973) elite, which comes from the social elite and is, according to him at least, destined for it, what Castells means by an 'elite' is neither the university system they are part of, or the social stratum they come from. *To be part of the sustainable elite in the informational world means to be self-programmable.* To be fair, the colonialists in Africa assumed that this top layer of the colonial elite would be trained back in the home institutions, hopefully to be inducted into self-programmability, as Castells has pointed out. But that was never likely to be a long-term solution after independence, yet another solution has simply not been planned for.

What this elaboration of differing senses of 'elite' has highlighted is the following: African universities have not only succumbed to the social function of letting in more students than they can cope with, which 'suffocates' the performance of the generative scientific and research function, they have also continued to produce an indigenous elite increasingly unsuited to the networked world and informational economy Africa is inexorably headed towards. In other words, African universities and their overseeing states have yet to recognise and respond to their historical mission in the emerging informational economy – to develop numbers of highly qualified labour that is essentially self-programmable. It is this quality of their teacher corps that distinguishes the teachers of Finland, say, who top the PISA and TIMSS performance tables, from teachers in more modestly-performing countries like Norway (Afdal 2012). This is the lesson that all high-performing developing countries have learnt.

CHAPTER 10 Muller, Cloete & Van Schalkwyk: Conclusion

Chapter 9 switches focus from functions to networks, a dimension so far little attended to in the previous three chapters. Yet the larger concern, that of mediating tensions, is the same. The chapter identifies two characteristic kinds of network that universities are involved in; the network with the scientific community, and the network with the world outside the university, often called 'engagement'. Each kind of network can act as a 'block' to the other. This is not for reasons of bad faith. The more that academics engage in high level research that will draw the attention of the international peer community, the more the work runs the risk of being so decontextualised as to make its relevance to local contexts difficult to describe and discern; this is the basis for the long-standing animus against the 'ivory tower'. The converse is also true; the more the work focuses on the local context only, the more that local context consumes its relevance, and the less the work will concern itself with relevance to a broader context – say, to the country, to regional Africa or to the scientific field. It is this potential conflict which must be mediated if the university is to be successful in both these key networks.

The particular focus in the chapter is on whether work which is directed to the local context is also directed to the scientific context, the tension above notwithstanding. The chapter finds examples of work that does both, and it is clear that careful design of the project at the outset is key. Certain academics are thus particularly adept at acting as 'switches' between the two networks. Equally, however, these are few and far between, and by and large few contextually directed projects also manage to contribute productively to the science function.

The conclusions of these chapters should not be taken as cataloguing the failure of African academia only. The intention is the opposite. We already know from international indicators that African universities do not perform well by comparison with their global peers. The question is why and how. This is the path opened by Castells's trilogy. His work shines a particularly powerful light on the developmental predicament, and is especially valuable in pointing to the many structural impediments that must be acknowledged and strategically accommodated if they are to be overcome.

Envoi

We ended our previous book on Castells with a reference to World Book Day on the 23 April 2001, which had the happy dividend of also paying tribute to Catalonia, Castells's spiritual and literal homeland. We end this volume on 18 July 2017, International Mandela Day, a day which saw some of the Mandela Elders[1] march through central Cape Town to launch the global project 'Walk together', to commemorate his 'Long walk to freedom'. Unhappily, this day of re-affirmation of our global hopes and dreams was also a day of anger, recrimination and fear as South African political elites continue to struggle for the power to determine the direction of the modernity of our country. The titanic struggle between the global and the local is not one easily ended, for all the reasons that Castells has given throughout his incomparably rich work. Yet the continent, and its higher education systems, is uncontestably in a better place than it was in 2001 when we ended the previous book, and the indices, also those shown in this book, are mostly on an upward trajectory. Castells has always enjoined us to take the long view, the basis for what Gramsci called the 'optimism of the will' and for any optimistic vision for the future. We hope to continue this intellectual adventure with him for a while yet.

---

1 The Mandela Elders are: Nelson Mandela (founder), Martti Ahtisaari, Kofi Annan, Ban Ki-moon, Ela Bhatt, Lakhdar Brahimi, Gro Harlem Brundtland, Fernando H Cardoso, Jimmy Carter, Hina Jilani, Ricardo Lagos, Graça Machel, Mary Robinson, Desmond Tutu & Ernesto Zedillo.

Afterword 2017

Manuel Castells

The analyses and policies on higher education and development compiled in this volume were elaborated and discussed in South Africa with the broader African context in mind. I add here a few considerations that take into account the social transformations that have taken place in the last decade in the world economy and in the global institutional environment.

Specifically, three major processes are changing the coordinates of the global political economy, and are thus the challenges and strategies to which higher education must respond. First, global financial markets are increasingly the core of national and international economies, and they are characterised by systemic volatility, as manifest in the 2008 to 2012 financial crisis and its aftershocks. Second, the social and political reactions to the inequality of the policies drafted in response to the financial crisis have deepened the crisis of political legitimacy everywhere, and brought the state, once again, to the forefront of social dynamics and policy-making once again. Third, the information technology revolution has accelerated, creating entire new economic sectors, particularly in biotechnology, biomedicine, energy, nanotechnology, internet-based social media, artificial intelligence, automation and informational education. In all these areas, the role of knowledge production and management is central, and so is the strategic positioning of higher education.

However, the most important feature of the new institutional landscape is that these three processes interact. Depending on the forms and outcomes of this interaction, a virtuous circle of development may be created, or new contradictions will emerge, leading to an impasse in policy-making. Allow me to elaborate.

First, the financial crisis, as I have shown elsewhere (Castells 2012; Castells 2017a), vindicated the role of the state as the ultimate guarantor of global capitalism. Without the decisive intervention of governments between 2008 and 2010 in the United States and Western Europe, there could have been a financial meltdown. Indeed, in terms of value destroyed in the financial markets, the impact of the crisis was greater than in the 1930s, even relative to GDP. However, in contrast with the undisputable primacy of public financial policies, the neoliberal mantra at the source of crisis (Engelen et al. 2011) continued to be preached and practiced in business circles and in academia. The reason is very simple: given that governments absorbed the shock of the crises by using public resources, what was a crisis for most, was in fact a bonanza for the business elites. The share of capital over labour in the GDP increased substantially, higher income groups appropriated more income and assets than ever, and inequality skyrocketed both within countries and between countries. The upper middle classes connected around the world forming new profitable markets while the lower income groups saw their relative, and sometimes absolute, social condition worsen. Class polarisation, aggravated by gender and race, emerged again as a fundamental feature of humanity.

The convergence of business interests and the interests of the political elites deepened the crisis of political legitimacy worldwide. In the gap of trust thus created in the political institutions, arose alternative social movements proposing alternative policies (Castells 2015; Castells 2017b), undermining even further the legitimacy of mainstream political parties. Furthermore, a new brand of demagogic politics, fed by xenophobia and racism, obtained significant social support, and introduced a new populist leadership that hinted at reversing globalisation in a move that was simply unthinkable a few years ago when globalisation came to be considered as a natural, unstoppable fact of life (Castells forthcoming). Trump and Brexit epitomised this movement precisely in the two countries, central in the world economy, that launched liberalisation and globalisation policies during the 1980s. With global capitalism suffering from economic uncertainty, social discontent and institutional turmoil, statist countries, such as China and Russia, came to play a hegemonic role in the global economic and the new geopolitics. The end of history preached by neoliberal ideologues became the re-run of history in which states used capitalism in their strategies of power-making, rather than submitting to the logic of capital. Therefore, the world became more interconnected and more fragmented at the same time.

In a different, but not unrelated development, the technological revolution that took shape in the 1970s accelerated in its three major components: the biological revolution, the information technology revolution, and the communication revolution. Entire realms of human activity are being transformed, and so new industries and new markets are being created in a globally interdependent dynamic. Education is one of the key sectors in this transformation, and the most promising market for many venture capitals as it represents a substantial share of employment, spending and investment in every country. However, because of the dominance of government, and of government bureaucracies, the technological and institutional transformation in the education sector is proceeding at a much slower pace than in the economy at large. Moreover, the penetration of a business logic in education is confining the transformation of education to education for the elites or, in the opposite direction, for mass education with a much lower quality for the majority of the population.

In this context, higher education is, at the same time, on the edge of economic and technological transformation, and a key engine of development in the transformation of society. As argued in this volume, knowledge and human resources are the source of productivity growth and competitiveness in our interdependent world. And at the root of these processes are the universities, in their multiple manifestations. This is now an accepted discourse in development policies in almost every country. Yet, a simple observation of the practice of higher education policies in teaching, research and management belies the actual priority given by governments to the developmental goal of higher education. In fact, the ideology of education for development often is used to feed the interests of the higher education establishment, inside and outside government, with some notable exceptions, some of which I have been able to observe in the South African and Latin American context.

The elements potentially conducive to a developmental higher education are presented in some of the chapters of this volume, and so I will not reiterate the discussion here. I simply want to emphasise that higher education institutions are essential for both economic growth and social justice. If we forget that the need for social, gender and racial equality is equally as important as innovation and growth, then higher education will sharpen social fragmentation, ultimately disabling the institutional capacity to manage universities and countries at large.

However, these considerations could apply equally to the situation in the last two decades. Do the changes in the world that I have summarised here affect the diagnosis and policies for higher education? No, if I refer to the definition of goals, because the developmental hopes for economic growth and social justice are still largely unfulfilled. But yes, if we consider the means to achieve these goals. This is because of the interaction between the three processes of transformation I presented here. Given the instability of the financial core of capitalism, the source of economic growth has to shift decisively to innovation and technological transformation spurred by entrepreneurship and venture capital; this is to say, to the productive economy in simplified language. Such a leap forward depends almost entirely on research and training in the universities, and on the quality of the labour force at large. This requires not only a greater share of resources devoted to higher education, but much smarter and more selective policies:

not socially selective policies, as this would increase social injustice, but pedagogically and institutionally selective.

Yet, for governments to play a legitimate role in this higher education transformation, they have to be legitimate themselves. And they are not. But this is not a catch-22. There is one way to re-establish legitimacy: to design and implement policies that truly have the public interest at heart. If governments continue to pillage public resources in the interest of politicians, then demagogues, such as Trump, will increase their popular appeal. And populist demagogues hate universities because they are, after all, the bastions of critical thinking and legitimate resistance to abuses and idiocy. But universities cannot simply mobilise against destructive politics; they also have to protect their mission as beacons of innovation, ideas and equality, without surrendering everything to activism. Ultimately, the convergence between the shift to a new form of economic organisation (Mason 2015), the acceleration of the technological revolution, and the re-legitimation of political institutions, has a site in society: higher education. This is why the university is simultaneously a decisive battlefield and our hope for a better future in the midst of the current darkness.

Appendix 1: Data on the academic cores of the eight HERANA universities (2001–2007)

Table 1: Academic core indicators: Scores and changes (2001–2007)

	% SET enrolments		Masters enrolments		Doctoral enrolments		Student:staff ratios		Student:staff ratios 2007		Doctoral graduates		Research publications		Research publication per academic	
	2001	2007	2001	2007	2001	2007	2001	2007	SET	BUS	2001	2007	2001	2007	2001	2007
Cape Town	40	42	2788	2906	706	1002	12	15	22	42	86	102	700	1017	0.92	1.14
Botswana	22	22	493	951	8	41	14	27	10	59	3	4	69	106	0.10	0.14
Dar es Salaam	52	36	609	2 165	54	190	11	14	14	22	10	20	49	70	0:12	0.07
Eduardo Mondlane*	61	48	0	420	0	3	10	13	12	51	0	0	0	11	0.03	0.03
Ghana	22	18	1344	1580	69	102	12	31	9	68	2	20	77	61	0.12	0.08
Makerere	16	32	1167	2767	28	32	15	18	11	96	11	23	72	139	0.07	0.20
Mauritius	51	43	350	859	114	193	24	16	12	34	7	10	23	36	0.12	0.13
Nairobi	33	31	3937	6145	190	62	12	18	8	42	26	32	143	136	0.12	0.11
NMMU	18	31	1100	1332	175	327	31	28	26	54	27	35	154	180	0.30	0.34

* 2001 figures for Eduardo Mondlane for masters and doctoral enrolments, and doctoral graduates and research publications, were not provided by the institution.

Appendices

Table 2: Academic core indicators: Ratings per university

	INPUT INDICATORS					OUTPUT INDICATORS		
PERIOD	Average for 2001–2007			2007 only		Average for 2001–2007		
INDICATOR	% SET enrolments	% masters and doctoral enrolments	Student: staff ratios	% academics with doctoral degrees	Research income / permanent academic (ppp$)	SET graduation rate	Doctoral graduates as % of permanent academics	Ratio of research publications per permanent academic
RATING	Strong: >39% Medium: 30–39% Weak: <30%	Strong: >9% Medium: 5–9% Weak: <5%	Strong: <20 Medium: 20–30 Weak: >30	Strong: >49% Medium: 30–49% Weak: <30%	Strong: >20 000 Medium: 10 000–20 000 Weak: <10 000	Strong: >20% Medium: 17–20% Weak: <17%	Strong: >10% Medium: 5–10% Weak: <5%	Strong: >0.5 Medium: 0.25–0.5 Weak: <0.25
Cape Town	41%	19%	13	58%	47 700	21%	15.00%	0.95
Botswana	22%	5%	15	31%	2 000	20%	0.66%	0.11
Dar es Salaam	43%	9%	14	50%	6 400	19%	2.18%	0.08
Eduardo Mondlane	54%	2%	12	24%	0	6%	0.00%	0.03
Ghana	19%	7%	22	47%	3 400	18%	0.17%	0.11
Makerere	24%	5%	16	31%	4 900	22%	1.63%	0.09
Mauritius	48%	13%	17	45%	3 000	26%	2.80%	0.13
Nairobi	31%	16%	14	71%	5 300	17%	1.87%	0.09
NMMU	25%	6%	30	34%	12 300	18%	5.50%	0.31

Key: ■ Strong ■ Medium ☐ Weak

Table 3: Academic core indicators for nine African universities: Average annual growth rates, 2001–2007

University	SET enrolments	Masters enrolments	Doctoral enrolments	Doctoral graduates	Research publications
Cape Town	3.1%	0.7%	6.0%	2.9%	6.4%
Botswana	5.3%	11.6%	31.3%	4.9%	7.4%
Dar es Salaam	8.3%	23.5%	23.3%	12.2%	6.1%
Eduardo Mondlane	6.6%	n/a	n/a	n/a	n/a
Ghana	12.9%	2.7%	6.7%	46.8%	-3.8%
Makerere	16.3%	15.5%	2.3%	13.1%	11.6%
Mauritius	2.2%	16.1%	9.2%	6.1%	7.8%
Nairobi	7.6%	7.7%	-17.0%	3.5%	-0.8%
NMMU	3.7%	3.2%	11.0%	4.4%	2.6%

Note: Annual growth rates for Eduardo Mondlane are not available in the table above for masters and doctoral enrolments, and doctoral graduates and research publications, because the institution could not provide us with this information for 2001.

203

Appendix 2: Data on research output and related indicators at seven HERANA universities (2001–2014)

Table 1: Changes in head count enrolments over 14-year period

	Average annual increase in total enrolments: 2001 to 2014	Head count enrolment total 2014	Change in head count enrolments: 2014 compared to 2001
Eduardo Mondlane University	12.8%	36 800	+29 100
University of Nairobi	11.9%	68 900	+52 900
University of Ghana	10.2%	40 200	+28 800
Makerere University	4.1%	36 400	+14 700
University of Cape Town	3.0%	24 700	+7 900
University of Botswana	3.4%	18 200	+6 500
University of Mauritius	3.4%	12 200	+6 700
Average/totals	**7.7%**	**237 400**	**+146 800**

Figure 1: Student enrolments and academic staff: 2001–2014

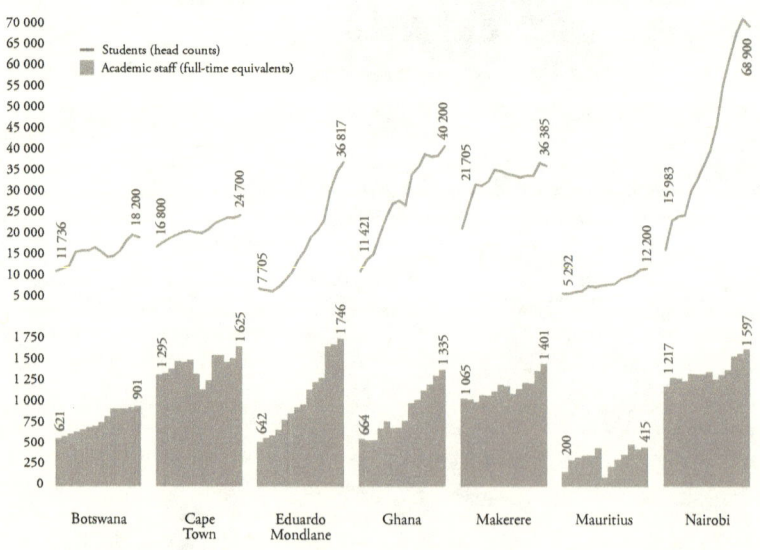

Appendices

Figure 2: % of undergraduate enrolments: 2001 vs 2014

Figure 3: Proportion of permanent senior academics and academics with doctoral degrees, 2014

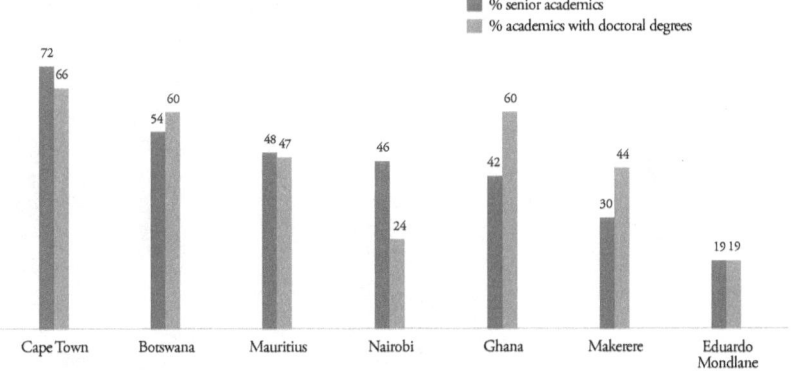

Figure 4: Percentage of academic staff with PhDs: 2001 vs 2014

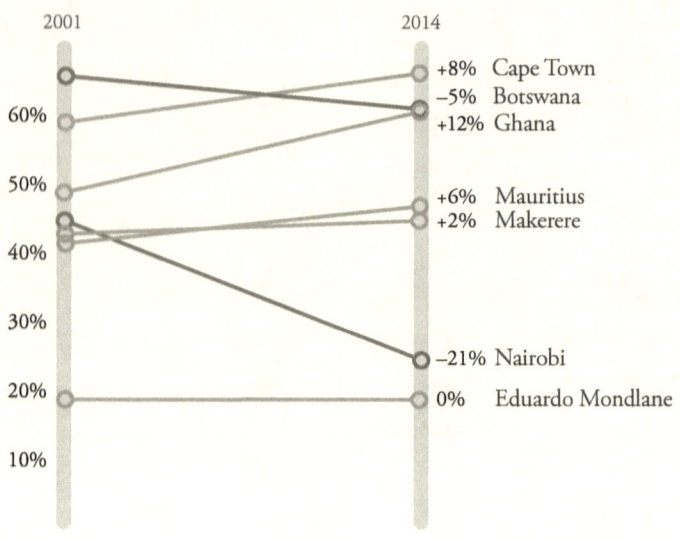

Figure 5: Doctoral graduates: 2001, 2009, 2014

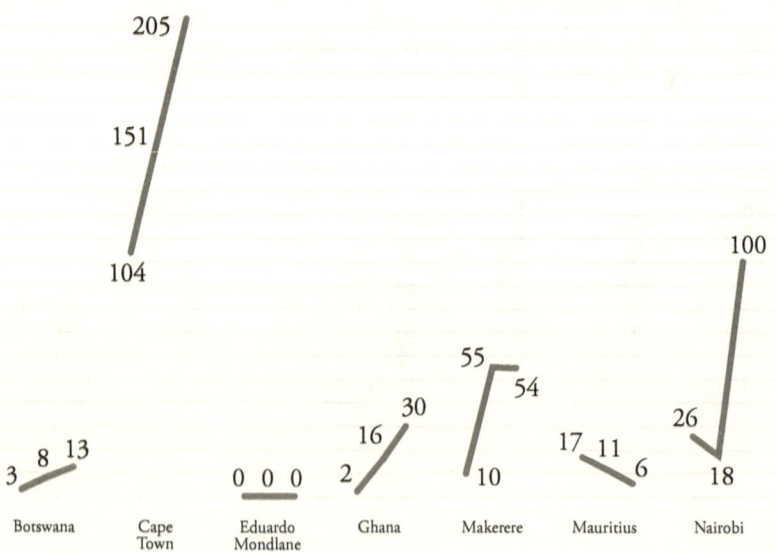

Appendix 3: Interconnectedness

Table 1: Indicators of interconnectedness and scores per indicator

	Articulation indicators	Score	Max score
A1	Alignment between project and university strategic objectives	For each project objective in alignment with university mission/vision = 0.25	1.0
A2	Initiation/agenda-setting	Self-initiated = 1	1.0
		Proposal more than one author = 0.5	0.5
		Project plan/terms of reference flexible = 1	1.0
		Advisory group and meets at least once per annum = 0.5	0.5
A3	Links to external stakeholders (non-academic) and to implementation agencies	For each link to an external stakeholder = 0.25 (max = 1)	1.0
		Direct link to implementation agency = 2 OR Indirect link to implementation agency = 1 OR Self-implemented = 1	2.0
A4	Funding	For each source of funding = 0.25 (max = 1)	1.0
		Long-term funding (more than three years) = 0.5	0.5
		Renewable funding (at least one source) = 0.5	0.5

	Academic core indicators	Score	Max score
C1	Generates new knowledge or product	New knowledge or product = 1.25 OR New data = 0.5	1.25
		Publicly available = 0.25	0.25
		PhDs linked to project = 0.5	0.5
C2	Dissemination	For each publication/presentation listed = 0.25	2.0
C3a	Teaching/curriculum development	Changes to courses/modules = 1 OR New courses/modules/programmes = 2	2.0
C3b	Formal teaching/learning of students	Students involved = 0.5	0.5
		Participation in project is course requirement = 1	1.0
		Other roles for students in project = 0.25 per role	0.5
C4	Links to academic networks	Links to academics from other universities = 1	1.0

References

Afdal H (2012) Constructing knowledge for the teaching profession: A comparative analysis of policy-making, curriculum content, and novice teachers' knowledge relations in the cases of Finland and Norway. Oslo: Faculty of Educational Sciences, University of Oslo

African Observatory for Science, Technology and Innovation (2013) *Assessment of Scientific Production in the African Union Member States 2005–2010*. Malabo: African Observatory for Science, Technology and Innovation. http://aosti.org/index.php/report/finish/5-report/15-assessment-of-scientific-production-in-the-african-union-2005-2010

Africa Progress Panel (2014) Grain, fish, money: Financing Africa's green and blue revolutions. *Africa Progress Report 2014*. Geneva: Africa Progress Panel. http://www.africaprogresspanel.org

Altbach P (2013) Advancing the national and global knowledge economy: The role of research universities in developing countries. *Studies in Higher Education* 38(3): 316–330

Altbach PG & Balán J (eds) (2007) *World Class Worldwide: Transforming research universities in Asia and Latin America*. Baltimore: Johns Hopkins University Press

Anderson MS (2001) The complex relations between the academy and industry: Views from the literature. *The Journal of Higher Education* 72(2): 226–246

Asquith Commission Report (1945) Report of the Commision on Higher Education in the Colonies, cmd. 6647. London: His Majesty's Stationery Office

Bailey T (2015) Roles of national councils and commissions in African higher education governance. In: Cloete N, Maassen P & Bailey T (eds), *Knowledge Production and Contradictory Functions in Higher Education*. Cape Town: African Minds. pp. 171–202

Basset RM & Maldonado-Maldonado A (eds) (2009) *International Organisations and Higher Education Policy: Thinking Globally, Acting Locally?* London: Routledge

Beauchesne O (2014) Map of scientific collaboration (Redux!). Blog post. http://olihb.com/2014/08/11/map-of-scientific-collaboration-redux/

Benner M & Sandstrom U (2000) Institutionalizing the triple helix: Research funding and norms in the academic system. *Research Policy* 29: 291–301

Bloom D, Canning D & Chan K (2006) *Higher Education and Economic Development in Africa*. Washington DC: The World Bank

Bourdieu P (1970) *La Reproduction*. Paris: Minuit

Bourdieu P (1973) *Cultural Reproduction and Social Reproduction in Knowledge, Education and Cultural Change*. London: Tavistock

Bourdieu P & Passeron J (1990) *Reproduction in Education, Society and Culture* (2nd edn). London: Sage

Braun D (2008) Organising political coordination of knowledge and innovation policies. *Science and Public Policy* 35(4): 227– 239

Brock-Utne B (2002) Formulating higher education policies in Africa: The pressure from external forces and the neo-liberal agenda. *Journal of Higher Education in Africa* 1(1): 24–56

Bunting I (2013) Differentiation in the South African public university system. Presentation at the Differentiation Seminar: Components of a Framework, Southern Sun Hotel, Cape Town, 24 January 2013. http://www.chet.org.za/files/resources/Ian%20Bunting%20Differentiation%20Slides%2024%20Jan%202013.pdf

Bunting I & Cloete N (2011) *Cross-national Performance Indicators: A case study of eight African universities.* Cape Town: CHET. http://www.chet.org.za/books/cross-national-performance-indicators

Bunting I & Cloete N (2015) Data trends and institutional performance: An overview of seven HERANA universities. Unpublished paper. Cape Town: CHET.

Bunting I, Cloete N, Kam Wah H & Nakayiwa-Mayega F (2015) Assessing the performance of African flagship universities. In: N Cloete, P Maassen & T Bailey (eds), *Knowledge Production and Contradictory Functions in African Higher Education.* Cape Town: African Minds. pp. 32–61

Bunting I, Cloete N & Van Schalkwyk F (2014) *An Empirical Overview of Eight Flagship Universities in Africa: 2001–2011.* Cape Town: Centre for Higher Education Transformation

Bunting I, Sheppard C, Cloete N & Belding L (2010) *Performance Indicators in South African Higher Education 2000–2008.* Cape Town: CHET. http://www.chet.org.za/books/performance-indicators-south-african-higher-education-2000%E2%80%932008

Carnoy M, Castells M, Cohen S & Cardoso F (1993) *The New Global Economy in the Information Age: Reflections on our changing world.* University Park: Pennsylvania State University Press

Carnoy M, Loyalka P, Dobryakova M, Dossani R, Froumin I, Kuhns K, Tilak J & Wang R (2013) *University Expansion in a Changing Global Economy: Triumph of the BRICS?* Stanford CA: Stanford University Press

Castells M (forthcoming) *Rupture: The crisis of liberal democracy.* Madrid: Alianza & Cambridge: Polity

Castells M, Bouin O, Caraca J, Cardoso G, Thompson J & Wieviorka M (eds) (2017a) *Europe's Crisis.* Cambridge: Polity

Castells M et al. (2017b) *Another Economy is Possible.* Cambridge: Polity

Castells M (2015) *Networks of Outrage and Hope: Social movements in the internet age.* Cambridge: Polity

Castells M (ed.) (2012) *Aftermath: The cultures of the economic crisis.* Oxford: Oxford University Press

Castells M (2010) *The Rise of the Network Society. The Information Age: Economy, society & culture.* Volume 1 (revised edition). Oxford: Blackwell

Castells M (2009) *Communication Power.* Oxford: Oxford University Press

Castells M (2001) Universities as dynamic systems of contradictory functions. In: J Muller, N Cloete & S Badat (eds), *Challenges of Globalisation: South African debates with Manuel Castells.* Cape Town: Maskew Miller Longman. pp. 206–223

Castells M (1998) *End of Millennium. The Information Age: Economy, society & culture.* Volume 3. Oxford: Blackwell

Castells M (1997) *The Power of Identity. The Information Age: Economy, society & culture.* Volume 2. Oxford: Blackwell

Castells M (1996) *The Rise of the Network Society. The Information Age: Economy, society & culture.* Volume 1. Oxford: Blackwell

Castells M (1991) The university system: Engine of development in the new world economy. In: A Ransom, S-M Khoo & V Selvaratnam (eds), *Improving Higher Education in Developing Countries.* Washington DC: The World Bank. pp. 65–80

Castells M (1989) *The Informational City: Information technology, economic restructuring, and urban regional process.* Oxford: Blackwell

Castells M & Himanen P (eds) (2014) *Reconceptualising Development in the Information Age.* Oxford: Oxford University Press

Chachon I (2014) Pacifism, human development, and the information model. In: M Castells M & P Himanen (eds), *Reconceptualising Development in the Information Age.* Oxford: Oxford University Press

CHET (2010) Cross-national Higher Education Performance Indicators. Draft report. Cape Town: Centre for Higher Education Transformation

Clark B (1998) *Creating Entrepreneurial Universities: Organisational pathways of transformation.* Oxford: Pergamon-IAU Press

Clark B (1983) *The Higher Education Systems: Academic organization in cross-national perspective.* Berkeley: University of California Press

Cloete N, Bailey T, Pillay P, Bunting I & Maassen P (2011) *Universities and Economic Development in Africa.* Cape Town: Centre for Higher Education Transformation

Cloete N & Gilwald A (2014) South African informational development and human development: Rights vs. capabilities. In: M Castells & P Himanen (eds), *Reconceptualising Development in the Global Information Age.* Oxford: Oxford University Press

Cloete N & Maassen P (2015) Roles of universities and the African context. In: N Cloete, P Maassen & T Bailey T (eds), *Knowledge Production and Contradictory Functions in Higher Education.* Cape Town: African Minds. pp. 1–17

Cloete N, Maassen P & Bailey T (eds) (2015) *Knowledge Production and Contradictory Functions in Higher Education.* Cape Town: African Minds

Cloete N, Maassen P, Fehnel R, Moja T, Gibbon T & Perold H (eds) (2006) *Transformation in Higher Education: Global pressures and local realities.* Dordrecht: Springer

Cloete N & Muller J (1998) South African higher education reform: What comes after post-colonialism?. *European Review* 6(4): 526–542

Cloete N, Muller J, Makgoba MW & Ekong D (eds) (1997) *Knowledge, Identity and Curriculum Transformation in Africa.* Cape Town: Maskew Miller Longman

Corbett A & Gordon C (2017) Universities must push for an 'intelligent Brexit'. *University World News* 446. http://www.universityworldnews.com/article.php?story=20170207210511508

References

Cross M, Cloete N, Beckham E, Harper A, Indiresan J & Musil C (eds) (1999) *Diversity and Unity: The role of higher education in building democracy.* Cape Town: Centre for Higher Education Transformation

Department of Higher Education and Training (DHET) (2013) *White Paper for Post-School Education and Training: Building an expanded, effective and integrated post-school system.* Pretoria: Department of Higher Education and Training

Douglass JA (2007) *The Conditions for Admission: Access, equity and the social contract of public universities.* Redwood City, CA: Stanford University Press

Douglass JA, King CJ & Feller I (2009) *Globalization's Muse: Universities and higher education systems in a changing world.* Berkeley: Public Policy Press, Center for Studies in Higher Education, Institute of Governmental Studies

Eder K (1999) Societies learn, and yet the world is hard to change. *European Journal of Social Theory* 2(2): 195–215

Elken M (2016) Standardizing Education? The Development of the European Qualifications Framework and National Qualifications Frameworks. Oslo: Faculty of Educational Sciences, University of Oslo

Engelen P, Ertürk I, Froud J, Johal S, Leaver A, Moran M, Nilsson A & Williams K (2011) *After the Great Complacence: Financial crisis and the politics of reform.* Oxford: Oxford University Press

Etzkowitz H, Webster A & Healey P (1998) *Capitalizing Knowledge: New intersections of industry and academia.* Albany NY: State University of New York Press

Evans P & Rauch JE (1999) Bureaucracy and growth: A cross-national analysis of the effects of 'Weberian' state structures on economic growth. *American Sociological Review* 64(5): 748–765

French Academy of Sciences (2006) Science and developing countries: Sub-Saharan Africa. RST 21, March. Paris: *Académie des sciences*

Gibbons M, Limoges C, Nowotny H, Schwartzman S, Scott P & Trow M (1994) *The New Production of Knowledge: The dynamics of science and research in contemporary societies.* London: Sage

Giddens A (1979) *Studies in Social and Political Theory.* London: Hutchinson

Gilwald A (2009) Wire less: A decade of telecommunications reform in South Africa. Unpublished doctoral thesis, University of the Witwatersrand

Gornitzka Å (2007) The Lisbon Process: A supranational policy perspective. In: P Maassen & J Olsen (eds), *University Dynamics and European Integration.* Dordrecht: Springer. pp. 155–181

Gornitzka A & Maassen P (2007) An instrument for national political agendas: The hierarchical vision. In: P Maassen & JP Olsen (eds), *University Dynamics and European Integration.* Dordrecht: Springer. pp. 81–98

Gornitzka A, Maassen P, Olsen J & Stensaker B (2007) 'Europe of knowledge': Search for a new pact. In P Maassen & J Olsen (eds), *University Dynamics and European Integration*, Dordrecht: Springer. pp. 181–214

Grace J, Kenny C, Qiang C, Lui J & Reynolds T (2001) *Information and Communications Technology and Broad-based Development: A partial review of evidence.* Washington DC: World Bank

Greenwood R & Suddaby R (2006) Institutional entrepreneurship in mature fields. *Academy of Management Journal* 49(1): 27-48

Gui X (2017) Which path the world might take: When Trump asserts 'America First' but Xi advocates global cooperation. *Chinese Sociological Dialogue* 2(1/2): 67–74

Hardy C & Maguire S (2008) Institutional entrepreneurship. In R Greenwood, C Oliver, R Suddaby & A Sahlin-Andersson (eds), *The Sage Handbook of Organizational Institutionalism*. Thousand Oaks, CA: Sage. pp. 198–217

Hayward FM (2008) Strategic planning for higher education in developing countries: Challenges and lessons. *Planning for Higher Education*. Society for College and University Planning (SCUP)

Hayward FM (1994) *Higher Education in Africa: Hearing before the subcommittee on African affairs*. 17 May 1993. Washington DC: US Government Printing Office

Hayward FM & Ncayiyana DJ (2014) Confronting the challenges of graduate education in sub-Saharan Africa and prospects for the future. *International Journal of African Higher Education* 1(1): 173–216

Heeks R (2002) I-development not e-development: Special issue on ICTs and development. *Journal of International Development* 14: 1–11

Huntington SP (2006) *Political Order in Changing Societies*. New Haven CT: Yale University Press

Jensen P, Rouquier J-B, Kreimer P & Croissant Y (2008) Scientists who engage with society perform better academically. *Science and Public Policy* 35(7): 527–541

Juma C & Yee-Cheong L (2005) *Innovation: Applying knowledge in development*. London: Earthscan

Kamara A & Nyende L (2007) Growing a knowledge-based economy: Public expenditure on education in Africa. *Economic Research Working Paper* No. 88. Tunisia: African Development Bank

Kapur D & Crowley M (2008) Beyond the ABCs: Higher education and developing countries. *CDG Working Paper* No. 139. February 2008. Washington DC: Center for Global Development. http://www.cgdev.org/content/publications/detail/15310

Kerr C (1991) *The Great Transformation in Higher Education, 1960–1980*. Albany: State University of New York Press

Langa PV (2010) Disciplines and engagement in African universities: A study of scientific capital and academic networking in the social sciences. Unpublished PhD Dissertation, University of Cape Town

Luescher T & Mugume T (2014) Student representation and multiparty politics in African high education. *Studies in Higher Education*, 39(3): 500-515

Lukes S (2005) *Power: A radical view* (2nd edn). Basingstoke: Palgrave Macmillan

Maassen P & Cloete N (2009) Higher education, donor organizations, nation states and development: The public donor dimension in Africa. In: RM Basset & A Maldonado-Maldonado (eds), *International Organizations and Higher Education Policy: Thinking globally, acting locally*. New York: Routledge. pp. 251–279

Maassen P & Olsen JP (eds) (2007) *University Dynamics and European Integration*. Dordrecht: Springer

Maassen P, Pinheiro R & Cloete N (2007) *Bilateral Country Investments and Foundations Partnership Projects Support Higher Education across Africa*. Report commissioned by the US Partnership for Higher Education in Africa. Cape Town: CHET. http://chet.org.za/papers/bilateral-country-investments-and-foundations-partnership-projects-support-higher-education

MacGregor K (2010, 2 May) Higher education a driver of the MDGs. *University World News* 122. http://www.universityworldnews.com/article.php?story=20100501081126465

MacGregor K (2009, 22 March) Africa: Call for higher education support fund. *University World News* 25. http://www.universityworldnews.com/article.php?story=20090322082237425

MacGregor K (2008, 29 January) Expansion in Africa delivers more of the same. *University World News: Special Africa Edition* 1. http://www.universityworldnews.com/article.php?story=20080129100837125

MacGregor K & Makoni M (2010, 2 May) Universities must be citadels not silos. *University World News* 122. http://www.universityworldnews.com/article.php?story=20100502103801345

Makerere University (2013) *Makerere University Self-Assessment Report: October 2013*. Kampala: Makerere University Directorate of Quality Assurance

Mamdani M (2016) Undoing the effects of neoliberal reform. In: T Halvorsen & J Nossum (eds), *North–South Knowledge Networks: Towards equitable collaboration between academics, donors and universities*. Cape Town: African Minds. pp. 109–133.

Mamdani M (2008) *Scholars in the Marketplace: The dilemmas of neo-liberal reform at Makerere University 1989–2005*. Pretoria: HSRC Press

Mamdani M (1993) University crisis and reform: A reflection on the African experience. *Review of African Political Economy* 58: 7–19

Mason P (2015) *Post-Capitalism*. London: Routledge

Maton K (2014) *Knowledge and Knowers: Towards a realist sociology of education*. Abingdon: Routledge

Mazzacuto M (2013) *The Entrepreneurial State: Debunking public vs. private sector myths*. London: Anthem

Miéville C (2009) *The City and The City*. London: Macmillan

Mkandawire T (2011) Running while others walk: Knowledge and the challenge of Africa's development. *Africa Development* 36(2): 1–36

Moja T, Muller J & Cloete N (1996) Towards new forms of regulation in higher education: The case of South Africa. *Higher Education* 32: 129–155

Mouton J, Gaillard J & Van Lill M (2015) Functions of science granting councils in Sub-Saharan Africa. In: Cloete N, Maassen P & Bailey T (eds), *Knowledge Production and Contradictory Functions in Higher Education*. Cape Town: African Minds. pp. 148–170

Muller J (2010) Engagements with engagement: A response to Martin Hall. *Kagisano 6: Community Engagement in South African Higher Education*. Pretoria: Council on Higher Education. pp. 68–88

Muller J (2003) Knowledge and the limits of institutional restructuring: The case of South African higher education. *Journal of Education* 30: 101–126

Muller J (1997) Citizenship and curriculum. In: N Cloete, J Muller, MW Makgoba & D Ekong (eds), *Knowledge, Identity and Curriculum Transformation in Africa*. Cape Town: Maskew Miller Longman. pp. 181–202

Muller J, Cloete N & Badat S (eds) (2001) *Challenges of Globalisation: South African debates with Manuel Castells*. Cape Town: Maskew Miller Longman

Nassif R, Rama G & Tedesco JC (1984) *El sistema educativo en America Latina*. Buenos Aires: Unesco-CEPAL, Kapeluz

National Planning Commission (2012) *National Development Plan 2030: Our future – make it work*. Pretoria: The Presidency, Republic of South Africa

Ng'ethe N, Subotzky G & Afeti G (2008) *Differentiation and Articulation in Tertiary Education Systems: A study of twelve countries*. Washington DC: The World Bank

Nye J (1990) *Bound to Lead: The changing nature of American power*. New York: Public Affairs

Nye J (2011) *The Future of Power*. New York: Public Affairs

Olsen J (2007) The institutional dynamics of the European university. In: P Maassen & J Olsen (eds), *University Dynamics and European Integration*. Dordrecht: Springer. pp. 25–54

Olsson Å & Cooke N (2013) *The Evolving Path for Strengthening Research and Innovation Policy for Development*. Paris: Organisation for Economic Cooperation and Development

Peper S (1984) *China's Universities: Post-Mao enrolment policies and their impact on the structure of secondary education*. Ann Arbor: Centre for Chinese Studies, University of Michigan

Pillay P (2010) *Linking Higher Education and Economic Development: Implications for Africa from three successful systems*. Cape Town: Centre for Higher Education Transformation

Pityana B (2009) The revitalisation of higher education: Access, equity and quality. http://www.unisa.ac.za/contents/about/principle/docs/Unesco_speech_30Jun09.pdf

Portland Communications (2015, 2016) *The Soft Power 30: A global ranking*. https://portland-communications.com/publications/a-global-ranking-of-soft-power/

Psacharopoulos G, Tan JP & Jimenez E (1986) *The Financing of Education in Developing Countries: Exploration of policy options*. Washington DC: The World Bank

Salmi J (2002) *Constructing Knowledge Societies: New challenges for tertiary education*. Washington DC: The World Bank

Sawyerr A (2004) Challenges facing African universities: Selected issues. *African Studies Review* 47(1): 1–59

Schemm Y (2013, December) Africa doubles research output over past decade, moves towards a knowledge-based economy. *Research Trends* 35. https://www.researchtrends.com/issue-35-december-2013/africa-doubles-research-output/

Scott P (1995) *The Meaning of Mass Higher Education*. Buckingham: Open University Press

Scott W (2001) *Institutions and Organizations* (2nd edn). Thousand Oaks CA: Sage

Shaplin J (2014, 5 May) University endowments, education and social mobility by Thomas Piketty. http://http://johnshaplin.blogspot.nl/2014/05/university-endowments-education-and.html

References

Sherman MAB (1990) The university in modern Africa: Toward the 21st century. *Journal of Higher Education* 61(4): 363–385

Solari A (1988) Sentido y function de la universidad. *Revista de la CEPAL* 35: August

Stalder F (2006) *Manuel Castells: The theory of the network society.* Cambridge: Polity

Steerpike (2016, 17 October) Science must fall: It's time to decolonise science. *The Spectator*

Swanson EB & Ramiller NC (2004) Innovating mindfully with information technology. *MIS Quarterly* 26(4): 553-583.

Swanson EB & Ramiller NC (1997) The organizing vision in information systems innovation. *Organization Science* 8(5): 458-474

Times Higher Education (2017) *World University Ranking 2017.* https://www.timeshighereducation.com/world-university-rankings/2017/world-ranking#!/page/0/length/25/sort_by/rank/sort_order/asc/cols/stats

Times Higher Education (2016) *BRICS and Emerging Economies Rankings 2016.* https://www.timeshighereducation.com/world-university-rankings/2016/brics-and-emerging-economies-0#!/page/0/length/25/sort_by/rank/sort_order/asc/cols/stats

Touraine A (1972) *Universite et Societe aux Etats-Unis.* Paris: Seuil

Trow M (1973) Problems in the transition from elite to mass higher education. Carnegie Commission on Higher Education, Berkeley, California

Trow M (2007) Reflections on the transition from elite to mass to universal access: Forms and phases of higher education in modern societies since WWII. In: J Forest & P Altbach (eds), *Springer International Handbook of Education* (SIHE, vol. 18). Dordrect: Springer. pp. 243–280

University of Botswana (2008) *University Research Strategy.* Gaborone: University of Botswana

Van Schalkwyk F (2015) University engagement as interconnectedness: Indicators and insights. In: N Cloete, P Maassen & T Bailey (eds), *Knowledge Production and Contradictory Functions in Higher Education.* Cape Town: African Minds. pp. 203–229

Van Schalkwyk F (2011) Responsiveness and its institutionalisation in higher education. Masters thesis, Department of Education, University of the Western Cape. https://www.academia.edu/1539185/Responsiveness_and_its_Institutionalisation_in_Higher_Education

Veysey LR (1965) *The Emergence of the American University.* Chicago: University of Chicago Press

Van Vught F (2007) Diversity and differentiation in higher education systems. Paper presented at the CHET 10th Anniversary Conference, Cape Town, 16 November

Vossen M (2015) *Wereldwijde Armoede in de Media.* Amsterdam: Kaleidos Research

Wangenege-Ouma G, Lutomiah A & Langa P (2015) Academic incentives for knowledge production in Africa: Case studies of Mozambique and Kenya. In N Cloete, P Maassen & T Bailey (eds), *Knowledge Production and Contradictory Functions in African Higher Education.* Cape Town: African Minds. pp. 128–147

Watson P (2010) *The German Genius: Europe's third renaissance, the second scientific revolution and the twentieth century.* London: Simon & Schuster

Wolfe DL (1972) *The Home of Science: The role of the university*. Chicago: Carnegie Commission on Higher Education; New York: McGraw Hill

World Bank (1999) *Knowledge for Development. World Development Report 1998/99*. The World Bank Group. Oxford: Oxford University Press

World Bank (2007) *The Knowledge Economy*. Washington DC: The World Bank

World Bank (2009) *Accelerating Catch-up: Tertiary education for growth in sub-Saharan Africa*. Washington DC: The World Bank

World Economic Forum (2012) *The Global Competitiveness Report 2012–2013*. Geneva: World Economic Forum

Xi J (2017, 17 January) President Xi's speech to Davos in full. World Economic Forum. https://www.weforum.org/agenda/2017/01/chinas-xi-jinping-defends-globalization-from-the-davos-stage/

Yesufu TM (ed.) (1973) *Creating the African University: Emerging issues in the 1970s*. Ibadan: Oxford University Press

Zeleza P (2014) The development of STEM in Africa: Mobilizing the potential of the diaspora. Paper presented at the third annual conference on 'Effective US Strategies for African STEM Collaborations, Capacity Building, and Diaspora Engagement', University of Michigan, 1–4 April

Index

Page numbers in *italics* indicate figures and tables.

academic core
  dimension of interconnectedness 171
  HERANA universities 120–122
  training/research functions 171, 178
academic core indicators
  HERANA universities 122–132, *129*, 140–151, *143*, *145*, 189, *202–206*
  interconnectedness 171–176, *173*, *174*, *207*
academic disciplines
  globalisation/fragmentation of 6
  importance of interdisciplinarity 47–48, 63–64
  independence of science disciplines 176–177
academic knowledge 6
academic networks 131
academic staff
  administrative 141
  concept of interconnectedness 170
  with doctoral degrees 123, 126, *129*, 143–144, 147, 149, 150, *203*, *205*, *206*
  foreign faculty 46, 50–51
  growth rate 142
  lack of trained faculty 45
  and network switching 179–182, 186, 195
  participation in global/local networks 164–166, 168, 175, 195
  permanent staff 141, 142
  preference for overseas universities 46–47, 105, 140
  proportion of senior/doctoral 143–144, *205*
  recruitment/training of 46, 50–51
  research income 123, *129*, 130
  rival visions of the university 192
  rotation between different institutions 52
  service staff 141
  student/staff growth 142, *143*, 147, *204*

    student–staff ratios 123, 125, 128, *129*, 147, *202, 203*
    supplementary teaching 131
    temporary staff 141
    in Third World university context 44
accountability 156, 163
Accra Declaration 103
adaptability 29
Africa
    ministers support for higher education 109
    research constraints/challenges 82, 139, 140, 152
    research publications output 105, 139
    state as actor for development 89–90
Africa Action Plan 108
Africa Higher Education Summit (Dakar) 14, 106
African Development Bank 110
African Minds 15
African Ministerial Council on Science and Technology 112
African Research Universities Alliance 14
African Union
    AU/NEPAD platform for science 112
    AU/NEPAD report 107
    research publication output 139
African universities
    call for revitalisation of 105–109, 110–111, 114, 188
    competing ideologies 102
    contribution to development 13–14, 102–104, 109–112, 116–120
    focus on elite formation/training 13, 28, 135, 188, 190, 193
    focus on ideology/political function 28, 188, 190, 193
    global rankings 138
    lack of development signposting 190–191
    need for focus on research/knowledge production 12, 13–14, 162
    negative stories told about 112
    as overcrowded elite systems 102, 194
    participation rates 101
    research/science function 12, 13, 103, 105, 133, 135, 138–139, 152, 162
    as self-governing institution 103–104, 117, 118, 119
    student politics 19, 36, 47, 192
    support for communities 106–107, 111, 112, 117, 118, 171
    tensions between contradictory functions 105, 140, 190
    training/education function 13, 28, 102, 194
    see also academic staff; developmental university; HERANA universities

Index

agencies, government 156–157
agency
  in global research networks 180
  and implementation of development 75, 88
agricultural schools 40, 59, 99
aid programmes *see* donor funding
Alibaba (Chinese company) 78
Altbach, P 137
American universities
  entrepreneurial universities 60
  Land Grant universities 38, 59, 98–99, 98n1
  professional universities 40, 59
  public/private universities 38, 64
  research-oriented universities 38–39, 59
  selection of elite 37, 58, 97
animal rights 70, 74, 87
Annan, Kofi 90, 110, 111, 114, 196n1
Appiah, Kwame Anthony 5
Argentina 80, 83
articulation
  as dimension of interconnectedness 170
  indicators 170, 171–176, *173, 174*, 185
Asian Tigers 26, 61, 190
Asian universities 102
Asquith Commission 43, 101
Association of African Universities 103, 108
Association of Commonwealth Universities 111
autonomy
  of government agencies 156–157
  spaces of autonomy 87–88
  of universities 65, 119, 155

Bawa, Ahmed 5
Berkeley University 59, 64, 98n1
Bhutan Happiness Index 71
Bolivia 78, 81, 83
Bourdieu, Pierre 36, 187, 194
Brazil
  exchange rates 79
  far-reaching changes in higher education 106
  network business model 80

219

as newly industrialising country 77
   participation in global research networks 168
   protests/social movements 85–86, 91–92
   THE's ranking of universities 138
Brexit 18, 21, 30
BRICS & Emerging Economies Rankings 137–138, 138n1, 138n2
BRICS countries *see* Brazil; China; India; Russia; South Africa
bureaucracy, training of *see* civil service training
business sector *see* private sector

Caltech 38, 59
Cambridge University 36, 58, 64, 96, 97, 193
capacity building 118, 156
capacity, lack of 128, 132, 156
Capital in the Twentieth Century 82
capitalism
   creation of oligarchs 82
   global informational capitalism 77
   see also economic growth
Cardoso, Fernando Henrique 90
Carnoy, Martin 6, 7
Castells, Manuel
   concept of academic core 171
   concept of network society 159–162, 166, 167
   concept of 'powerful' universities 168
   contradictory functions of universities 12, 29, 47, 100, 105, 117, 133, 151–152, 163–164
   definition of development 68
   definition of 'elite' 194
   distinction between forms of labour 24–25
   'engine of development' notion 11, 111, 114, 117
   ICT as prerequisite for development 8
   importance of relative quality of universities 154
   importance of research/science function 162
   knowledge as productive capacity 23
   one of most cited social scientists 7
   theory of power 20, 21, 22–23, 30
   trilogy of books 6
   university participation in research networks 164
   views on globalisation 7–8, 17
   visit to SA (2000) 7–8, 10–11, 17

visit to SA (2009) 12–13
visit to SA (2011) 9, 13
visit to SA (2014) 14
warns against massification 11, 18–19, 97
Centre for Higher Education Transformation (CHET)
    compilation of data on African universities 122
    establishment of 3
    invites Castells to SA 6–7
    management of HERANA 115
    from NGO to networked organisation 14–15
    series of seminars and presentations 5
    work post-Castells 2000 visit 11–12
Challenges of Globalisation: South African Debates with Manuel Castells 11, 15, 17n1, 95
Chile 78, 79, 89
China
    economic miracle 88–89
    and globalisation 78–79
    Intel moving to 85
    investment in education 46, 106, 114
    new model of growth 80–81
    as newly industrialising country 77
    participation in global research networks 168
    proportion of research universities 136
    THE's ranking of universities 138
    use of high technology 78
    Xi Jinping's views on globalisation 30–31
Chinese university system 39, 43, 48, 98, 106
Church-based universities 35, 39
Cisco Systems 8, 9
citation indexes 141
citizenship skills 5
civil service training 28, 37, 39, 102, 117, 193
Clark, Burton 120
Cloete, Nico 3, 6, 16
CODESRIA 106
collaboration, research 138, *169*
colleges (Makerere University) *173*, 177, 178
colonialism
    colonial foundations of university system 43–44, 193
    gross underdevelopment of universities 102

universities as extensions of Western models 101
university production of imperial values 58, 96
Columbia 88
communication, access to 83–84, 87
communication skills 28
communities
    and development mission of universities 106–107, 111, 112, 117, 118
    see also university–community engagement
competitiveness 40, 73–74
conservative ideologies 36, 99, 102
Constructing Knowledge Societies: New Challenges for Tertiary Education 109
consultancy work 130, 131, 132, 165, 192
corruption 89, 91, 92
Costa Rica 84–85
crime 80, 87
cultural identity 44, 47, 102
curricula, outcomes-based 24

Data Trends and Institutional Performance: An Overview of Seven HERANA Universities 146
democratisation
    disconnection between citizens/governments 90
    focus of NCHE framework 4
    and holistic concept of development 74
    universities as source of 57, 96
Department for International Development 108–109
Department of Education 3, 4
Department of Higher Education and Training 184
deregulation 75, 88
developed countries
    'engine of development' discourse 111, 114
    and meanings of term 'development' 68
developing countries
    importance of higher education in development 111, 114
    obstacles to scientific/technical training 45–46
    research/science universities 136–137
    role of distance education 62
    state's role in ICT 9
    see also newly industrialising countries
development
    Castells's definition of 68

centrality of knowledge/information 10–11
in context of global knowledge economy 75
dimension of economic growth 69, 70–71, 72–74, 76–86
dimension of human dignity 70, 74, 86–87
dimension of human well-being 69, 71
dimension of sustainability 69–70, 74, 86
growing pains of developmentalism 30
has multiple meanings 67–68
holistic concept of 74
investment in human capital 61
link to tertiary participation rates 114
mode of development 10, 25–26, 161, 189
must include tertiary transformation 48
NCHE's framework 4–5
need for a new world order 53–54
neo-developmentalism 88
role of markets 88
and self-determination 90–91
and university functions 18
development cooperation *see* donor funding
developmental university
    embraced by World Bank 109–110
    failure of Third World universities 48
    mediation of contradictory university functions 29
    post-colonial development discourse 103–104, 188
    university as development tool 110–112, 188–189
differentiation
    differentiated universities 97, 125–126, 137, 140, 152–155, 154n6, 192–193
    of research/teaching functions 178–179
dignity of humans 70, 74, 86–87
disciplinary valency 176–178
distance education 62, 64–65
doctoral enrolments
    % masters and doctorates *129*
    Eduardo Mondlane University *202, 203*
    Makerere University 127, 150, *202, 203*
    masters, ratio to doctoral enrolments 127
    NMMU *202, 203*
    University of Botswana *202, 203*
    University of Cape Town 131, *202, 203*

University of Dar es Salaam 131, *202*, *203*
University of Ghana *202*, *203*
University of Mauritius 147, *202*, *203*
University of Nairobi 126, 148–149, *202*, *203*
doctoral graduates
    Eduardo Mondlane University 126, 144, *202*, *203*
    increase/decrease in 144
    Makerere University 126, 144, 151, *202*, *203*
    need for increase in 123
    NMMU 126, *202*, *203*
    University of Botswana 126, *202*, *203*
    University of Cape Town 126, 129, *129*, 144, *202*, *203*
    University of Dar es Salaam 126, 129, *129*, *202*, *203*
    University of Ghana 126, 129, *129*, *202*, *203*
    University of Mauritius 126, 144, *202*, *203*
    University of Nairobi 126, 144, 149, *202*, *203*
doctorates
    component of university ranking 138
    correlation with research output 125–126
    PhD supervision vs supplementary teaching 131
    as proportion of academic staff 123, 126, *129*, 143–144, 147, 149, 150, *203*, *205*, *206*
    summit of self-programmability 27
donor funding
    channelled to national institutions 52, 53
    main sponsors of consultancies 192
    need for selective aid 12, 48–49
    research prerogatives of funding agencies 165
    support for skilled faculty 50
    universities as institutional enclaves 113
    for university research 166, 172, 176
    see also World Bank
Duesberg, Peter 9

e-commerce companies 78
e-learning 62, 64–65
East Asia 61, 77, 88, 101, 191
Eastern Cape Province 167
École Polytechnique 37
economic growth
    access to communication 84

on the basis of ICT 77, 78, 79–80
dependencies theories of 26
vs ecological conservation 53
and financial crises 71, 77
and human development 71–72, 74, 86
ignored in NCHE's framework 4, 5
importance of higher education 100, 111, 135–136
and macro-economic destabilisation 78
massification vs economy's requirements 11, 18, 41
measured by GDP 69, 70–71
in newly industrialising countries 77–82, 84–85
not a focus of developmental university 112
separate from technological development 161
economists' view of knowledge 23, 24
economy, global 53–55
Ecuador 78
Eduardo Mondlane University
    changes in head count enrolments *204*
    doctoral enrolments *202, 203*
    doctoral graduates 126, 144, *202, 203*
    doctoral staff *203, 205, 206*
    masters enrolments *202, 203*
    masters, ratio to doctoral enrolments 127
    part of HERANA network 115
    research income per permanent academic *203*
    research publications *145, 202, 203*
    SET enrolments *202*
    SET graduation rates 126, *203*
    strength of academic core rating 124, 125
    student/staff growth 142, *143, 204*
    total enrolments 142
    undergraduate enrolments *205*
education function *see* training/education function
education systems
    East Asian countries 26, 61
    Finland 62
    legacy of colonialism 4
educators
    and quality of education system 61–62
    views on knowledge 23–24
Ekong, Donald 5

elites, selection/formation of
    historical overview 36–37, 58, 96–97
    in context of massification 97
    different notions of 'elite' 193–194
    in First World universities 193
    focus of African universities 13, 28, 135, 188, 190, 193
    main function of Third World universities 44, 45, 101
    one of four main university functions 41
    in public/private universities 64
Empirical Overview of Eight Flagship Universities in Africa 141
End of Millennium 6
engagement *see* university–community engagement
'engine of development' notion
    Annan's development tool 110, 111
    Castells' concept of 11, 111, 114, 117
    HERANA's analytical framework 118, 118–119, 120, 189
engineering schools 38, 40, 41, 59, 98
enrolments
    doctoral *see* doctoral enrolments *129*
    and higher education funding 154
    masters *see* masters enrolments
    masters vs doctoral 127, 131
    postgraduate 123, 142, 143
    SET fields 122, 128, *202*
    student/staff growth 142, *143*, *204*
    substantial growth in 44–45, 142
    undergraduate 142, 143, 147, 149, 150, 157, 189, *205*
    undergraduate vs postgraduate 143
entrepreneurial universities 60
equity
    focus of transformation discourse 4, 13
    within holistic concept of development 74
    university contribution to 57, 96
Estonia 21
European Commission 114
European Qualifications Framework 20–21, 24, 30
expenditure
    per student 104, 113
    on research and development 138
extension units (NMMU) 182–183

Faculties (NMMU) *174*, 177–178, 182
faculty staff *see* academic staff
financial crisis (2008) 71, 77
Finland 62, 74, 116, 194
First World
    vs African universities 193
    and connectivity 76
    and 'non-global' global crisis 77
flexible personalities 63, 96
flows of information *see* information flows
foreign faculty 46, 50–51
France
    colonial view of universities 101
    dominance of state over private sector 37
    grandes écoles 37, 58, 97, 98, 193
    Napoleonic model of university 39, 98
functions of universities *see* elites, selection/formation of; ideology/political function; research/science function; training/education function
funding
    from industry 166–167, 175–176
    research prerogatives of funding agencies 165
    research/science 130, 140, 157
    and total student enrolments 154
    university–community projects 170, 172, 176, 184
    see also donor funding

G8 summits 108
GDP (gross domestic product) 69, 70–71, 80, 110
gender equality 74, 86–87
generalist universities 59–60, 97
generic labour 24–25, 26–27, 193–194
German universities 37–38, 39, 59, 98
Giddens, A 22
Gleneagles G8 summit 108
global economy 53–54
global informational capitalism 77
global knowledge economy
    characterised by globalisation 75
    and development process 75
    functions of the university 57, 95–96
    importance of research/innovation 61, 100

see also knowledge
global research collaboration 138, *169*
global research networks
　agency of individuals 180
　existence of mega-nodes 168, *169*
　and information flows 166, 168
　vs local networks 49–50, 161, 164–166, 167, 168, 185, 195
　and newly industrialising countries 81
　no overlap with ICT networks 161–162
　university participation in 18, 60–61, 164
globalisation
　anti-globalisation wave 17
　Castells's views on 7–8, 17
　centrality of knowledge/information 10–11
　as global networks 75–76
　impact on state/society 9–10
　state loss of power 20
　Xi Jinping's views on 30–31
governance
　Castells's theory of power 20
　institutional governance 154
government policies
　concept of pact with universities 191
　and development discourse 103–104, 103n5
　factors constraining government agencies 156–157
　homogenisation of universities 153–154, 155
　investment in education systems 26, 61
　supervisory approach to higher education governance 155–156
　universities as 'engine of development' 120
　see also state
graduation rates
　masters 127, 148, 150
　SET fields 123, 126, 128, *129, 203*
　see also doctoral graduates
grandes écoles 37, 58, 97, 98, 193
gross domestic product (GDP) 69, 70–71, 80, 110
Gross National Happiness Index 71

Harvard University 58, 64, 96
healthcare 73, 82, 117, 118
HERANA universities

background/overview 12, 14, 115–116
academic core 120–122
academic core indicators 122–132, *129*, 140–151, *143*, *145*, 189, *202–206*
analytical framework 116–120, 188–189
Universities and Economic Development in Africa 13–14
see also under individual universities
higher education councils 155–156
HIV/Aids Presidential Advisory Panel 9
holistic development 74
homogenisation of universities 153–154, 155
see also differentiated universities
Hong Kong 43, 61
Huawei 78
human capital
 'brain circulation' 81
 Castells' definition of 72–73
 example of Asian Tigers 26, 61
 improving quality of universities 50–51
 university production of 102, 119
human development
 deterioration in living conditions 91
 and economic growth 71–72, 74, 86
 in newly industrialising countries 82–83, 85–86
Human Development Index 71
human dignity 70, 74, 86–87
human rights 74, 87, 110
human well-being 68, 69, 70, 71

ideology/political function
 historical overview 35–36, 58, 96
 colonial-era universities 43–44, 188
 conservative and radical ideologies 36, 99, 102
 focus of African universities 28, 188, 190, 193
 fundamental role of universities 35, 96
 one of four main university functions 41
 plurality of manifestations 35–36
 tensions with research/science function 47, 102, 105
 tensions with training/education function 102, 140, 190
India
 far-reaching changes in higher education 106

229

investment in education 114
as newly industrialising country 77, 80
participation in global research networks 168
THE's ranking of universities 138
state as actor in development process 89
Indonesia 52, 77, 79–80, 80, 89
industrial era
creation of large-scale organisations 75
industrialism to post-industrial mode 25
to state's role in informational era 10
industrialisation
role of structured industries 80
role of the professional university 40, 59, 98
role of the research university 38–39, 98–99
training of the labour force 39–40
inequality
under apartheid 3, 4
economic 53, 54, 57, 82–83, 84, 96
influence 20, 21
information
digitisation of 76
link to productivity 10–11, 54, 73–74, 76–77
see also information flows; information processing
Information Age 38, 48, 75, 76, 160, 165
Information Age: Economy, Society and Culture 9
information and communications technology (ICT)
allows for global digital networks 75–76, 159–160
digitisation of information 76
and economic growth 77, 78, 79–80
impact on universities 57–58, 64–65
and knowledge economy 72
Mbeki's initiatives 8–9
no overlap with science/research networks 161–162
potential for development 8, 9, 10
see also technology
information flows
community engagement projects 175–176, 180, 183–184, 186
direction of 166, 183–184
in global research networks 168, 183
intersection of flows and spaces 183
space of flows 159, 160–161, 164, 167, 180, 183

information processing
   and capacity of the human mind 72, 76
   of flows of information 160–161
   society based on 57, 95
   source of productivity 10
Information Society and the Welfare State: The Finnish Model 74
informational development 13, 73, 76–77
informationalism
   based on ICT 76
   importance of training/research functions 28–29
   as mode of development 25–26
   self-programmable vs generic labour 27, 193–194
innovation
   Africa lagging on key indicators 138
   driver of technological development 161
   focus of entrepreneurial universities 60
   ignored in NCHE's framework 4, 5
   not a focus of developmental university 112
   and research productivity 28
   self-programmable vs generic labour 25
   university contribution to 100–101, 136
   vital in global knowledge economy 61, 100
institutional convergence 193
institutional governance 154
institutional reforms 50, 100
institutions, lack of trust in 91
instrumentalist role of universities 110–111, 188, 189
Intel 85
interconnectedness
   academic core indicators 171–176, *173*, *174*, 185, *207*
   articulation indicators 170, 171–176, *173*, *174*, 185, *207*
   bi-directional flow of information 183–184, 186
   definition of 169–170
   disciplinary valency 176–178
   switching between networks 179–183, 186
interdisciplinarity 47–48, 63–64
International Organisations and Higher Education Policy 12
international universities 52
internet, uses of 61, 62, 64–65, 88
Ivy League universities 37, 58, 97

Japan 38, 68, 168
Johns Hopkins University 38, 59
Juma, Calestous 111

Kerr, Clark 96, 99
knowledge
    Castells accused of not taking seriously 23
    central to production and development 10–11
    educators' vs economists' view of 23–24
    has always been important 72
    'learning to learn' 11, 29, 62, 98
    see also global knowledge economy
Knowledge, Identity and Curriculum Transformation in Africa 5, 6
knowledge production
    confers specialised capacity to its holders 22
    in the global economy 60–61, 100
    ignored in NCHE's framework 4–5
    input/output indicators 122–123, 141
    lacking in African universities 132–133
    not a unitary process 178–179
    promoted by HERANA 14
    university vs industry roles 101
    see also research/science function
Knowledge Production and Contradictory Functions in African Higher Education 14, 95
Korea 39, 42, 61, 114
Kotecha, Piyushi 111
Kuznets, Simon 69

labour power
    and government investment in education 26, 61
    human ability to generate/produce 73
    perception of cheap labour in China 78
    quality depends on educators 61
    university role in producing high-quality labour 57, 61, 62, 95, 114, 136, 153
    see also self-programmable labour
Land Grant universities (USA) 38, 40, 59, 98–99, 98n1
Latin America
    access to communication 83–84
    colonial foundations of university system 43–44

Index

Costa Rica 84–85
economic growth 77, 78, 79–80, 81, 88, 89
and human development 85–86
poverty 83
public spending 78
'learning to learn' 11, 29, 62, 98
Lenovo 78
liberal arts colleges 35, 36
lithium production 78, 81
local networks
   vs global research networks 49–50, 161, 164–166, 167, 168, 185, 195
   switching between networks 159–160
   and university–community engagement 167–168
Louvanium University Centre 43
Lukes, Steven 21–22

Makerere University
   changes in head count enrolments *204*
   commercialisation of 105, 107
   commitment to strengthening research 149–150, 157, 166
   community engagement projects 166–167, 172–176, *173*, 177, 178, 184
   development priorities vs research function 168
   doctoral enrolments 127, 150, *202*, *203*
   doctoral graduates 126, 144, 151, *202*, *203*
   doctoral staff 126, 144, 150, *203*, *205*, *206*
   foreign donor funding 166, 172, 176
   low proportion of senior academics 150–151
   masters enrolments 127, 150, *202*, *203*
   masters, ratio to doctoral enrolments 127
   not listed in the BRICS and Emerging Economies Rankings 138n2
   part of HERANA network 115
   research income per permanent academic *203*
   research publications 144, *145*, 151, *202*, *203*
   role of university in development/knowledge economy 119
   SET enrolments *202*
   SET graduation rates 126, *203*
   strength of academic core rating 124
   student/staff growth 142, *143*, *204*
   student–staff ratio 125
   training of elites 101
   undergraduate enrolments 157, *205*

Makgoba, Malegepuru 5
Malaysia 46
Mamdani, M 101, 106–107, 194
Mandela Elders 196, 196n1
Mandela, Nelson 3
Marianne and Marcus Wallenberg Foundation 13
markets 88–89
Massachusetts Institute of Technology 38, 60, 98n1
massification
    Castells's warning against 11, 18–19, 97
    consequences for universities 41–42, 194
    and 'generalist' universities 59–60, 97
    NCHE proposal 4
    Scott's analysis 5–6, 97
    social demand for university access 11, 18, 29, 41, 190
    and student–staff ratios 125
    vs university functions 29
    without resources 102, 194
masters enrolments
    Eduardo Mondlane University 127, *202*, *203*
    Makerere University 127, 150, *202*, *203*
    NMMU 127, *202*, *203*
    ratio of masters to doctoral enrolments 127
    University of Botswana 127, *202*, *203*
    University of Cape Town 127, *129*, 131, *202*, *203*
    University of Dar es Salaam 126–127, *129*, 131, *202*, *203*
    University of Ghana 127, *129*, *202*, *203*
    University of Mauritius 127, 147, *202*, *203*
    University of Nairobi 127, 148, *202*, *203*
masters graduates 127, 148, 150
material production 73
Mauritius 101n3, 146–147, 147–148
Mazzucato, M 101
Mbeki, President 7, 8, 9
Meaning of Mass Higher Education 5
Miéville, China 159
military technology 39
Millennium Development Goals 69, 90, 108, 111
mission and vision statements 119, 121, 125, 132, 172, 188–189
mobile phones 83, 87
mode of development 10, 25–26, 161, 189

mode of production
    in context of network society 161
    informational mode of 189, 194
    vs mode of development 25
    and use of technology 10, 79
money laundering 80
Muller, Johan 5, 6, 16

Napoleonic model of university 39, 98
nation state 10, 20, 75
National Commission on Higher Education (NCHE)
    establishment of/TOR 3–4
    transformation proposals 4–5, 5–6, 13
National Development Plan (SA) 191–192
national identity 117
Nelson Mandela Bay Metropolitan Municipality 167
Nelson Mandela Metropolitan University
    community engagement projects 166–167, 167–169, 172–176, *174*, 181–183, 184
    doctoral enrolments *202, 203*
    doctoral graduates 126, *202, 203*
    doctoral staff 126, *203*
    masters enrolments 127, *202, 203*
    masters, ratio to doctoral enrolments 127
    mix of research and teaching 166
    participation in HERANA network 115n1
    research income per permanent academic *203*
    research publications 127, *202, 203*
    role of university in development 119
    SET enrolments *202*
    SET graduation rates *203*
    sources of research funding 166–167, 175–176
    staff participation in local/global networks 168
    strength of academic core rating 124
    student–staff ratio 125
neo-developmentalism 88
neoclassical economics 26
NEPAD 107, 112
network business model 80
network society
    capacity to 'learn to learn' 29

existence of multiple networks 161–162, 167
influence on personal/collective identity 11
made possible by ICT 75–76, 159–160
modes of production/development 161
Rise of the Network Society 6
self-programmable vs generic labour 24–25
space of flows 159, 160–161, 164, 167, 180, 183–184
space of places 161, 164–165, 167–168, 180, 183, 184, 185
see also global research networks; interconnectedness; local networks
network switching
allows cooperation between networks 162
both complex and contradictory 159–160
power of switchers 21, 23
practised by academic staff 179–182, 186, 195
'networked state' 10
networks, academic 131
networks, social 36, 96–97
New Dynamics on Higher Education and Research: Strategies for Change and Development 109
New Production of Knowledge 5
newly industrialising countries
access to communication 83–84
economic growth 77–82, 84–85
and human development 82–83, 85–86
see also developing countries
Ng'ethe, Njuguna 153–154, 154n6
Nigeria 52, 69
non-governmental organisations 90
NORAD 12, 115
North Carolina 116
Norway 21, 79, 194
Nye, J 21

Ocean Turtle Task Force Project (NMMU) 181–182
OECD
development of the Third World 54
dominant development discourse 114
guidelines on performance indicators 141
OECD/IHERD report 136
Oxford University 36, 58, 64, 96, 97, 193

performance indicators 122–123, 141
Peruvian cholera epidemic 54
Piketty, Thomas 82, 97
post-colonial universities
    as extensions of Western models 43
    ideological/elite socialisation functions 43, 188
    production of human capital 102, 119
postgraduate enrolments 123, 142, 143
    see also doctoral enrolments; masters enrolments
postgraduate training 130
potentia/potestas (Spinoza) 22
poverty 53, 54, 82–83, 84
poverty reduction 111, 112, 118
power
    Castells's theory of 20, 21, 22–23, 30
    Lukes' theories of 21–22
Power of Identity 6
predatory states 89–90, 91
Presidential ICT Advisory Council 8–9
Presidential National Commission on Information Society and Development 9
primary education 73, 81, 104, 113, 117
private sector
    distrust of university research 38
    dominance of French state over 37
    establishment of joint research centres 51
    and increased access to higher education 101
    industry funding for universities 166–167, 175–176
    investment in R&D 139
    support for training/education function 51
    and tertiary institutional reforms 50
    university support for small business 118
private universities
    budget-maximising behaviour 155
    France 37
    introduce a level of differentiation 154
    selection of elites 64
    supplementary teaching at 131
    USA 38
production of knowledge *see* knowledge production
productive power 19, 30

productivity
    enhanced by research/science universities 40
    and human development 84
    and information development 10–11, 54, 73–74, 76–77
professional universities 39, 40, 42, 59, 98
programming power 21, 23
public spending 78
public universities 38, 59, 64, 105, 107, 155

qualifications frameworks 20–21, 24, 30

racism 87
radical ideologies 36, 99, 102
rankings of universities 30, 137–138, 138n1
Reconceptualising Development in the Information Age 13, 14
regional development 121, 172, 175
regional universities 52
Renewal of Higher Education in Africa 107
Report of the Commission for Africa 108
research
    engaged research 165, 195
    funding for 130, 140, 157
    funding per academic 123, *129, 203*
    ignored in NCHE's framework 4–5
    in private sector 38
    relationship with consultancy work 131
research and development
    central factor of production 81
    gross domestic expenditure on 138
    low level in Sub-Saharan Africa 157
    private sector investment in 139
research capacity 27, 108, 138
research centres 38, 50, 51, 59–60, 60, 100, 164
research collaboration 138, *169*
research publications
    Africa's share of output 105, 139
    University of Botswana *145, 202, 203*
    correlation with doctoral qualification 125–126
    Eduardo Mondlane University *145, 202, 203*
    University of Ghana 129, *129,* 144, *145, 202, 203*
    incentives to publish 130, 131–132, 192

    as index of contribution to innovation economy 28
    Makerere University 144, *145*, 151, *202, 203*
    University of Nairobi *145*, 149, *202, 203*
    NMMU 127, *202, 203*
    output as academic core indicator 123, 127
    Sub-Saharan African output 128
    University of Cape Town 127, 129, *129*, 144, *145*, 146, *202, 203*
    University of Dar es Salaam 129, *129, 202, 203*
    University of Mauritius 127, *145*, 147, *202, 203*
research/science function
    historical overview 37–39, 59, 98–99
    in African universities 12, 13, 103, 105, 133, 135, 138–139, 152, 162
    consequences of massification 18–19
    constrained by teaching commitments 190
    in context of development 42, 120, 168, 171
    development of capacity 28
    importance of interdisciplinarity 47–48
    lagging in Third World universities 46–47
    and massification 194
    national and global research 49–50
    need for military technology 39
    vs needs of society 163–164
    one of four main university functions 41
    part of academic core 171, 178
    separation between teaching and research 38
    strong at UCT 13, 135
    students' loss of respect for 19, 47, 192
    tensions with ideology/political function 47, 102, 105
    training function, linked to 28–29, 40–41
    training function, tensions with 133, 148, 157, 190, 194
    University of Botswana's strategy 121
research/science networks *see* global research networks
research/science universities
    global rankings 137–138
    historical development 37–39, 40, 59, 98
    OECD/IHERD report 136
    small percentage of tertiary sector 38, 39, 98, 136
Revitalisation of Higher Education: Access, equity and quality 108
revitalisation of universities 105–109, 110–111, 114, 188
Revitalizing Higher Education in Sub-Saharan Africa 108
Rhodes University 130

Rise of the Network Society 6
Russia 25, 77, 106, 138, 139

Salmi, Jamil 6, 110, 114
salmon farming 79
Saxenian, AnnaLee 81
Schneider, Carol 5
School of Lausanne 59
school teachers 45, 49, 61–62, 194
science, engineering and technology (SET)
 % SET majors *129*
 enrolments 122, 128, *202*
 graduation rates 123, 126, 128, *129*, *203*
 student–staff ratios 125, 148
science function *see* research/science function
science networks *see* global research networks
science universities *see* research/science universities
Scott, Peter 5–6, 18, 97
sea turtles 181
self-programmable labour
 vs generic labour 24–25, 26–27, 193
 and 'learning to learn' 29, 62, 98
 part of the sustainable elite 194
 university role in production of 28, 114
Sen, Amartya 70
Shuttleworth, Mark 8
SIDA grants 144
Silicon Valley 38, 81
Singapore 14, 46, 60, 61, 67
small business development 118
social mobility 41, 97, 153
social movements 90, 91
social networks 36, 96–97
socialist countries 40–41
societal needs
 demand for higher education 11, 18–19, 29, 41, 190
 NCHE framework 4
 see also communities; university–community engagement
soft power 22
South Africa
 correlation between doctorates and research publications 125

    corruption 89
    differentiated universities 140, 193
    National Development Plan 191–192
    potential of distance education 62
    subsidies for research publications 130
    Top 20 university rankings 138
South Asia 88
South East Asia 77
South East Asian Institute of Technology 52
South Korea 14, 46, 116
Southern African Regional Universities Association 111
space of flows 159, 160–161, 164, 167, 180, 183
space of places 161, 164–165, 167–168, 180, 183, 184, 185
spaces of autonomy 87–88
specialisation 49, 105, 153, 179
Spinoza, Baruch 22
staff *see* academic staff
Stanford University 38, 40, 60, 64
state
    as actor in development process 89–90
    and exercise of power 20
    impact of globalisation on 9–10
    intervention in economic development 26
    and investment in education 10, 26, 61
    and massive corruption 89
    neo-developmental role 88
    see also government policies
Stellenbosch Institute of Advanced Studies (STIAS) 12–13
structured industries 80
student politics 19, 36, 47, 192
Sub-Saharan Africa
    engaged research 165
    expenditure per student 104, 113
    higher education participation rate 101
    low investment in R&D 157
    policies driving university dynamics 112
    rankings of universities 138
    research publications output 128
    state supervisory approach to higher education governance 155–156
subsidies
    for developing countries 67

    for research publications 130
supplementary teaching 131
sustainable development 69–70, 74, 86, 121
Sweden 144
switches *see* network switching
symbolic manipulation skills 27, 28

Taiwan 46, 61, 138
teachers 45, 49, 61–62, 194
technical training 45–46, 47, 48, 102
technology
    also driven by non-economic factors 161
    capacity of societies to transform 10
    and information processing 72, 76
    and meanings of term 'development' 68
    military technology 39
    in newly industrialising countries 78–80
    see also information and communications technology (ICT)
technology institutes 42, 46, 99
Thailand 43
The City and The City 159
theological schools 35, 36, 58, 96
Third World countries
    integration into world economy 54
    lack of connectedness 76
    poverty and underdevelopment 53–54
Third World universities
    expansion of university enrolment 44–45
    failing to perform developmental function 48
    historically rooted in colonial past 43–44
    loss of skilled staff 44, 46–47
    policies to improve quality 50–51
    recruitment of elites 44, 45, 101
    role of specialised organisations 182
    tensions between ideology/science functions 47
    training/education function 44–46
Times Higher Education rankings 137–138, 138n1, 138n2
Touraine, Alain 36, 187
training/education function
    historical overview 39–41, 59, 60, 98
    in African universities 13, 28, 102, 194

Index

Asian universities 102
civil service training 28, 37, 39, 102, 117, 193
in context of development 102, 120, 163–164, 171
different levels of training 49
ideology function, tensions with 102, 140, 190
one of four main university functions 41
part of academic core 171, 178
postgraduate training 130
production of skilled labour force 57, 61, 62, 95, 114, 136, 153, 194
required by industrialisation 39–40, 59
research/science function, linked with 28–29, 40–41
research/science function, tensions with 133, 148, 157, 190, 194
in Third World universities 44–46
training educators 61–62
young faculty and doctoral students 50
transformation discourse 4–5
Transformation in Higher Education: Global Pressures and Local Realities 11
transparency 156, 163
Turok, Ben 7
turtles, protection of 181

UN Millennium Project Task Force on Science, Technology and Innovation 111–112
undergraduate enrolments 142, 143, 147, 149, 150, 157, 189, *205*
UNESCO
conferences 103, 108, 109, 115
demands for university revitalisation 110
devalues the status of higher education 109
United Kingdom
Brexit 18, 21, 30
colonial view of universities 101
education system 4
proportion of research universities 136
United Nations 90, 110
United Nations Environment Programme 181
United Nations University report 108
United States of America *see* American universities
universities
Castells's concept of 'powerful' universities 168
Castells questions durability of 19
in context of network society 160

critical role in effecting 'new society' 27
disconnected from development cooperation 12
as driver for economic growth 100, 111, 135–136
importance of relative quality of 154
institutional reforms 50, 100
must be complete systems 48, 49, 58
participation in global networks 18, 60–61, 164
role in context of knowledge economy 57, 95–96, 100
and technological change 57–58, 64–65
see also African universities; developmental university; HERANA universities; Third World universities
universities, access to
  differentiated universities 152
  and parental income 97
  role of private sector 101
  social demands for 11, 18–19, 29, 41, 190
  see also massification
Universities and Economic Development in Africa 13–14, 95
universities, functions of
  historical overview 35–41, 58–60, 96–99
  combined in different ways 60
  formation of flexible personalities 63, 96
  in global knowledge economy 57, 95–96
  HERANA's analytical framework 116–120
  need for cross-fertilisation of disciplines 47–48
  take place simultaneously 42–43, 99, 146, 188
  tensions between contradictory functions 12, 29, 47, 99–100, 105, 133, 151–152, 163–164, 187–188
  see also elites, selection/formation of; ideology/political function; research/science function; training/education function
university–community engagement
  academic core indicators 171–176, *173, 174, 207*
  academic dividends of 163
  articulation indicators 170, 171–176, *173, 174,* 185
  differentiating academic core functions 178–179
  disciplinary valency 176–178
  flows of information 175–176, 180, 183–184, 186
  vs knowledge-production activities 163–164
  Makerere University projects 166–167, 172–176, *173,* 177, 178, 184
  NMMU projects 166–167, 167–169, 172–176, *174,* 181–183, 184
  switches between networks 179–182, 186, 195

Index

University of Botswana
    changes in head count enrolments *204*
    doctoral enrolments *202*, *203*
    doctoral graduates 126, *202*, *203*
    doctoral/senior staff 143–144, *205*
    doctoral staff *203*, *205*, *206*
    'engine of development' notion 119
    higher education participation rate 101
    masters enrolments 127, *202*, *203*
    masters, ratio to doctoral enrolments 127
    part of HERANA network 115
    research income per permanent academic *203*
    research publications *145*, *202*, *203*
    research strategy 121
    SET enrolments *202*
    SET graduation rates 126, *203*
    strength of academic core rating 124
    student/staff growth 142, *143*, *204*
    student–staff ratio 125
    undergraduate enrolments *205*
University of California 9, 63–64, 64, 98n1
University of Cape Town
    % masters and doctorates *129*
    changes in head count enrolments *204*
    doctoral enrolments 131, *202*, *203*
    doctoral graduates 126, 129, *129*, 144, *202*, *203*
    doctoral/senior staff 143–144, *205*
    doctoral staff 126, 128, 129, *129*, *203*, *205*, *206*
    highest ranked university in SA 115n1
    masters enrolments 127, *129*, 131, *202*, *203*
    masters, ratio to doctoral enrolments 127
    part of HERANA network 115, 115n1
    postgraduate enrolment 128
    research income per permanent academic 128, *129*, *203*
    research publications 127, 129, *129*, 144, *145*, 146, *202*, *203*
    THE's ranking of universities 138
    SET enrolments 128, *129*, *202*
    SET graduation rates 126, 129, *129*, *203*
    strong academic core rating 124, 189
    strong research/science function 13, 135
    student/staff growth 142, *143*, *204*

student–staff ratio 125, 128, *129*
subsidies for research publications 130
undergraduate enrolments 150, *205*
University of Central America 52
University of Dar es Salaam
  % masters and doctorates *129*
  development role of university 119
  doctoral enrolments 131, *202, 203*
  doctoral graduates 126, 129, *129, 202, 203*
  doctoral staff 126, 128, 129, *129, 203*
  masters enrolments 126–127, *129*, 131, *202, 203*
  masters, ratio to doctoral enrolments 127
  part of HERANA network 115
  postgraduate enrolment 128
  research income per permanent academic 128, *129, 203*
  research publications 129, *129, 202, 203*
  SET enrolments 128, *129, 202*
  SET graduation rates 126, 129, *129, 203*
  strength of academic core rating 124
  student–staff ratio 125, 128, *129*
  unable to meet data requirements for HERANA Phase 3 140n3
University of Ghana
  % masters and doctorates *129*
  changes in head count enrolments *204*
  doctoral enrolments *202, 203*
  doctoral graduates 126, 129, *129, 202, 203*
  doctoral staff 126, 129, *129*, 144, *203, 205, 206*
  masters enrolments *129, 202, 203*
  masters, ratio to doctoral enrolments 127
  part of HERANA network 115
  postgraduate enrolment 128
  research income per permanent academic 128, *129, 203*
  research publications 129, *129*, 144, *145, 202, 203*
  role of university in development 119
  THE's ranking of universities 138
  SET enrolments *129, 202*
  SET graduation rates *129, 203*
  strength of academic core rating 124, 125
  student/staff growth *143, 204*
  student–staff ratio 125, *129*
  total enrolments 142

undergraduate enrolments *205*
University of Hong Kong 43
University of Ibadan 138
University of Louvain 37, 43
University of Mauritius
     changes in head count enrolments *204*
     doctoral enrolments 147, *202, 203*
     doctoral graduates 126, 144, *202, 203*
     doctoral staff 126, 144, 147, *203, 205, 206*
     higher education participation rate 101
     masters enrolments 127, 147, *202, 203*
     masters, ratio to doctoral enrolments 127
     needs commitment to differentiation 157
     part of HERANA network 115
     research income per permanent academic *203*
     research publications 127, *145*, 147, *202, 203*
     role of university in development/knowledge economy 119, 146, 191
     SET enrolments *202*
     SET graduation rates 126, *203*
     strength of academic core rating 124
     student/staff growth *143*, 147, *204*
     student–staff ratio 125, 147
     undergraduate enrolments 147, *205*
University of Moscow 37
University of Nairobi
     changes in head count enrolments *204*
     commitment to strengthening research 148, 157
     doctoral enrolments 126, 148–149, *202, 203*
     doctoral graduates 126, 144, 149, *202, 203*
     doctoral staff 126, 144, 149, *203, 205, 206*
     enrolment growth 142, 144, 149
     masters enrolments 127, 148, *202, 203*
     masters, ratio to doctoral enrolments 127
     part of HERANA network 115
     research income per permanent academic *203*
     research publications *145*, 149, *202, 203*
     THE's ranking of universities 138
     SET enrolments *202*
     SET graduation rates *203*
     strength of academic core rating 124
     student/staff growth 142, *143*, *204*

student–staff ratio 125, 148, 149
tension between research/teaching functions 190
undergraduate enrolments 157, *205*
University of South Africa (Unisa) 62
University of the Witwatersrand 138
US Foundation Partnership for Higher Education in Africa 12, 115

valency, disciplinary 176–178
values
   and development goals 69
   and meanings of term 'development' 68
   university shaping of 63, 96
   see also ideology/political function
Venezuela 89
vision and mission statements 119, 121, 125, 132, 172, 188–189

Web of Science journals 123, 127, 141, *145*
welfare states 85, 89
well-being of humans 68, 69, 70, 71
West African International University 52
White Paper for Post-School Education and Training 184
World Bank
   markets as key to development 88
   policy on higher education 104–105, 109, 109–110, 114
World Cup (FIFA) 91–92
World Economic Forum 147
World University Rankings 138n1

xenophobia 87
Xi Jinping 30–31

Zaire 43
Zeleza, P 138–140
Zuma, Deputy President 9